DAMANHUR

Social Alchemy, Magical Temples and the Superindividual

JEFF MERRIFIELD

WATKINS

Sharing Wisdom Since 1893

This edition first published in the UK and USA in 2021
by Watkins, an imprint of Watkins Media Limited
Unit 11, Shepperton House
89–93 Shepperton Road
London
N1 3DF

enquiries@watkinspublishing.com

Design and typography copyright © Watkins Media Limited 2021

Text copyright © Jeff Merrifield 2021

1 3 5 7 9 10 8 6 4 2

Designed and typeset by JCS Publishing Services Ltd

Printed and bound in the UK by TJ Books Ltd

A CIP record for this book is available from the British Library

ISBN: 978-1-78678-370-7
www.watkinspublishing.com

For Dawn.

CONTENTS

BY WAY OF ACKNOWLEDGEMENT

I wrote a book, over 20 years ago, about a remarkable community I came across, in a synchronistic way, in the Italian Alps. That community was named Damanhur and it has enriched my life in unimaginable ways.

Thank you, Damanhur. Thank you very much. I have been fascinated and utterly intrigued by your deeds and exploits for almost a quarter of a century. I've visited the community on countless occasions, yet the story of Damanhur, the social structure, the philosophy, including its esoteric or "reserved" aspects, are so intricately developed and decidedly complex that try as I might, as an outsider, I have had to struggle to fully comprehend everything. The deeper understanding of the initiate requires a strength of character and level of involvement that I found difficult to match.

This book is very much my story of revisiting Damanhur with the purpose of exploring the community two decades on, in the wake of the much-valued time and my many encounters there. However, my understanding of Damanhur, examined yet incomplete as it may be as an outside observer, could not have been possible without a considerable amount of help from a host of Damanhurians, many of whom have become friends over the years. Conversations, chats, discussions, sharing, informal interviews and many rich encounters have made for a most enjoyable and enlightening process. Whatever the level of language appreciation, something always seems to get lost in translation and I am grateful to all those who helped me through.

Without doubt, my meetings with the acknowledged founder of the community, Oberto Airaudi, were one of the highlights of my life. Oberto was his name for most of the time I knew him. He was latterly known as Falco Tarassaco, and he was an inspiration and without doubt the most kindly, enigmatic and deeply spiritual man I have ever met. Damanhur is his legacy and we are all blessed for that.

Many people had long travelled the journey with Falco, and I am also profoundly grateful for their wisdom and solace. The serenity of Sirena Ninfea, guardian of a deeply contemplated spiritual awareness; the insightful spiritual perceptions of Condor Girasole; the well-researched treasure chest of Selfic magic embraced by Cicogna Giunco; the calm dignity and considered insights of Caimano Salice; the radiant spirituality of Orango Riso; and the caring community consciousness and legal insights of Cormorano Sicomoro. These sages charged with guiding the future pathways of Damanhur have had an important influence on the writing of this book, and over the years, through their wise advice and shared contemplations.

Others have counselled with selfless introspections and shared experiences. Coboldo Melo, whose grasp of the social structure of Damanhur compared to ancient civilizations and internalized historical archives were invaluable to me; Capra Carruba, who arrived at Damanhur the same time I made my first visit and who has remained a friend and confidant ever since; Gazza Solidago, who is another long-time friend and source of some wiser discoveries about Damanhur; Anaconda Papaya gave me a perspective about Damanhur that was over and above the received wisdom; we shared adventures and laughed a lot. And of course, the intuitions elucidated by Piovra Caffè were invaluable in helping me understand the deeper meanings of the temples and other artwork.

Respect to a few further friends, Facocero Radicchio for alerts about the superindividual, Capra Carruba for sharing her education initiatives, Betsy Poole and Formica Coriandolo for their inspired encouragement. Bertuccia Bietola, who was my valuable guide, interpreter, motivator and patient organizer. She headed a managing team that included Giaguaro Scilla and Coboldo Melo. Many thanks are also due to the Damanhur Foundation, for looking after me during my many visits, particularly to Rinoceronte Giuggiolo and Manta Max Ramaciotti, who helped sort out a few wrinkles along the way.

Damanhur's international ambassador, Esperide Ananas, was my veritable champion of deeper meanings and better understandings. She was a hard taskmaster, true to her own intentions, and at times I found it frustrating to convey that those outside the tent often find it difficult to grasp an equivalent level of understanding as initiates. However, her passion and commitment for her community are immeasurable, and I'm beyond grateful for the help she gave me, also immeasurable. I'm sure both our intents were sincere and genuine. And there was much love within the chafing.

My early researches into Damanhur, way back, were shared with the members of the McKee Group, a collaborative collection of writers, including Ken Campbell, Irving Rappaport, John Joyce, John Constable, Suzie Crawley, Janet Fielding and Daisy Campbell, all of whom had taken the Robert McKee Story Structure course. This group was an invaluable inspiration and greatly helped me in my writing endeavours. The late Ken Campbell was a mentor, guide, source of inspiration and loyal friend for over four decades. I miss him so much.

Another person who heavily influenced my thinking and for whom I held the most enormous respect, is the late Sir Ken Robinson. I worked with Ken for a number of years on a project called Artswork and I am indebted to him for helping me to find, in his terminology, "being in my own Element". Ken, it's a great place to be and I thank you.

At Watkins Books, I am eternally grateful for the confidence in me shown by owner Etan Ilfeld. He shared my desire to spread the word about Damanhur. Adam Gordon, my editor, was a tower of strength in seeing the project through COVID-19 lockdown and other unforeseen interruptions, whilst remaining cordial and supportive. Copy editor Steve Marshall proved to be an enthusiastic participant in the Damanhur phenomenon, pushing me to deeper understanding and greater clarity. I appreciated his enthusiasm greatly. Managing editor Daniel Culver put the icing on the cake, so to speak.

Finally, my rock, my anchor, my soul-mate and most reliable friend and partner Dawn Merrifield, whose inspiration and support I cannot measure, it being of infinite supply. Thank you for your faith and encouragement.

FOREWORD

Damanhur has been an inspiration in my life for nearly three decades. And I have Jeff Merrifield to thank.

It all began the day that two very unusual people walked into my London office (and life). One was Ken Campbell – all eyebrows, growl and creative mischief. The other, in his wake, slightly out of breath and grinning, was Jeff.

They'd come to see my partner and I to pitch a creative project. Radical sex education theatre for schools was sadly beyond our expertise but as Jeff was closing his briefcase a flash of colour caught my eye. It was a beautifully illustrated catalogue for a food company called Compagnia della Buona Terra based somewhere called Damanhur. Where was that? Jeff's eyes lit up. He and Ken had just been visiting and he had returned with tales to tell.

Jeff, as you will discover in this book, is a man who can *really* tell a story. And this one had me spellbound. He talked about the origins of the project, the early days in the mountains, the first pioneers, how the community had grown and the amazing things they'd achieved in so little time. The puzzling thing was that, the more he told me about this extraordinary living experiment, the more familiar it seemed. But when he began to describe the underground temples, the hairs stood up on the back of my neck. Because the scene he was painting was one I already knew.

Seven years earlier, feeling lost and seeking some direction in my life, I had attended an immersive self-development course. In one guided meditation we had been encouraged to imagine an ideal living place for ourselves. It could be anywhere in the cosmos; at any time in history or the future. This was a challenge to think the unthinkable, to let our creativity fly. So, I was a little disappointed to find myself projected to what looked like a battered farm door somewhere in the foothills of the mountains in Italy. It was present day and it was snowing. Over the next two hours, guided by the facilitator, I dutifully constructed a place for myself in my mind; a beautiful fiction of intricate design and improbable technology. Except it wasn't fiction.

As Jeff spoke I realized that what I thought I had imagined all those years before was actually real.

I stopped him in mid-sentence and began quizzing him about specifics, offering details that not even he knew about. For example, that barn door I had seen was the one which the Damanhurians used to pass through to do their initial excavations. By hand. Using buckets.

Now it was Jeff's turn to be entranced.

Within days I was in Italy, walking up the path to Damanhur's reception centre and throwing my arms around our mutual friend Esperide – someone I was, technically, meeting for the first time, but who I felt I had known for ever.

Mysterious? Wildly synchronistic? Magically real?

That's Damanhur.

I have learned since that many people have had similarly charmed introductions to this extraordinary place. Ever since Falco and his friends first started chipping into the Alpine rock, it has been magnetizing people towards it.

But I have huge gratitude for Jeff. He was my spirit guide in human form that connected me with this fascinating living experiment. And now, with this book, he is going to be yours.

Enjoy the journey. And who knows, maybe we'll meet at Damanhur some time.

David Pearl

David Pearl is an innovator who works in business, the arts, and social change. He also runs the world's only improvising opera company, Impropera.

INTRODUCTION

You are not wrong, who deem
That my days have been a dream;
Yet if hope has flown away
In a night, or in a day,
In a vision, or in none,
Is it therefore the less gone?

(Edgar Allan Poe,
A Dream Within a Dream)

There are not many places in the world that you can visit, then not go back for many years, but on returning find so many familiar faces, get a welcoming reception, literally feel the love; where people readily recall your name and things about you, and where you are made to feel fully at home. And where magic happens. Such a place is Damanhur.

For over 40 years, a group of special people have been beavering into an Alpine mountain in the Piedmont region of Italy, creating the stunning Temples of Humankind, one of the most profoundly monumental achievements of artistic and spiritual accomplishment. The stunningly decorated subterranean chambers are now internationally celebrated, attracting thousands of interested people to visit, to share the visual and spiritual experiences with the people who created them, and to marvel at their accomplishments.

The people involved in this precious work have moulded themselves into a tightly knit community, learning how to live together, share life's experiences, do amazing common endeavours and, most importantly, become an entity known as *il Popolo*, the People, that extends far beyond the Italian Alps. Over the decades, they have developed a shared way of living that enhances the existences of the individuals involved. They have set up international groups in many countries, established a university of esoteric and related subjects, developed their own ongoing constitution and guidelines for living, devised a uniquely independent currency, known as the "Credito", and attracted media and public attention from many parts of the world. Currently, they are exploring a concept of the "superindividual", where individuals within a group act together as one; simultaneously, they are dreaming of opening up their ideas, thoughts, secrets, mysteries and confidences to the whole wide world.

On recent visits, I found much evident energy, a strong sense of renewal, resurgence and restructuring. A new governance was in place with a positive attitude and a determined purpose. This is a community bursting with positive potential. Despite causing mild consternation for some long-term community members, change has always been a fundamental aspect of Damanhurian life. Monumental change needs to be absorbed and even appreciated.

Damanhur's philosophy was the inspiration of its prime founder Oberto Airaudi, later known as Falco Tarassaco. The foundation of this philosophy is based on positive thinking, active change and the idea that every individual has a desire to leave something of themselves to others and make a contribution to the evolution of humanity.

Neither a cult nor a religion, the practical spiritual message of Damanhur invites everyone to seek their own answers to life's fundamental questions within themselves, through personal introspection and by way of exchange, discussion and shared experiences with others. Through community life, the values shared are solidarity, sharing, mutual love and respect for the environment.

Damanhurians define themselves as *il Popolo*, the People, a relatively simple word, but used here in a way that is both more subtle and more complex. The People is comprised of different ethnicities and cultures, united by shared ideals and 40 years' experiential life together. An intricate and articulated social model based on solidarity, mutual trust and respect, Damanhur is a steady community with a long, stable history that is quite unique for such a group.

Moving closer to this goal can deeply transform each individual.

Recognizing themselves in others, they learn to follow a common rhythm, to think together without losing individuality. On the contrary, they value it even more, with positive practical steps to realize what has been termed the "superindividual". The word, like much of Damanhur's philosophy, has a complex meaning, not used in the sense of Marvel cartoon characters with superhuman powers, nor is it akin to the existential superiority of the Nietzschean Übermensch.

On the contrary, the emergence of this idea of a superindividual is probably the most important recent philosophical aspect of Damanhur, where spirituality gives meaning to and recognizes significance in every aspect of life.

My friend Facocero Radicchio first alerted me to this concept. Over dinner, he told me that the superindividual concept had developed as a significant influence in the community. It had become their definitive goal. "Love is the crucial aspect in this idea. To love one another, to love oneself. This is the realization of all we work for." The notion is of a group, a collective, a community with capability to unite together in love and mutual respect, to obtain a result that is greater than a sum of individual characteristics, to achieve dreams that would otherwise be impossible. The concept is explored more extensively later in this book. For now, just suppose it to be so.

Suppose there was a new way of thinking, a new way of doing, a new way of living, a new way of reawakening awareness. Suppose there were no limits to human achievement, suppose imagination was limitless. One person, who I was honoured to call a friend, and who influenced my life more than anyone else, was the late Ken Campbell, probably the sharpest innovator the British theatre has seen in modern times. He was a "supposing" man. If anyone asked him if he believed something, he would say: "This whole thing about belief seems nuts ... it's a kind of blinkering thing. But if you can suppose a thing, it just means, 'can you put your mind around it, just for the moment?' That seems to be a mind-widening business."

A broadcaster named David Bramwell had heard on the grapevine that Ken knew something about a place called Damanhur and was intrigued, so he rang him. A while into his questioning he said: "You don't believe all of the things they claim, do you?" He was edging round the subject of time travel, of course. "I don't believe in anything..." said Ken, "but I'm happy to suppose in it. I suggest you do too." He suggested that Bramwell ring me. "Jeff knows lots of stuff about Damanhur."

When the call came, Bramwell only seemed interested in one topic, time travel. In spite of all the wonderful achievements in constructing the superb Temples of Humankind and creating a sustainable community, people just seem fascinated in time travel. "I'm open-minded about it," I said, "but the Damanhurians don't make a big feature of it in their lives." I wanted to nail it, so I paused. "Look," I said, "either they didn't do it and made up a daft story, or it's real and was done for a specific purpose. But when you've achieved so many remarkable things as the Damanhurians have, why make up a such a story?" Suppose on that, I thought.

There is a much-appreciated significance in supposing. Thinking or assuming that something is true or probable, but without definite proof or absolute certain knowledge. Matthew Lyons supposed his *Impossible Journeys* (Folio Edition, London, 2009), a sort of Chaucer's Tales of the imaginary and fantastical, and I, for one, loved them. You see, mind-widening. In the days of yore, the seasons, the night sky, stories told of their ancient ancestors were the everyday happenstance of common folk, providing a firm foundation for understanding and relating to the world. In an age dominated by reason, by dogma, by quasi-scientific thinking, by the ever-increasing reliance on celebrity, many, if not most, of the old life principles have been subjugated and forgotten.

As well as Ken Campbell, there was another Ken who was an inspiration in my life. The late Sir Ken Robinson contributed the most-watched TED talk ever. It was about education. We shared a profound love of a book called *Education Through Art* by Sir Herbert Read (Faber & Faber, 1967) and we worked on a project called Artswork for several years in the 1990s. He had a well-founded concept of "being in your Element" as one of the cornerstones of creativity. When you are fully in your Element, time is irrelevant and may even stand still, you are consumed by your involvement in a creative process, be it writing a book, composing a poem or dancing a dance. He also led me to the work of Warren Bennis and Pat Ward Biederman (*Organizing Genius: The Secrets of Creative Collaboration*; Ingram Publishers, 1997), who write about "Great Groups", collections of people with similar interests who create something much greater than any of them could have created individually. "A Great Group", they say, "can be a goad, a check, a sounding board, and a source of inspiration, even love." Dr Robinson rechristened this concept as "the Alchemy of Synergy". If any group captured the Alchemy of Synergy in an astonishing and extraordinary way, it is the people of Damanhur, such is their profound supposing.

Perhaps supposition brought me here, to this point in my book. One morning back in 2017, I awoke and in my drowsing reverie I became acutely aware of a shaft of bright light, a brilliant sunbeam that came through the curtains and struck me in the middle of my forehead. I don't quite know why, but I had a strong recollection of Damanhur, a flash of a thought, which passed in a flicker. It had been many years since I visited the celebrated community. I had been there, of course, for the funeral of Falco in 2013, where grief was abundant. Now, in a strange, convoluted, synchronistic way, I was again drawn back to Damanhur within months, this book being a consequence.

Life is a journey, not only in the sense of a journey through life, but a journey towards self-awareness, and alludes to the most fundamental questions that can be discovered within. Such personal growth flourishes through exchange and dialogue with companions on the path of inner transformation. Life as a game, the Game of Life being one of the fundamental pillars of Damanhur. There is an awareness of embracing a sense of humour and a serious light-heartedness, along with a desire to change staid behaviours and unproductive habits.

Anyone wishing to share in this spirit of research may join *Popolo Spirituale*, a unification of peoples from around the world, connected to human, spiritual and universal values. I consider myself a "friend of Damanhur", so I guess I could be considered one of the "Spiritual People".

For nearly 50 years I've been intrigued by a painting. Don't ask me why. But from the moment I first saw it, I was obsessed. I had a large print, framed in ornate gold, and it looked splendid on my wall. I made a student film in the 1970s and this painting was not only the structure but featured as a presence throughout the film. The painting was *Where Do We Come From? What Are We? Where Are We Going?* by French artist Paul Gauguin (*see* Plate 1). He inscribed the original French title in the upper left corner: *D'où Venons Nous / Que Sommes Nous / Où Allons Nous*.

The idea of "where we come from, who we are, where are we going" is a theme that philosophers have long reconnoitred. Gauguin attempted to give form to it, as he lived an exotic life in the beautiful climes of Tahiti. I thought long and hard, eventually deciding that I would use this painting as a structure for the book. Three parts of a whole. Not as might be obvious – as three parts that look at past, present and future – but as a process where all interviews and researches were conducted with this visual philosophical concept in mind.

Falco was a great storyteller. His books, his talks, his community guidance were all enhanced by the telling of tales, gleaned from a wide variety of sources, ancient and modern, science and science fiction. Most cultures have a creation myth and Damanhur is no exception. The "myth of the mirror" is a basis of the Damanhurian magic-esoteric school. It illustrates both the origin and direction of the human soul which, in turn, represents the nucleus around which the entire framework of the future philosophic structure is then developed:

Many aeons ago, the primeval divinity known as humankind decided to explore the universe of forms. In order to enter this dimension, characterized by multiplicity and continuous transformation, it had to divide itself into a myriad of fragments, like a mirror that shatters into shards.

The Mirror of Humankind shattered into millions, billions, trillions of pieces. The bigger pieces became divinities, the smaller pieces became human beings, animals, vegetables and plants, down to the smallest form existing. Since that time, it has been the essential purpose of humans to attempt to draw back together the shattered unity of consciousness. The challenge, indeed, is to recognize ourselves and all forms in the universe as one within diversity.

Creation stories are universally important. In the work of Carl Gustav Jung on "archetypes" and Joseph Campbell on mythology, you can find the universal pattern that connects with creation stories, and other myths such as the hero's journey, of slaying the dragon, of good versus evil and the various kinds of mythological motifs that we encounter. Joni Mitchell sang that "we are stardust", and I've just seen our own television professor, Brian Cox, in a programme called *Stardust* (BBC 4 series, *Wonders of the Universe*, episode 2), saying that his creation story is the account of how we are part of something far bigger than we can really comprehend:

My creation story is that the path to enlightenment is not about our own lives and deaths but about the lives and deaths of the stars. It tells us how we were made by the universe. It explains how every atom in our bodies was formed, not on Earth, but created in the depths of space, through the epic life cycle of the stars.

You will often hear reference to a "divine spark" in the context of Damanhurian philosophy, the shards of the mythical broken mirror, a little of the divine that is in everything. We, as humans, are aware of this, and can transcend purely material endeavours, thus making our lives the richer. For me, in some respects, this divine element might be thought of as life itself, real life, the fundamental life force.

It reminds me of Giordano Bruno's concept of "nature", his way of describing what others, including the church authorities that tried to eradicate his ideas, defined as "God". (See *The Pope and the Heretic: The True Story of Giordano Bruno, the Man Who Dared to Defy the Roman Inquisition* by Michael White, Harper Perennial, 2003.) He paid dearly for his thinking with seven years of torture and a ghastly and gruesome end at the stake. We owe him a great debt.

Another Damanhur concept referenced in the books and the online media of Damanhur is the idea of "separation of the planes of existence". The legendary history says that the time in which we live today is not the present. It is an extraordinary opportunity offered to humankind to change the tragic and catastrophic events that led to the destruction of life on Earth, approximately around the year 2,613. Therefore, a plane of reality already exists that led to a tragic ending. But a new plane of probability has been "grafted" on the original one, which is growing at a completely different angle. This means, we all have a chance to create a different future: we are all time travelling on this new plane to create a new history. If the awareness of the inhabitants of our planet is able to grow enough to provoke different, positive and lasting events, this "test time" of ours will eventually be solid enough to substitute completely the time plane that has already passed. Otherwise, it will be re-absorbed within the original flow. In order for this to happen it is truly necessary for each single individual to help achieve a critical mass which is able to reverse the trend. Damanhur is actively committed to this plan for salvation, which is also supported by extra-planetary intelligences and forces. Our planet has been isolated for thousands of years from other intelligent worlds, but it actually belongs to a vast galactic alliance. The doors which link us with the more evolved worlds will open again only when humanity reaches an adequate level of spiritual, social and material growth.

A crucial point in this legendary history relates to a situation, probably around the year 1990, the year of the first Gulf War, codenamed "Operation Desert Storm". It was a time in which the old plane was pulling strongly on the new one, which was at risk of collapsing.

At the time it appeared to us mere mortals that the world might just be on the cusp of a mighty conflagration that would start in the Middle East and then spread wider. According to Damanhur, the Galactic Council were ahead of the game and met in a galactic fluid year around 2550 in Earth years, in the midst of a serious emerging crisis on Earth. The council consisted of 13 members who supervised the development and the maturation of human souls on the different living planets, whatever physical form they take. A situation of extreme crisis had arisen, as the human species on Earth risked losing its soul. The Earthlings had forgotten their divine origin, and selfishness, hatred and violence reigned on the planet, suggesting an impending annihilation.

One of the ways in which Damanhur has chosen to tell the world about itself is through comic books. These graphic storybooks, originally published in Italian in two separate volumes, are now translated into English as *The Stories of Damanhur: The Chest of Memories* and *Checkmate to Time* in one volume (Esperide Ananas and Stambecco Pesco, publishing under their original names Silvia Buffagni and Silvio Palombo, Devodama, 2016). In the latter, Damanhur's mythical story of the separation of the planes is revealed. The Galactic Council was meeting on a timeship at a point close to a sun in a small corner of the Milky Way:

> The Sun, a meeting point of synchronic lines, the rivers of energy that unravel from our star to link all living planets, carrying thoughts, dreams, and... souls. Any soul that is to reach Earth must start its journey here.

A heated discussion ensued regarding the perilous situation on Earth. There was general agreement that the situation on Earth was "an extreme emergency".

For some it was too late: Earth was doomed. They considered that "Earthlings have lost their ability to create their reality and interpret everything through a few limited senses and fragmented memories." They felt that there was no chance to change things now. On the other hand, some pointed out the great achievements of the past: that Atlantis was for millennia the pride of the whole galactic civilization; the flowering of the Renaissance in Italy, a glorious artistic achievement, though the enemy of humankind had eventually snuffed that out. It was from then on that the decline had started.

One of the council members offered to adopt a drastic measure, to mount a rescue mission, by one of them travelling back through the synchronic lines as a divine spark and take a local body, find a way to bring back ancient teaching and to create a new current of time, a new civilization.

And so, the concept of the separation of the planes of existence came into being. The dates are significant. The year 2550 is 600 years from 1950, the date that Signor e Signora Airaudi gave birth to a son, who they named Oberto, after his grandfather. According to the story told in the *Checkmate in Time* comic book, when his father, Giuseppe, a war hero and partisan, was asked by a neighbour if the boy would follow in his footsteps and become a hero, his father said: "No. He will have a normal life." Well, as we all now know, he would have far from a "normal" life.

As for the significance of the timescale, Earth had approximately 600 years before environmental disasters and wars would wipe humanity as we know it off the planet. The separation of the planes started in 1967, when a new, more positive, possible future for humanity started being created. That was the year The Doors released their first album, the Black Panthers tried valiantly to show us that black lives matter, and the Vietnam War trundled on. Going back to "Desert Storm", had the planes of reality not been separated at this point, the Gulf War would have been the start of a situation that would unleash a prolonged series of catastrophic events.

And that is why Damanhur exists, as part of a global, or rather galactic, plan to save the planet we live on from future catastrophe. Damanhur is not alone in this. Similar initiatives take place around the planet, laborious efforts to keep the planes apart long enough to avoid disaster. The action to rectify climate change and desperate measure to reduce plastics and pollution are just part of such necessary and vital efforts. Climate, consumption, new viruses and possible pandemics, and human population growth. A dawning awareness, a collective consciousness.

Keeping the planes actively separated requires strenuous efforts in a myriad of ways. Prayer, meditation, concentrated efforts, action, change, fulfilling remarkable projects. For the last four decades, Damanhurians have toiled to construct the Temples of Humankind, to concentrate on environmental priorities, such as an active forestry regeneration initiative, creating a sustainable community, and building networks of analogous groups around the planet. That is why Damanhur is so important. That is one of the major ways in which the planes are kept separate.

CHAPTER I
TIME OF THE PEOPLE

Since its beginnings in 1976, Damanhur has existed as a dedicated community with a Path of Initiation at its core and an artistic approach to its spiritual researches. Originally, it was called School of Meditation, but in 2019 the name was changed into Medit-Action, to underline the practical approach to spirituality of Damanhur's Initiation Path. The community has been relatively stable in all this time, attracting the attention of eminent sociologists by its stability and durability. In his book *Damanhur: Popolo e comunità* (Editrice ElleDiCi, Torino, 1998), Luigi Berzano, a distinguished professor in the Department of Cultures, Politic and Society of the University of Turin, described Damanhur as "one of the largest communities of the Age of Aquarius; just outside Turin, 400 residents, as well as more than 300 sympathizers participate assiduously in its activities".

Other distinguished sociologists have visited Damanhur, including Eileen Barker from the London School of Economics, a renowned specialist in New Age movements, who described the temples as "quite remarkable" and found the community to be amicable and benign in its nature, particularly in its regard to raising children (*Methodological Innovations Online* 6.1, 2011, 18–39); Massimo Introvigne, director of CESNUR, the Centre for Studies on New Religions, said: "Damanhur is, arguably, the largest communal group in the world today, or at least, the largest communal group in the ancient wisdom-magical tradition"; and Maria Immacolata Macioti, who has written about "entering into a fairy tale", observed that, although rituals are performed in the temple, it is thought that the most important ritual has been – for the past 16 years – the construction of the temple itself (both of these quoted in

1

"Damanhur: A Magical Community in Italy", *Journal of the Communal Studies Association* 16, 1996).

The participant numbers have grown considerably since he published his study at the turn of the millennium. Berzano expressed admiration for the constant nature of the community, comparing it with other groups who he regarded as "revolving door" communities, with participants regularly coming and going over time. Damanhur's constancy is due in no small part to the role that artistic expression plays in their everyday and spiritual life. The other stabilizing factor has been the organized citizenship of Damanhur and the participation of such citizens in the Path of Initiation.

Like the esoteric schools from ancient times, it is a reserved institution, with initiates who progress through a series of stages, identified by the wearing of a specific colour of robe for ritualistic activities. This has served the community well, enhancing the relevance of participation, bringing the group together in common purpose from the earliest times.

Damanhur has established a positive reputation for its environmental and sustainability work, being an active member of the Global Eco-village Network (GEN), Italian Eco-village Network (RIVE) and Conacreis (National Coordination of Associations and Communities of Ethical Spiritual Research). The community has been able to positively demonstrate that new forms of environmental society are possible and achievable.

Living in a community means being open to the world, being part of a social and political system that can respond to the needs of its citizens, with a sense of service to society. After building the internal structures, the project will continue with dedicated environmental restoration, an intention to give back harmony to the expansive area of wooded hills. Major projects of Damanhur have largely been made possible thanks to the contributing groups and individuals who have felt an affinity with these projects and wished to support their realization, either through their direct efforts or through donations. The work has been undertaken thanks to the technical and specialized design collaborations already in place within and affiliated to the community.

On 23 June 2013, the citizens of Damanhur shared a very sad evening. Their founder, spiritual guide and innovative inspirational source, Falco Tarassaco, left his physical body and passed away in his Damanhurian home. Synchronously, in Damanhur's Open Temple, the Ritual of the Oracle was taking place. It was the night of the full moon, actually a super moon that month. Many Damanhurians felt Falco had chosen

2

that moment for his passage. His death was a moment of truth for a community that had relied so much on his invaluable guidance, it was a time to reflect and assess. In the months leading up to his demise, Falco expressed his desire for the idea of Damanhur to become more open, more determined in reaching out, more inclusive of people from the wider world. This meant opening out some of the benefits of their Initiation School, most of which were secretly preserved for initiates. This marked a radical departure. The community had always been welcoming of people coming into the group, participating in its activities, but now the community was to be more outgoing, with the concept of "the People" being much enlarged.

The idea of the superindividual – a collective consciousness emerging from deep connection between individuals, and helping them in turn reach a higher evolutionary step – had been germinating for a few years by this time. In September 2017, Damanhur staged a piece of musical theatre entitled Vajne Tujl, dedicated to the superindividual project. Art is one of the most important elements in Damanhur. Art, in all its aspects, is a way of living and, through art, meaning is brought to their lives and the environment. For the Damanhurians, it is important that art is shared and created together by many people.

This new musical was a collaboration with musicians, actors, directors, filmmakers, writers, altogether more than 150 people. Members of the cast wrote about it later on their website:

There are so many emotions, among both those who participated on stage and those who witnessed this complex theatrical work. It is a collective emotion that has raised the temperature of the Popolo, reaching a level of fusion among the people, moving directly from the heart of each one of us.

Vajne (pronounced "Vi-ney") means the programme of evolution of the human species. Humanity evolves spiritually according to this "programme of the species". We are not here by accident: there is a path which humanity is on, which is not just for this planet. Throughout human history, stories were created to make sense of the world we live in, to give meaning to life, to inspire dreams.

Mystical traditions say that in every epoch there is a group of people who protect the ageless wisdom and the alliance between humanity and the gods, holding the vision for the future of humanity, remembering the world to come. This is the story of Damanhur, its aim the freedom and reawakening of the human being as a divine, spiritual and material principle.

On this planet, there are many other species connected within Vajne. Many more in the universe. Vajne is the reconnection of humans, plants, animals and minerals, beings and intelligences of other worlds, divine forces at all levels, so that the resident species on this planet can all reach a higher stage of consciousness, together. Vajne is based on the exalted principles of love and divine intelligence and is supported by extra-planetary intelligences and forces. We may all participate and evolve within Vajne through many lifetimes.

As Esperide Ananas Ametista said to me:

> Everyone in Damanhur has an awareness that we are part of a programme for the awakening of humanity. We know there will be other appointments to be met. The one in approximately 600 years' time, from where Falco's consciousness returned, when the myth started, but we also have another scheduled stop in-between. So, all Damanhurians, if we can do things well, we are going to meet together in-between these times, in about 300 years.

The people of Damanhur sought a perspective where it's okay to talk about lofty ideas, but Esperide felt that if radical action was not taken in practical form, restructuring the economy, creating the new Temple projects, Damanhur would not progress as it should, in order to play its role for humanity. If they wish to continue within the Vajne project, to be the ones at the spearhead of Vajne on planet Earth, then they have not only to survive, take care of their economy, of their agriculture, of the environment. "Our plan is to thrive so that we can reach our spiritual objectives."

On Damanhur New Year last year, 31 August 2018, those chosen as sages and others got together and created a booklet to help the citizens of Damanhur define and focus more on Vajne. As a part of the steps towards the actualization of Vajne, in 2019 every initiate belonging to the Initiation Path of Damanhur, anywhere in the world, started to be considered a Vajne citizen. This was a big philosophical revolution, as for the first time Damanhur recognized its presence in the world, while giving all initiates the same status, no matter where they choose to live. Living communally is still considered – and always will be – the best way to grow together with others, but there are now many different ways of being a Damanhurian citizen.

This also means that every initiate will be able to use the Temple as only Damanhurian residents did before. Esperide was clear about this:

> We feel this is a completely new way of thinking and is important that you write this in your book. Because, when you came here, even two months ago this was not the case. Now, everything is changing. This is a major rethink. This is like, why are we on this planet? Before, we felt we were here because we needed to build Damanhur and the temples. Now, we feel that, as we continue building, it is just as important to share Damanhur's knowledge and the temples. A new, more complete perspective.

Every initiate, resident or not, is now a Vajne citizen. They are citizens of the world as part of the Vajne project, a different idea from being a citizen of Damanhur. It is now clear that they are citizens of this planet and the Vajne project is a direction in which to take humanity.

The Damanhurian unit of currency, the Credito, is significant in the scheme of things. Last year, the Vajne project was announced. This year, it has just been announced that every citizen, here or elsewhere, will be given a special Credito coin with a hole in it and a little cord. Esperide explained:

We are going to ask everyone to wear this special pendant. The specific coins are being energetically prepared right now by Sirena Ninfea, at the Baita, one of Damanhur's most sacred places, and in the temples. They will have two major functions. First, to help prosperity. So, everyone who is part of our project will be in the flow of prosperity, which can support the concept and aims of Damanhur. Second is changing the frequency to money. The idea is, by wearing this coin we will be able to purify money.

With the Vajne project, this special Credito becomes a magical tool, like a catalyst for a new way of thinking. Once Damanhurians have adopted the coins, the next step will be to offer everyone in the world who feels a connection with the energy of Damanhur the opportunity to purchase the specially activated Credito in a range of values, at the face-value of the coin, plus a little extra for the activation and the cord. Magically prepared, they become a magical catalyst. Also, people around the globe will be offered the chance to become an initiate, so they might attain more personal energy to contribute towards creating the new timeline. More and more people with awareness are needed, to help in keeping the plane of existence separated.

Of course, the Credito will continue to be used as the official complementary currency of Damanhur. It is still accepted by some of the businesses outside and around Damanhur, but not on a scale comparable to previous times, due to restrictions of new European legislation. As Esperide told me: "That is one of the reasons we want to return the Credito to the level of a magical instrument, as it was when it was first introduced."

It's an old cliché that "the love of money is the root of all evil", but there can be little doubt in the minds of reasonable thinking people that money is at the core of what all the evil powers are using to destroy the planet. Maybe the time is right to take back the realistic value of money, as a means of fair exchange. Magic money, it may be, but it is a way to revalue our own thinking. In Britain, we have long had a joke about "the magic money tree", being the means by which governments seem able to find money to suit their own ends, and the ends of those with mutual financial interests, but not for the general good of the population.

This readjustment of the frequency of human values, especially in regard to money and its consequences, is one of the reasons the Federation of Damanhur was originally created.

Looking around at what is happening in the world – the conflicts, the lack of trust between peoples, the political manipulation, the explosion of greed, the exploitation of financial systems, the lack of concern for the environment and the limited resources of the planet, the attacks on indigenous populations, the burning of the rainforest for financial gain – it is plain to see that all is not well with the world. In truth, the planes of existence are becoming very close, and we risk falling back into the timeline that we are trying to substitute. Esperide continued:

> The meaning of Vajne: everyone on board. And the temples, not just as Falco used to say, an example of what a small group of people can do. That is a part of it, an important part, but now the temples are going to be even more active as an activator. Throughout history, civilizations have built sacred spaces to receive information and energy coming from the cosmos to vibrationally guide the evolution of souls, peoples and planets. The Temples of Humankind are one of these antennas. They are a receiving point for the cosmic energies, and because this is a receiving point, these energies can be redistributed. And if many more people can be supported in their spiritual awakenings, many more people will be making conscious choices that will help reinforce the new, positive plane of reality. This is one of the ways in which the Damanhurians feel the temples are in service to humanity.

Maintaining the temples – let alone creating new artworks – costs a fortune, and Damanhurians have no sponsors. For this reason, visitors are charged a fee to visit the temples. But to make them accessible also to those who might have financial challenges, once a month the underground complex can be visited for a minimal offering.

There are other important changes taking place. The story that the Damanhurians now wish to tell is more complex and complete that it was before. The new emphasis is that in the Labyrinth it is possible to catch a glimpse of a possible, positive new future, with the idea of all the gods and goddesses of all times interacting in harmony and sharing their stories with each other. In this way, they are creating a new narrative for humans. In this new story, the gods that were violent, like the gods of war, become subdued, because their qualities mix with those of the forces of love, for instance, and create a new balance. This story implies that, hopefully soon, there will be no more wars in the name of God, because the gods themselves are creating a different narrative that will lead humanity to honour the divine forces with higher and more elevated energies than those created by conflict and suffering. After leaving the Labyrinth, Esperide explained to me how the journey continues:

> In every tradition of the world, creation comes through the elements. From the union of the gods we represent in the Labyrinth, when we visit the other halls of the temples, we immerse ourselves in symbology dedicated to the elements. We have the Hall of the Earth, dedicated to the masculine principle, and connected to the Hall of Victory, representing Mother Earth, as masculine and feminine principles are both needed to create life. The Hall of Water, the feminine element, connects us to the ancient memories of humanity, the Hall of Metals, which is connected to fire. And what is fire? Transformation. And that is time. Because without time there is no history.

Esperide felt that the elements come to life through time. The Hall of Spheres, which is ether, an alchemical container, represents the purity – being covered with gold, the goal of the alchemist – to become the purest being they can, and therefore transform themselves into spiritual gold. And the Hall of Mirrors, of course, which is air and reflects the light and all images over and over to infinity.

> After having told the story of a new harmony among all the divine forces of Humanity, having contemplated creation through time, what is the next step? The unity of all the peoples of the world together. The West listening to the wisdom of the indigenous peoples, because they are the only ones who always kept a connection with the Earth alive. This is the theme of the Time of Peoples, where you can see all people here are represented with their traditional food, as it is in this way that we nourish ourselves of the experiences of all the fruit of the Earth: in this way we are planet Earth. Indigenous people have also kept the memory that we came from the stars; hopefully we will re-open a communication with our stellar family and through the gods of our space-time, go even beyond the universe as we know it today and continue exploring the higher levels until maybe one day we reach the Absolute. This is an important story that the temples tell today.

This Time of the Peoples chamber is, in my opinion, the most magnificent work of the Damanhurian painters to date. It is gloriously painted with all the panache and bravado the Damanhurian artists are noted for, but this time taken to a whole new level of beauty and excellence (see Plate 13). When I was first shown into this chamber, it fair took my breath away, creating a profound emotional impact. Artwork of a meticulous standard, the creation of a group of artists working in the same ways as the grand masters of old, but with a razor-sharp modern approach.

The ceiling is the largest domed structure ever built in the temples complex and is also the most beautifully painted, an astonishingly accomplished piece of artwork that illustrates just how far the Damanhurian painters have come in their artistic and creative endeavour. It tells the story of humanity from its earliest history and beyond. All races are represented in groupings of men, women and children, and their domestic animals. Also depicted are the creatures that enriched their lives, and in some instances from which they evolved, as are the many species of insects, fishes and wild animals that they have shared this planet with. Or should I say, *we* have shared, as this is our story, the story of us, of humankind. And it is awesome in its grandeur. There are depictions of the many, many families of humankind grouped, each in their particular races, from childhood to old age, covering a vast panoply of time.

Of all the people depicted, unlike in other parts of the temples, there is only one recognizable Damanhurian individual, Condor Girasole, who represents the whole community in this rich depiction of all human beings. Pictured above all the peoples of the world are a band of ethereal creatures of a nether world. Looking down from the pinnacle of the dome, through an opening in the fabric of space-time, are three godlike beings, those representatives of the Triad: Horus, Bastet and Pan.

I had the great honour to sit alone for some time in this chamber, to contemplate my feelings about the place and make notes on the artwork. It was an awesome experience, emotionally draining. Strange that, though the temperature appeared constant, as I was writing this description I became overwhelmed by the energy of the place. I let out a gentle cry and it echoed back at me. I felt quite hot, sweating profusely, and I was compelled, somewhat self-consciously, to take my shirt off, in order to continue writing.

First, the enormous cupola ceiling. The background is a beautifully calm light blue, a glorious sky with little fluffy clouds. Through an opening in the sky, we have a glimpse of a space beyond, with a vast darkness of void and hundreds of glittering stars, like a tear in the fabric of reality. Peering through this hole in the sky are the representatives of the Triad, Horus, Pan and Bastet (looking for all the world like a typical grinning cat!) observing what goes on below. Magic upon magic, evolution on progression, the growth of humanity, the sacredness of life itself. In the sky there are birds of many kinds, angelic spirits of many varieties, and several hot-air balloons, obviously representing humanity taking a first flight into the cosmos. Spirits of air, fire and water.

This is an overwhelming space, bursting with powerful energy. You lock onto that energy when you enter by placing your hand on a wall-painted hand, like the cave paintings of earliest people, and you give back the energy as you leave by touching a similar painted hand.

All round the vast perimeter of the ceiling are some of the most gorgeous paintings the Damanhurians have accomplished. These are paintings that could easily have come from the studios of the Renaissance masters, yet they are fresh, of our time and wonderfully characterize the diversity of the planet we inhabit. These are the representatives of the cultural people of the world in their myriad of diverse peoples. We are a human species with so much in common, yet with a wide spectrum of interests, creativity and spiritual perspectives.

Here are Africans, Australian aboriginals, Mayans, Mongols, Alaskan Inuits, Arabians, Nordics, Hawaiians, all with their families, their cultural instruments and adornments, their domesticated animals and those wilder animals that share their planetary environments. It is a glorious display of vibrant colours, perfectly painted portraiture, and celebration of humanity. Together, they rejoice in our planet and the ways in which it is valued, guarded and protected.

This is superinividualism at its finest. Here are the indigenous nations of humankind. The ones who want to preserve and protect traditions and cultural inheritances, the exact opposite of those who set out to exploit the resources of the planet for financial gain while destroying the environment without care and attention, motivated by greed. The peoples depicted here are the guardians of our world and, when they come together, they are indeed a supremely powerful grouping and force. Indomitable.

I had wondered about one section of this ceiling. It is the panel where Condor is seen, representing Damanhur in the whole panoramic depiction of humanity. He is the figure in a blue robe holding a chalice on the right of the picture.

The panel shows an indigenous grouping and at the centre is a table, with the food on top of a Damanhurian flag. Seated at the table partaking of the food are two people, a Tibetan and a white aristocratic looking man. I wondered who he was. I asked Esperide at a later time and she told me:

> That guy sitting there at the table is a war pilot from Northern Europe. He is sitting down with a Tibetan woman. The West has destroyed many indigenous people and cultures. The fact that they are eating food together on top of a Damanhurian flag represents Damanhur wishing to be a meeting point of cultures to create a new future, to facilitate a new understanding of peace and harmony.

We British have a lot to answer for, in regard to our imperialist past and our self-important Empire. The "colonies" were regarded as places to be looted and booted, subjected to the rule of despotic viceroys and unscrupulous business exploitation. I'm presently reading *Inglorious Empire* by Shashi Tharoor (Horst & Company, London, 2016) which explicitly explains how Britain ruthlessly exploited India and its people, financially, morally and unjustly. Not forgetting the butchery and exploitation of indigenous peoples in Australia, New Zealand, North America and large swathes of Africa. Turns out that our so-called Empire was nothing more than a cash cow, to be milked over and over again, without consequence or honour. We weren't the only European invaders, but I guess we were the worst, and so many of the world's ills can be traced back to these times. I'm glad I asked about this painted section, and am even more content with the answer I got. Esperide also told me that on the table in the centre of the picture are three chestnuts. This connects with the idea of food in the region around Damanhur and also alludes to something that Falco said in his book *Seven Scarlet Doors* (Oracle Institute Press, 2013), that in order to be healthy – in mind, body and spirit – you should eat three chestnuts a day. Nutritionists now recognize that chestnuts are rich in microelements and are wonderful food also for the brain and the nervous system.

Many indigenous people now visit this part of the temple and bring some of their own energy with them, as well as taking some of the collective energy away with them. Shamans from a wide range of countries have recently visited. They come to the Crystal Spiral of Damanhur and into this chamber.

On the floor there is a concave pattern representing water and the many water-related aspects of our existence. The floor space can be filled with water and becomes like a mirror, superimposing the figures from the ceiling on the watery world below. I'm told that it holds precisely 333 litres of water.

The walls were mostly painted by Falco. A supreme burst of energy that resonates and vibrates overwhelmingly. Without doubt, this is a deftly accomplished work, replete with sacred language and the iconography of spiritual vitality, like the walls he painted in the Hall of Water, but on a much grander scale and, I guess, of more penetrating significance. The walls are fashioned from the deeper meanings of a sacred language, long forgotten, but now revived and much revered at Damanhur. An archetypical language that dates to an era when humankind had mastery over the deepest meanings and values of life.

As different language groups migrated and reproduced among themselves, their own ethnic features became emphasized and were further influenced by geographical conditions. This caused the demise of the sacred language, later researched and revived by Falco. These mysteriously painted walls are a legacy beyond comprehension, a work of powerful productivity from the final throws of life. Awesome, invigorating and inspirational.

Also, round the walls are seven distinctive panels, depicting alien worlds, possibly linking to a future timescale for our planet? They are like the fruitful creations of a science fiction mind. The science fiction authors were always ahead of their times. Philip K Dick, Arthur C Clarke, Isaac Asimov, Robert Heinlein. They often wrote about a future that is slowly, yet relentlessly, coming to fruition. I guess that these are not directly from Falco's hand, the styles suggest not, but they are for sure from his inspiration and guidance. He often used science fiction stories to explain his ideas. A supreme form of the art of supposing.

Together with the artistic gathering of the indigenous peoples, these panels reach out to a distant future, where not only the planet we live on arrives at a superindividual oneness, but where the universe becomes as one. This is about LIFE beyond comprehension. It is almost impossible to describe the imagery of these seven panels. They are speculations about alien worlds we can only dream about, but where fruitfulness and diversity are paramount. These are the mirrors of our worlds and we must be aware of their reflections. I notice that the seven panels are each lit by the image of a falcon.

As I place my hand on the energy releasing painted hand and emerge from this wonderfully inspirational space, I notice a glass case with a small collection of indigenous instruments connected to shamanism that will no doubt grow over time into a full-blown exhibition of the cultural and spiritual diversity of our planet.

This will not be the end of the journey, once new plans are put into operation. Acknowledgement of indigenous peoples, so exquisitely celebrated in the Hall of Time of Peoples, will be developed in the Temples of Concordance and a Parliament of Peoples, in an area close to the Temples of Humankind and adjacent to the Sacred Woods of Damanhur (See also Plate 11).

This much-anticipated further construction of the Temples of Humankind, involves radical plans that will take the development of the temples complex to a whole new level. Strategies are now in place for this ambitious project to be built inside an old lime quarry that has been abandoned for over 60 years, in an area known as the "Buche".

The purchase and planning of this Buche area has been something of an ordeal, involving several decades of struggle. As with many other aspects of Damanhur the positives finally overcame the negatives, making determination stronger, and the project is now set fair.

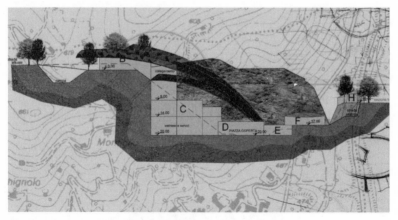

Above: Schematic diagram of the proposed new sections.
(F is the currect section).

To start the exchanges with different indigenous peoples even before having the space, a group of Damanhurians postulated the idea of inviting shamans to visit. Piovra Caffè created the Crystal Spiral, after Falco's death. He had left indications that they could make best use of this spiral by inviting shamans from all over the world "to perform their ceremonies here". When they perform ceremonies, the whole spiral gets activated, and through the energies of the temple, utilized as an activator, the values of their people will be transmitted through the synchronic lines. Because this is done through the temple, the values that are transmitted are pure.

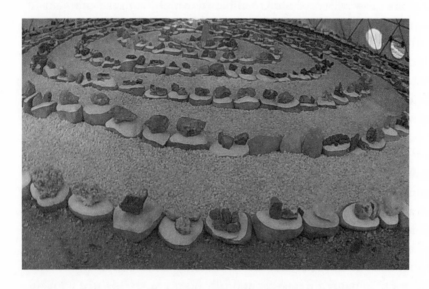

CHAPTER 2

REAWAKENING OF AWARENESS

Suppose a metaphor of "threads". Threads you can take, weave, unite and use in all manner of creative ways. Threads are used to weave fabrics, from silk to tapestry, from cotton to carpet. But threads are more than that. We have now conceived of a "fabric of reality", woven from the threads of cosmological theory. We have notions of the "rich tapestry of life", woven from the incidents we live as individuals and communities. We assume the idea of threads to convey packages of energy; threads that connect plants, animals, the distant, the deceased; threads that unite experiences, capacities and people. Threads that connect human beings often get tangled but could still be used to unite. Awareness facilitates access to infinite potentials of reading signs, weaving threads and an ability to see their beauty and usefulness. A related ancient metaphor tells us that: "Thought is a thread, and the raconteur is a spinner of yarns – but the true storyteller, the poet, is a weaver." (From an Old North French text of the 12th century, cited in Robert Bringhurst's *The Elements of Typographic Style*, Hartley & Marks Publishers, Dublin, 1993).

Scribes in ancient times made many an old and oral abstraction into a new and visible fact. After long practice, their work took on such an even flexible texture that they called the written page a textus, denoting cloth, textiles, something woven. It can also mean a connection. The best way to galvanize such threads is to connect with others, to support them, to think of them, to listen to them, to understand them. The threads that connect us do not only depend on space and time, but on connectivity and change. If two points are destined to touch each other, the universe will find a way to put them into connection; this is a component of what we know as synchronicity. Untangling a synchronic thread of some intrigue, years ago, led me to my own discovery of Damanhur.

At Damanhur, you may encounter stories of quantum physics, where scholars and practitioners are pursuing the borders of matter and energy, with claims to have penetrated those information codes underlying human DNA, or where psychic technicians speak of travelling Earth's planetary energy lines, espousing synergy and synchronicity, slipping backward in time to adjust and set events in motion that are destined to change the course of a distant future. These are the essential synchronicities that have spawned the community of Damanhur and kept it vibrant for over four decades.

I think it safe to say that, to my knowledge, Damanhur represents one of the most structured communities in the world in current times, yet its story contains many initiatives and events of universal significance. The book you are holding in your hand appears, again with help from a reflective synchronistic source, at a time when the community is undergoing a radical restructuring and is launching itself on a new trajectory of openness and outreach to a wider world. What has germinated over decades is now being tested on a world struggling with its own foibles and difficulties, where those things learned and developed in a closely managed artistic-spiritual reality might just be the answer to the many prayers and yearnings of the greater family of humankind.

The story of Damanhur can be summarized as falling into five major phases: an incubation period of growth for a community project; the physical creation and settling of the community in Valchiusella; the direct effort of the founders consolidating the community, discovering ways to make it constructive, hiding a secret of building a temple inside a mountain; the rapid expansion, achieving considerable international fame for Damanhur; and the later growth, in some respects more carefully

thought out than in the preceding period, with a focal point in 2013, when what could have been an apocalyptic catastrophe occurred with its founder's death.

If ever there was an individual who typified the conception of imaginative supposing, it must rest firmly with Oberto Airaudi, the founder of Damanhur and its spiritual guide, latterly to be known as Falco Tarassaco.

He was a dreamer, a visionary, an intrepid explorer of mind, body and spirit. It was his vision, his energetic encouragement, his inspiration, his constant researches, that drove Damanhur; his enthusiasm and stimulations were its beating heart and its source of nourishment.

For most of the time that I personally knew him, he was Oberto, but from now on, I will refer to him as Falco, his own chosen Damanhurian name. For sure, he was key to the advancement and prosperity of the community, though he never assumed the role of leader. He left such matters to other colleagues. However, there is little doubt that he was a spiritual guide and the main source of motivation for Damanhur. There was sometimes a concern about what might happen if he were suddenly not there. He would, from time to time, tease the community with such ideas. This was probably more to keep them on their toes, organization wise, rather than expressing narcissistic reasoning.

Through all these developmental stages, these extraordinary adventures, the ups, the downs, the good and the bad, the figure of Falco Tarassaco had stood firm. He seemed adept at turning negative energies into positive ones and it was such fortitude that invariably saved Damanhur in their hours of greatest need. It is no easy matter keeping a community functioning, and sociologists say they expect that a newly formed communal group would normally burn out within ten years. This community has survived over 40 years and has ridden some of the most tempestuous times with the sort of determination Falco initially instilled in them.

On Sunday 23 June 2013 at 11:12 pm, as the people of Damanhur were celebrating the summer solstice, as well as an "Oracle rite" associated with a full moon, Falco left his physical body and passed away from this life, aged 63. After a life lived fully, intensely and with great joyfulness, he had now forged ahead with his death. In March 2013, he had found out that he was terminally ill, but in typical Falco style, he was not dismayed by the news.

Esperide told me that Falco had been saying for over three years that he was going to leave. Everybody in the community thought he meant he would go and start a new Damanhur somewhere else. Nobody thought he meant his time on earth was coming to an end. In retrospect, in the last few years of his life, it is possible to see how he was preparing to leave behind all the necessary tools for Damanhur to continue without him. He gave a huge impulse to the development of Selfica – Damanhur's own spiritual technology – he taught many new courses, was available also online for meetings with groups and people around the world and encouraged more and more people to take direct responsibility in the management of the community. People who knew him well recall him saying that, as a healer, he could help others but not himself. He

died of a particularly virulent type of intestinal cancer that attacked his liver: once it had taken hold, it took over the body in irreparable ways. Falco chose not to take any drugs, nor did any course of therapy. He was managing his pain in natural ways, and was available for heart to heart, spiritual farewell meetings with all the Damanhurians till very shortly before dying. His very moving last message, given to the community and the world by Skype when he could not leave his bed anymore was: Love each other!

The people of Damanhur stopped holding their breath as they had since the first bad news of March, and a cry rent the air in the calm Valchiusella, a cry for the pain of the separation, as well as for the joy of the richness they held in their hearts. It was a moment that many had anticipated for months, some more forcefully than others, yet the shock of the moment was nonetheless raw and despondent. He had tried to dispel any doubts about the future of the community, the continuation of their valuable contribution to humankind, yet there could be no doubting the shudder of the loss and the uncertainty it represented.

They organized a wonderful send-off for their spiritual guide in the place that he had inspired them to create. There was a service of ritual remembrance at the Open Temple site in Damjl. Some 2,000 citizens and friends of Damanhur, from many parts of the world, including this writer, came to pay their final sincere respects. But whatever their grief for their departed visionary, this was not the end of the story. The end of a chapter maybe, but the dream of Damanhur remained as vibrant as ever. He had made sure of that.

When I went back to Damanhur two years after Falco had passed away, that optimistic, vibrant spirit was still there. And more so. The vision was ever present and developing. The community was still constructing inside the temple and beyond. Indeed, more so. There was a profound sense of loss for their spiritual guide, and some feared for the future, yet there was a feeling that his guidance was still on hand.

He had placed in the hands of certain people specific instructions that would help things along at relevant times. Such instructions were in the form of letters, letters that wove particular threads to keep the community on its right tracks. This was the highest order of supposing. The threads of the letters were proving fruitful and Damanhur was just as pulsating, just as engaging, as enigmatic, as it ever was. Falco had left the messages, to be read posthumously, some even months or years after his death. There is one that has been described as "most dear" to the Damanhurians and traces the path for the future of the community. It is even more significant keeping in mind that Falco was a painter and I guess it is a pertinent message for all of us:

Work for your dreams, love each other for mine. Together, create the most beautiful picture I have ever made.

Another memory came to mind. On Thursday, 19 March 2015, at 10 pm, I was in a Damanhurian community meeting at which one of the special letters Falco had left was read out. These were normally sessions for Damanhurians only, but tonight was an open session and those from outside the community could attend. There was talk in the letter about bees and the way they pulled together in adverse times and where the individual bee is less important than the group. This was the genesis of the idea of the superindividual, though I was not aware of this at the time.

There was also talk of the Temples of Humankind being more open and more welcoming to those from outside the community. There was a lovely moment where packets of seeds were given out, entirely according to

Falco's instructions, not only to the Damanhurian community groupings, but also to all the visitors from many parts of the world who were present. People from Colorado, Texas and California took their seeds back to the US; people from Sweden, Denmark and Norway, Brazil, Austria, Germany, Spain, Ireland, Russia, China and Japan, Australia and Switzerland took seeds back to their respective countries.

I had not visited Damanhur since Falco's funeral, nearly two years before, and got a fond reception and a substantial round of applause and cheering when I went to collect my seeds, which were to be taken out of a chalice. When I said, "These are going up near the North Pole", there was an even bigger cheer. A memorable night amongst a fine community of people that left me  with a warm glow inside. Back home we planted our seeds and helped the bee population of the cool northern climes to thrive and survive. The picture shows their blossoming growths sitting outside our back porch in Sandwick, Shetland Islands.

From the time that Falco left his physical body, the Damanhurians became engaged in a series of transformations based on their collective experience and the determination arising from wide-ranging international relations. At what might well have been a low point, the future now appeared more promising. One of the most important elements of this reinvigorated activity was the idea of Damanhur moving away from a social situation built on esoteric, secret and closed doctrine, to a more open way of thinking, where the 40 years of meditational growth were to be made readily available to people from outside the community. This was a radical idea. This was extremely powerful supposing.

CHAPTER 3
THE OTHER 90 PER CENT

"Digging into the mountain as a metaphor for digging into our own souls" was invariably the driving force embraced by most people who originally formed Damanhur or joined it along the way. The magnificent temples they built are probably what bring most people to Damanhur. Their artistic beauty and audacious construction are now recognized as a renowned monumental achievement. I recall when I first visited the temples in 1997, it was like shock and awe, the memory of first seeing the artwork and the cavernous space is still as vibrant as when I was first there standing inside the structures.

The scale of the project is phenomenal. Constructed into the foothills of the Italian Alps, behind a private residence in the heights of Vidracco village, the temples are created like a three-dimensional book, narrating the history of humanity. Here, 30 metres (100 feet) down and hidden from public view, lies this astonishing complex of chambers that have drawn comparisons with the fabled city of Atlantis and has been referred to as a "modern wonder of the world" alongside the likes of Gaudi's Sagrada Família in Barcelona, the Wieliczka Salt Mine Chambers in Krakow, and the Djenné Mud Mosque in the Niger Delta of central Mali. Weaving their way beneath the Vidracco hillside are the nine sumptuous temples, on five levels, whose scale and magnificence take the breath away and place them squarely among the other modern wonders.

It had all begun in the early 1960s, when Falco, then Oberto Airaudi, was aged about ten. From this early age, he claims to have experienced visions of what he believed to be a past life, in which there were amazing temples. Around these temples, he dreamed there lived a highly evolved community in which people were conscious, loving and worked for the common good.

He also appeared to have another supernatural ability: the gift of "remote viewing", the ability to travel in his mind's eye and to describe in detail the contents of any building. "My goal", he said, "was to recreate the temples from my visions." He began digging a trial hole under his parent's home to better understand the principals of excavation.

Following several years of preparatory work, studying the Earth's synchronic lines, flows of energy that envelop the planet and link its peoples, in 1977, together with other visionaries that shared his dream, he bought land in a secluded valley in Piedmont. That area is today considered the capital of Damanhur. In 1978 he selected a remote hillside where he felt the hard rock would sustain the sort of structures he had in mind.

After receiving the green light from the universe, in the shape of a shooting star on an August night, using hammers and picks, they began their dig to create the temples of Damanhur, meaning City of Light and named after the Egyptian city, now heavily industrialized, where legend has it that there used to be a complex of underground temples, in which many of the great initiates of the past were instructed.

As no planning permission could be asked, due to the absence of Italian legislative norms regulating underground constructions – let alone temples of that ambitious scale – they had to share their plan only with like-minded people. As the community grew in size, the secret work being carried out inside the mountain was eventually revealed to those recently arrived. Taken inside, blindfolded, they were dumbfounded at what they saw, the monumental scale and visual magnificence of the temple artwork. They then worked, for the next 16 years with no specific building skills, no formal plans other than Oberto's sketches, ideas and visions, and no doubts about their intentions. They were creating a sacred space, connecting to universal wisdom.

I am happy to be back here, in the beautiful Temples of Humankind. I have been here many times and I feel at home here, as if the temples have become a part of my life. The walls are decorated with glass and stone mosaics, paintings, sculptures, inlays in wood and copper, embossed. You can follow articulated pathways, discovering again the seven rooms of the temples, each one dedicated to an element and characterized by its own mysticism. The Hall of Mirrors is dedicated to light, air, sky and the sun. It has a huge Tiffany glass dome, which has now become one of the most recognizable symbols of Damanhur, and a superb granite and marble floor. The Hall of Water is dedicated to the feminine principle and divine forces. It is enriched by another Tiffany glass dome and on a stone altar, a glass sphere is illuminated by a candle whose flame is always lit. The Hall of Spheres is entirely covered with gold leaf. It represents the heart of the temples, the name is given by the nine spheres along the walls, which contain alchemical liquids of different colours, where you make contact with the synchronic lines. And then, the mighty Labyrinth, in which the history of humanity and the stories of the gods are traced through paintings and beautiful windows along all the walls and where some of the most impressive artwork of the temples has recently been achieved.

I recall a time, around 1997, when I spent a whole night in the Hall of the Earth, freely writing, totally inspired by the surroundings. At that time, I entered into the Hall of the Earth, via a spiral staircase, the umbilical cord from the womb of the Hall of Water. This is a place with which I particularly identified. The following is from the notes I wrote at the time.

*   *   *

Sitting in the Hall of the Earth in the Temples of Humankind, writing about the temples in the temples. Eight white columns, rising from floor to ceiling, all individual, while all in the same style – gold embossed images in relief on white china glaze ceramic. Sacred symbols, divine images – serpents, birds, a scorpion; mermaids, statuesque figures, mythical symbolism. Crowning the columns are capitals, each with its own specific imagery.

These columns stand majestic, symbols in themselves of the steadfastness, firmness, solidity of this Hall of the Earth and of the people who built it. As I sit writing this, I am aware of a hammer drill in another part of the temples, as the construction work goes on. Only 10 per cent built, with an age of construction work ahead, as further doors are opened into the soul, into the universal psyche of humankind.

The walls of the temples are meant to be read in much the same way as you would read a deck of tarot cards, to be read, interpreted and meditated upon. I look up. The ceiling is a fabulous splash of colour – six circular bands of rich variety. I have been told that everyone at Damanhur had a hand in painting it. That is important. Falco had told me that there are many paintings underneath the paintings that can currently be seen and that the Temples of Humankind are not just the artwork that is on the surface, but that which is under the surface and never revealed. Like the ancient Egyptians, who always painted the reverse side of the sarcophagus, underneath the Damanhurian frescoes the whole history of Damanhur is painted, no less potent for no longer being seen.

The outer ceiling ring is orange, save for the places where the columns meet, the capitals, where it fades to white. An intricate design has been painted into this orange ring, interlocking circles of red, green and gold. A piece of the roof, left in its original state of bared craggy rock, cuts into the orange band, as well as into the next band of deep purple. This is the reminder of the cutting into the bare earth, a point of spiritual contact between the temples, those who built them and those who come to share them.

The purple is a darker, more prominent colour. Painted into this ring are diamond and angular shapes. The next band is a deep green, at the blue and turquoise end of the scale. This is the widest of all the bands of colour with six rings within it, mostly of a red colour, like berries in abundant foliage, and including a prominent band of intricate red heart shapes. Inside this, separated by a band of equally intricate red diamond shapes, is a strong band of royal blue, a lush, vibrant colour, with lotus flower shapes painted into it. And, finally, a band of rich red completes the design, a maroon red with star shapes and leafy patterns.

They tell me that the symbols in the design of this ceiling are actually ideograms in the sacred language, spelling out the words of a song: *ERIJA BET LEBAJ* (We arrive at the awakening). The whole of the song is carved into the marble all around the room. It is a song to the reawakening in a new body, with all the memories of former lives.

The final band is multi-coloured and is in illuminated Tiffany glass. Green and purplish blue, it culminates in rippling bands of colour. And in the centre of all these rippling bands, a montage of seven faces, and in the centre of them, the sun. Who are these faces? Surely, they are divine…

The gods… The gods… The gods – those who are about to fall asleep – reunite. They know that, for them, the large wheel of the Kali Yuga draws near, at nightfall, and that, for a long time, victory will go to the black god of the stellar vortices. The great major god of the superior circle, three times Ra, summons those three gods who are still awake, who are allied to humankind: Horo, the goddess of the waters and the mysterious god. These three immense gods sit down shoulder to shoulder, as if in the centre of a great arena, and they look outwards, into the eye of the great god of the superior circle. It is so vast that all three gods, whose own sight is exceptional, perceive only the pupil that fixes on them, bathing them with benevolence and respect.

A mighty voice tells them that they will awaken again only if a new city rises up out of the alliance between gods and humankind, on that point where, one day, thousands of years in the future, new vortices, knots and synchronic lines will pass; a city which will be able to save humankind, who will, in the meantime, be tried and tempered to see if it is worthy of its destiny.

And only with the awakening of the gods, will humankind undertake the right way. The times will have to be precise and perfect and be born from the desire and the force of humankind.

This future sacred place of this alliance between humankind, the gods of humankind, and the god of the superior circle, is land now entrusted to a small gnome called Soffio. The alliance will be possible only if the masculine and feminine principles unite, tantrically producing the androgen among humankind. Horo goes north, to the land entrusted to the small Soffio. He is tired of the journey, of the multi-millennia struggle, and is getting weaker and weaker. He digs a handful out of the mountain, as if it were fresh snow, making a comfortable seat; and he settles down, reclining his head, resting it on the palm of his left hand, and falls asleep.

The goddess of the waters, in order to rest in the same place, turns herself into three sources. Where she places her knees, large lakes are formed, and where she places the fingers of her hands, small lakes are made. Where she places her head becomes the sea. Now, to the gods, only the dreams are left, for giving substance to their maya, towards humankind, their protected. Only the dreams are left… Only the dreams…

I shake myself, as if awakening from a deep sleep. I am looking up at the ceiling and contemplating the rich flow of life, the ripples we make on the surface of reality. My eyes are drawn to seven faces in the centre of the concentric bands of colour. My dream thoughts have been drifting around one of the Damanhurian legends, "The Myth of the Sapphire Masks" (Oberto Airaudi, *The Myth of the Sapphire Masks*, Federazione Damanhur, Baldissero Canavese, 2001).

Now I remember these seven faces staring down at me represent the seven original races of Earth. The sleeping gods are to be reawakened here in this place, through this work. This ceiling symbolizes the dedication, the diligence and the sense of purpose of the Damanhurians. What binds them together is what keeps them together. The interlocking structure of the ceiling painting is a reflection of the close and interlocking nature of their lives.

From behind one column, I see Time peeping out at me. He is tall and dignified, with long grey hair and beard. At his side, the four seasons are represented: the way in which we perceive the passage and the cycles of time. A little further to his left, there are the important monuments of the past civilizations of our planet, and high above, a golden city that represents a future, new golden age for humanity.

As I gaze around the hall, the next large figure I see is female. Maybe she is Mother Earth. Or maybe she is the Goddess bringing life into the universe. She is certainly pregnant. Her almost naked body is draped in a turquoise chiffon garment, transparently covering her shoulders and part of her torso. Great waves of flowing bright red hair, with strands of beads and shells woven into it, enhance her beauty. Her arms are outstretched, one palm facing up, the other down. On top of her hands, a scene of destruction. The Damanhurians have told me that this is a sacred dance movement: this woman/Goddess is separating the planes of existence, making sure the old line of destruction does not happen. Indeed, she is stepping into a scene of truly epic proportions, the conflict between humankind and the anti-life principle, the conflict of Damanhurians overcoming adversity.

Grey forms of the anti-life principle are represented in vast numbers of oncoming figures, and they have the same faces of the Damanhurians, pitched against them in battle. This represents an inner battle against their own limitations they are fighting, not an external enemy. And the awakening of the feminine's values in every human being is indispensable to overcome one's shadow. I recognize some of the Damanhurians. These are the people who have become friends on my many visits. Look, there is Tapiro, and there is Fenice. There are Caimano and Gau and Ara. There Coboldo and Antilope. I notice Condor with the body of Superman, and I have a quiet laugh to myself.

The battle is raging, but the Damanhurians all have smiling, laughing faces as well as an expression of determination. These are people who will win, with joy and humour; they will not let their inner darkness overcome them, not allow anti-life negativity, their own limitations to be the victor in this conflict. This is a fight for life, no less!

The scene representing universal darkness, a grim warning painted over the chiffoned shoulder of the Earth Mother-to-be is what could happen if humanity fails in its task. But the smiles and the determination on the faces of the Damanhurians show you that they will fight until their last breath. These are a people of joy, of pride, of resilience, of fortitude, of a determined optimism (see also Plate 6).

Another female figure looks at the battle scene, her hands also in a gesture of sacred dance. She is completely naked, save for flowers and ribbons entwined in her hair. On her body, her arms, her thighs, are painted – like tattoos – animal figures that represent the Damanhurians, all close together, as the Damanhurians themselves are. Above the woman's head, suspended, is a grail chalice, floating on a silken yellow cloth. The second figure in this grouping is a large androgynous being, the golden body of humankind, the tallest figure in the whole chamber at around 5.5 metres (18 feet) tall. Without hair or defined sexual organs, at a first glance it looks more like a man, but the outline of a woman is painted over it in a special fluorescent paint that can only be seen in ultraviolet light.

On the lower level of the walls, a series of painted panels depicts the spiritual paths of Damanhur, the "ways". Each of the Damanhurians follows a particular spiritual path associated with their own interests and it seems only natural to represent these in the temples.

It still intrigues me to see people I know well depicted on the walls of the temples. First, a panel that depicts a group of children, children from all the nations and continents of the world. They are holding hands in a dance of union. In the distance, a couple stand face to face, their hands outstretched in front of them, touching. This is the spiritual path of education, of caring and nurturing, dedicated to the union of the world's children.

The next panel shows the atmospheric Open Temple, bathed in blue moonlight. Sirena Ninfea stands at the fire altar, conducting a ritual ceremony for the Way of the Oracle, the spiritual path of communication with divine forces. Next is a picture of builders in the temples transporting the many buckets of earth, a human chain of high-powered action. There is Picchio, and there is Alce. These people are on the Way of the Knights, they have taken on a specific responsibility for construction in the temples and for security in Damanhur. The Way of the Monks is represented by a scene of meditation and ritual in the temples, showing Cicogna Giunco and other monks, both male and female, in devout spiritual contemplation. In another dominantly blue panel, Gabbiano sits, book in hand, profoundly explaining the finer points of Damanhurian philosophy to a seated circle of avid listeners. This represents the Way of the Word.

*   *   *

As I rewrote the above section from my notes, memories came flooding back. One particular time I was visiting, there was one place in the Hall of the Earth that was just solid rock. When I went back there some time later, not only had this solid rock been dug out to form another huge chamber, connected to this one like an infinity symbol, but it was painted, mosaiced, given a column that represented the tree of life and a ceiling with the actual starlight that had been recorded on the night that Damanhur was founded. This is now called the Hall of Victory (see Plate 1).

The question I have been most asked over the years is: "Where did they get the money from?" The answer is: from endeavour. They largely funded the purchase of materials for the scheme by setting up small businesses to serve the local community. Alongside this, Falco devoted his time, his skills and his total devotion towards raising monies to fund the temples. He was a prolific painter and developed a unique style of "Selfic art". Painting several pictures before breakfast every morning filled a gallery with top-selling works. He was a pranatherapist, a healer of extraordinary qualities, and apparently all the money he raised from this work was for the temple and other community projects. It was from a high level of organization, willpower and effort that the temples got built, generous donations from appreciative followers, and the unstinting contribution of those undertaking the actual construction. And the work continues to this day.

By 1991, the chambers were almost complete with stunning murals, mosaics, statues, secret doors and stained-glass domes, doors and windows. "They are to remind people that we are all capable of much more than we realize and that hidden treasures can be found within every one of us once you know how to access them," said Falco. But time was running out on the secret construction in the foothills of the Alps.

The Temples of Humankind have an adventurous history. Once the first excavations had begun, the temples remained a secret for 16 years. Only the Damanhurian artists, craftspeople and masons directly involved in the construction knew about it. The reasons for the secrecy are now obvious – planning laws. Even though the temples were on Damanhurian property, they were unauthorized because, in the Piedmont region of Italy, there were neither laws that regulated underground construction, nor authorities for the asking of permission.

Any planning permission was impossible.

The following year, a former member of Damanhur, mischievously egged on by a dubious lawyer, sent an anonymous letter to the local police station that affirmed the existence of "hidden temples". Armed police and explosive experts came to the house where the entrance to the chambers were located, on 3 July 1992 at seven in the morning. Falco and his friend Cormorano Sicomoro, one of Damanhur's lawyers, led the District Attorney of Ivrea and three police officers into the temple complex. A fourth person followed them inside with a camera to film the visit. An hour later, the men came out of the mountains, and they were deeply moved and touched by the beauty of what they saw as the first witnesses from outside of Damanhur to see the temples. Negative into positive.

The account of this incursion on the temple complex is more fully described in my previous book on Damanhur and is quoted in Alexia Parks' consciousness training book *Rapid Evolution* (The Education Exchange, Eldorado Springs, 2002), which goes on to say:

> Saving the Temple of Humankind took four more years, during which the citizens of Damanhur decided that to save their way of life and the temples from future attacks by suspicious people, they would have to become more open to the public.

Damanhur held the first press conference to announce the existence of the Temples of Humankind, and the next evening, images of the temples were transmitted in an exclusive broadcast on national television. The legal surveys carried on, and it wasn't until June 1996 that the existence of the Temples of Humankind was finally legalized. It meant that construction already completed was safe from any national or local government action, but any further work could not be undertaken until all the necessary stress tests, geophysical surveys and building regulations had been satisfied.

In November 1997, I interviewed Elena Rabbi, a geophysicist at Geodata, the respected Turin firm of consulting engineers called in by the government to survey the structural aspects of the temple. As part of the final legal rights for the preservation of the temple, the Damanhurians were required to provide conclusive evidence that the structure in the mountain was safe, secure and free from any ecological dysfunction. Geodata were given the brief to carry out this examination. Ms Rabbi explained to me how amazed the structural engineers were at the quality of the construction. They carried out a whole range of stress tests and seismic readings but could not fault the structure in any way. They could not believe that here was a structure built by this group of, well, just ordinary people. They were amazed at the quality of the building work and the overall safety of the structure, despite the fact that most of the people involved in the construction had little or no building training or experience.

Even more amazing was the geological survey. The Damanhurians had made a great deal of the place where the temple was situated, claiming it was specifically chosen for its extra-special energy qualities. Ms Rabbi had personally carried out the geophysical survey and she had identified that the temple was situated directly above the place where the large African and European tectonic plates met and crossed each other. At this place, over the millennia, violent collisions of rocky promontories produced upheavals of land surface resulting in the Alpine mountain range. However, what is most amazing is that a rare mineral, rich in energies and known as mylonite, is found precisely in this place. So precise, in fact, that the temple fits exactly into the narrow 45 metre (150 feet) seam of this rich mineral. Mylonite is formed from molten rock resulting from excessive friction and high pressure. It records an abundance of energy captured in the rock.

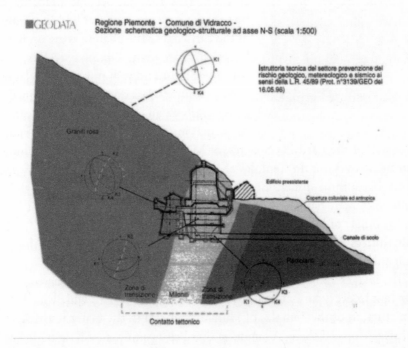

Elena Rabbi and her team had discovered the mylonite scientifically, but Damanhurians had discovered it, quite independently, without realizing it, through synchronic investigations. They had not even known what mylonite was. In the light of all the positive responses from the appointed structural engineers, Damanhurians had to then wait for the full legal permissions to be able to proceed onto the next 90 per cent of the construction work, as Falco had outlined, but secure in the knowledge that their work to date has been given official approval.

Full descriptions of the temple chambers and the construction that was already completed are contained in my earlier book (*Damanhur: The Story of the Extraordinary Italian Artistic and Spiritual Community*, Hanford Mead, 2002), so I shall not reiterate them in any expansive way here, but what follows is a brief description of some of those completed chambers.

Entrance to the temple is now through a conventional corridor, but initially entry was through a plain wooden door, situated in the courtyard of the house (now named Porta del Sol) leading down a labyrinth of passages into nine enormous chambers. It was a plain, nondescript door, not at all what you would expect as the entrance to such a magnificent creation. This door has become an iconic image for many of us who visited Damanhur in the early days. The chambers are on five levels, there are many linking corridors, wall paintings, floor and wall mosaics, two large Tiffany stained-glass domes, many stained-glass windows, all creating a subterranean construction of epic proportions. The Halls of Water, of the Earth, of Spheres, of Mirrors, of Metals, the Blue Temple, and the Labyrinth: the Temples of Humankind are an underground work of art, like a three-dimensional book with a narrative running through it, built entirely by hand and dedicated to the divine nature of humanity and the chronicle of humankind's history through all forms of art. The Labyrinth is the place where some of the most accomplished of all the Damanhurian artwork has now been attained.

The images and symbols aim at awakening the sense of the sacred inherent in every human being. A sacred language is used widely in the construction of the Temples of Humankind and in the many aesthetic rituals performed there. A language that belongs to the esoteric tradition,

an ancestral language existing since the time before languages began to specialize.

As was the case in the Renaissance, the building of a temple gave impulse to the development of many artistic workshops and craft-based activities, to the study of ancient techniques, to the creation of a place as a supreme collective of artistic expression. Damanhur's society grew and refined itself, founded on the basis of its culture and tradition. The development of such artistic skills not only served the purposes of the temple, but also supported it developmentally and financially. The highest quality work in glass, mosaic, ironwork, clay and china, fabrics, mural work and architecture emanated from its workshops, which are often commissioned by Italian architects for high-quality building work. These energetic and creative commercial enterprises provide Damanhur with some of its financial base, allowing work on the temple to proceed unabashed.

In 1997, the Italian Beaux Arts recognized the Temples of Humankind as an example of artwork of exceptional beauty. Damanhur also received a Global Human Settlements commendation from the United Nations, an award for sustainable communities. This honour, received in Shenzhen, China, by Bisonte Quercia, a Damanhur citizen who was then mayor of the local village of Vidracco, stated:

> We are pleased to inform you that Damanhur has been chosen to receive our 2005 Award for Sustainable Communities. Founded in

33

the early 1970s, Damanhur, Federation of Communities, in Italy is now an internationally recognized centre for artistic, ecological, spiritual and social research. Damanhur is an eco-society, a federation of communities and eco-villages composed of 20 small communities. A special characteristic is its connection with the neighbouring cities and villages... Damanhur has a well-organized system of economy and commerce, technological ability in the use of renewable energies; it constructs ecologically built dwellings and dedicates great attention to education. Congratulations!

In 2007, Damanhur was recognized as a model community from the Earth Charter Initiative, whose role is "to promote a transition to sustainable ways of living and a global society based on shared ethics, including respect for and attention to community life, ecological integrity, universal human rights, respect for diversity, economic justice, democracy and a culture of peace". The role of the Damanhur community is to promote a transition to sustainable ways of living and a global society based on shared ethics, including respect for and attention to community life, ecological integrity, universal human rights, respect for diversity, economic justice, democracy and a culture of peace. One of the key points of the Earth Charter Initiative is the dream of a more just world and the realization of a global governance. According to the Charter, Damanhur is "a rare example of a direct and responsible civic engagement". Ashok Khosla, former Indian Minister of the Environment and the president of the International Union for the Conservation of Nature, declared:

> Damanhur and the Temples of Humankind are for the 21st century what Assisi was in the time of Saint Francis in that both represent the deepest commitment to the well-being and the dignity of all our fellow human beings, and the highest respect for other living things and indeed for all of creation.

I recall my earlier visits to Damanhur and how invariably, at the end of each stay there, I would find out something amazing that blew my mind. I went away from such experiences with a lot to think about, with more understanding about what parallel universes really are. On one visit, I was interviewing Falco and mentioned that I had heard that only 10 per cent of the temple was built, wondering about what the other 90 per cent might entail. Falco's eyes sparkled. "Less than 10 per cent," he said, jumping up in a way that totally surprised me. "I will take you to see the new chamber in the temple right now, and you can continue the interview in the car."

As we got into Falco's Range Rover, I was in a state of flux, uncertainty and heightened anticipation. "So, an interview in a car," I said, "this is a good one." Trying to draw a distinction between the temple, and the work on the temple, and the work that has yet to be done, I ventured, "You know what the other 90 per cent of the temple looks like?" He smiled that beatific smile. "Of course, yes," he said. "Do you remember when Esperide showed you those big indentations in the land, going to Ogni Dove?" (the name of the house high on the hill situated near the temples). I did remember the big holes, large cave-like natural structures, that they called the Buche, literally "potholes".

"Imagine (suppose) that they are covered," he continued, "and imagine that there will be a cupola there about one and a half kilometres across..." He went on to further elaborate:

There will be a special electric train that will lead from the Labyrinth up to this big space. It will be on three underground floors and will be about 26 metres high. In the central part, you will enter in a sort of spiral, in the walls. And each one of these floors will be the size of a soccer field, about. We also want to have, in an underground space, a library of the largest collection of esoteric books in the world.

On top of this there will be all the art laboratories, all those that create work for the temple. And there will be a big space for conferences, for hundreds of people, and a space for the concerts we will have. There will be a cable car going up to the various levels. There did use to be a cable car here that was used to take away all the material excavated from the quarries around here. The cable car will take all the visitors inside this space, for the conferences, the concerts, and everything. It will be all interconnected with the temple, which will be like the diamond, and all this will be like the crown, in which the diamond is set.

He told me that the one big problem, at that moment, was the owner did not want to sell that piece of land, particularly to Damanhur. They had tried for years to buy it. I queried whether this might not be the only problem. "From the moment we buy the land," he pondered, "in maybe one and a half, two years maximum, we will realize it. Because a lot of the excavation is already done, there are already those big holes, indentations in the land."

I thanked him for that fantastic information about the future building plans, but asked if the more than 90 per cent of the big project that needs to be done is going to be a little harder than that?

"Naturally, it is a challenge," he said. "It is something that is considerably more stimulating." I asked him if he was happy with the way things were going. "Hmm," he pondered. "So-so. We are spending too much on the legal matters. These are not useful." At that very moment we passed the point at which the conference centre would be built. Falco stopped the car and wound down the window:

> This is the place where the centre will begin. The little train will go under the Sacred Wood to reach the temple. A person will go visit the temple and when they think that they have seen it all, they will be shocked, because they will find themselves on a train arriving somewhere that is twenty times bigger.

His smile was immense. Part of the plan was not to just have visitors coming to this new place. There were loftier ambitions. "The visits are our way of trying to teach that all small groups can create big things. A sort of stimulation, to think, if they made it why cannot we?"

That was then, this is now. I was taken to the Buche on a recent visit and it was quite an adventure. The way to it was up a long, rugged path, among really uninspiring surroundings. Further up the rough path, more desolate landscape and then through a heavy iron gate. We had entered into a tunnel that led to a huge cave, open to the elements on one of its sides. This was an enormous space into which there was to be set the ultimate project.

In Damanhur, the creation of sacred space is at the core of the community's experience. Damanhur is known mostly because of its Temples of Humankind. During the building, representing a high form of collective artistic expression, the community has grown, refining itself and establishing its own culture, myths and tradition. Over the years, other sacred spaces have been created, like the Sacred Wood, covering an area of approximately 3.5 square kilometres (350 hectares), with kilometres of stone spirals spread over the landscape. Now, the still embryonic Temple of Concordance with its Parliament of Peoples, dedicated to the wisdom and traditions of the indigenous peoples of the earth, is the next project. They are not to be thought of as monuments of the past, but rather an answer for the future of the world. They are sacred mirrors that amplify the inner light of every human being and reflect it from the Earth to the heavens.

The Temple of Concordance will be a place to rekindle hope for the future of humanity and the spiritual, artistic and social renaissance of our world. A place to reinforce faith in the profound ethical nature of human beings and from which to construct the path towards a future of peace. At its heart there will be the Parliament of Peoples, where indigenous leaders will be able to meet with each other, and with leaders of corresponding thought, political figures and agents of social transformation. In this way the ancient wisdom of those who never forgot the harmonious ways of Earth will not only be honoured, it will inspire policy makers and help solve some of the challenges of our future.

The complex as a whole will develop over an area of about 20,000 square metres (2 hectares). The total area of the intervention is about 9,000 square metres (97,000 square feet) for a volume of 70,000 cubic metres (2.5 million cubic feet) and a development in elevation up to 24 metres (80 feet), from the bottom of the already excavated quarry, consisting of two cavernous holes. The harmony of the natural landscape will be restored and exalted. In the spaces next to the Parliament of Peoples there will be:

- a physical and virtual museum to preserve texts, handicrafts and traditions of indigenous people
- an interactive library to gather, record and share languages, songs and traditional stories of indigenous people, as well as elements of their cultures

- a wellness centre for treatments and natural healing
- halls and spaces for seminars and studying
- a small boutique hotel
- cabins on stilts to sleep fully immersed in the canopy
- an organic restaurant to recuperate and preserve ancient recipes based on wild herbs and products of the territory

This is a complex project that requires innovative, ad-hoc architectural solutions. An immense challenge. Damanhur's associated architects have been tackling this challenge for over 15 years, many designs already seen, and they continue to evolve as new solutions and materials are developed.

The approach currently being explored is inspired by biomimicry. Biomimetic architecture seeks solutions not just by replicating natural forms, but by understanding the rules governing those forms, looking to recreate the resiliency, efficiency, utility and beauty of nature.

In this way, it will be possible not only to restore the natural environment destroyed by decades of quarrying, but also to create a completely sustainable structure, comfortable for humans and non-disruptive for the birds and the animals of the area. Part of the existing rock walls will be left untouched to create a special acoustic and energetic effect.

On a later visit, I was taken to a geodesic structure. I thought of Buckminster Fuller, the inventor of the geodesic dome and another of my inspirations. We went inside, and I was amazed to find a large spiral, made like similar spirals of laid-out stones, but on this one a large crystal had been positioned on each of the stones. In many traditions, such crystals are an instrument of contact with the energies of our planet. Indigenous peoples consider them as powerful tools for evolution and healing.

The Crystal Spiral was the opening salvo in this major creative undertaking to completely revolutionize the work of Damanhur. Piovra and Astore Baobab were commissioned to collect stones and crystals and begin to prepare the spiral, not saying anything to anyone. This was a method Falco frequently employed at the beginning of a project. The crystals were collected from initiates in many parts of the world. I can vouch for this, as I was in Damanhur when a crystal was brought from the newly established Damanhur centre in Australia. The crystals would then be prepared in the temples for more than a year, before being positioned in the spiral. Then they were connected to the stones holding them.

The Crystal Spiral is a place for collecting and amplifying this magical type of knowledge. Waiting for the Parliament of Peoples to be built, this special space is now dedicated to welcoming ceremonies of shamans from all over the world. In this way, Damanhur helps them affirm their existence and give strength to the values of their people. The orderly atomic structure of the crystals works like collectors and reservoirs of memories, in which the shamans can "deposit" a copy of their own knowledge, so that it can be preserved.

A group was formed to make arrangements for the indigenous people visits, including Esperide Ananas and Shama Viola. Some indigenous people are invited here, some come of their own accord. Visitors include people from the Hopi tribe and people representing a number of indigenous North American tribes, and shamanic people from Norway, Greenland, Hungary, Tuvan throat singers, people from the Basque country. Shama Viola and other Damanhurians recently made a pilgrimage to Australia, to meet with aboriginal people and make connections with their culture.

Representatives of these peoples come, walk the Crystal Spiral and, as they come out, focus on a particular crystal and unload their spiritual energies into that crystal. They often act out their own rituals and thus make contact with the many aspects of Damanhurian life as a shared experience. Some bring crystals with them. They are each encouraged to connect to particular crystals in the spiral and invest it with some of their own particular magic, a process of magical transformation on a global basis.

A typical visit to Damanhur these days, from a representative of indigenous people, was that made by Robert A Vars Gaup, shaman of the Sami people, who came to Damanhur to share his wisdom and transmit it through the synchronic lines, the great rivers of the energy of the world. The Sami are an indigenous population of about 75,000 people located in the northern part of Fennoscandia, extending from the Kola Peninsula to central Norway, including the northernmost regions of Finland and Sweden.

At Damanhur, with his traditional dress and ritual drum, the Sami shaman celebrated contact with the spiritual forces connected to his people, which was amplified and received in the spirals of the Sacred Wood temple. He lit a sacred fire and called his ancestors, the spirits connected with them and the forces of the north wind. After the ceremony, a falcon, which was the shaman's totem animal, hovered low in the sky, flying in circles around him and the group of Damanhurians who were there gathered near.

The falcon was giving a clear salutation before flying off towards the temples. The crystal that Vars Gaup brought with him was left in the spiral as a testimonial, perfectly integrated with one of the crystals already present, as if it had been waiting for the arrival of the Sami crystal for some time. The shaman was gifted a scarf that was handwoven in Damanhur, as an expression of the bond that unites their peoples in a living network of connection, orienting all of humanity towards respect for life and planet Earth, of which indigenous peoples have always been the caretakers.

When asked about his impressions of this visit, Vars Gaup said that he was impressed by the people, the beauty of the temples, and the mission they are enacting. He encouraged them to continue protecting the value of the diversity of the peoples, because this could be of great importance for the whole world.

The emotions that remain with the Damanhurians after having welcomed the representatives of various indigenous peoples from the world are hope, joy and the certainty that the magic of this profound sharing can germinate the seed of a new era. The human race is losing ever more diversity, and with it, the linking to an original spiritual matrix. Indigenous peoples have kept the lineage of their wisdom alive. Without them, it will be most difficult to bring humanity back on a path of sustainability and respect for all of life. The shamans of the indigenous peoples are now the spiritual mothers and fathers of all humanity. Inspired by their example, Damanhur aims to create an active network to orient humanity this way.

Other recent indigenous visitors have been:

- Venerable Abuela Nah Kin, who shared the exciting Mayan tradition with the community and offered meditations and a *despacho* ceremony and, in order to create an even stronger connection, planted seeds in Damanhur's soil
- Marza Millar, the last Grandmother of the Wind Creek Yavapai Tribe of Sedona to carry the medicine of the Emergence Door for the 4th Cycle of the Sun for the Yavapai People and to bridge the 5th Cycle of the Sun, and she was given permission and instructions by her elders to share the prophecies and healing techniques of the 5th Sun Cycle with the people of Damanhur
- Tibetan-Chinese shaman Yuan Miao, a singer, dancer, artist and author, she does not consider herself as a spiritual teacher but rather a transmitter of joy, sharing the wisdom of the Tibetan Nyingma Dakini lineage to work in harmony for the benefit of humankind, offering an inspired mantra singing workshop with the community

Obviously, such visits are financially problematical to organize, often people have to persuade them to come to Damanhur when they are already coming to Europe. One visitor with important indigenous connections was Dr Will Taegel, professor and writer, former dean of Wisdom University, and founder of the nature-based spirituality group Earthtribe. He weds his Native American background and traditional training in shamanic circles with his 30-year practice of psychotherapy. He balances his academic interest in evolution and trauma with the spiritual practice of rainwater collection, solar and wind energy, and environmental restoration. He reported:

> For me Damanhur is a remarkable flaring forth of creative genius. I have visited the prominent art museums of the world, and I thought I was familiar with the transformative power of art, and I thought I knew something of the impact of creative expression. And I did know. Still, my various times in the Temples of Humankind took me to an entirely different level of human possibility. The creators of the Damanurian works of art are from our generation. Every generation has to create its own narrative. If such a narrative were a book for our generation, the Temples of Humankind would be the cover.

The first seeds have been sown of the next big developments at Damanhur, the opening out of the community to the rest of the world and major advances in constructing the next 90 per cent of the temple complex.

The Parliament of Peoples is a new space, at the heart of the Temple of Concordance. It will be the meeting point between the wisdom of the past and the first steps of a new, harmonious future. With such actions and choices, the community are getting more and more confident that they can make that future come true.

The basis of Damanhur's philosophy is the understanding that everything physical, as well as spiritual, is organized as an interconnected ecosystem. After creating a temple dedicated to a new, harmonious relationship between humans and transcendental forces, the time seems right to build a space for preserving, sharing and amplifying all the voices of wisdom of our planet.

The Parliament of Peoples, once completed, will be the ultimate setting for extended meetings and ceremonies with indigenous and other spiritual people from all parts of the planet. The plans are ready, the funds are being raised, the dream is being realized. This will be the most monumental achievement of Damanhur. There are ways you can help (see Appendix 2 on the Damanhur Foundation) and there is already a prodigious effort underway.

CHAPTER 4

THE DAMANHUR
WAY OF LIFE

We live in a historical period in which we consume a lot, and we reveal next to nothing about our capacity to think, which is what distinguishes humans from other creatures on the planet. We live from our memories, often incomplete and inaccurate ones, unconnected with one another according to a logical thread of events that happen over time.

Damanhur does not exist in isolation. It is a remarkable example of an alternate social living experiment that has co-existed within an established local, national and international system for many years. Damanhur exists during the start of the human adventure in the Anthropocene era, which is the first era in which humankind has had such a significant impact on the planet. We all need to have an obligation to ensure this impact is not too disastrous. Without doubt, this is one of Damanhur's aims, but it has not always been easy, and they have not always been helped.

When I first went to Damanhur, around 1997, I met with the press officer at the time, Coboldo Melo. He showed me the filing cabinets full of antagonistic press cuttings, with headlines that screamed powerful invective comments about Damanhur and Oberto Airaudi. For example, the hard-line Cardinal Saldarini was sent from the Vatican to sort out the Turin region, which was thought to have become a resting-place for many groups with Satanic leanings, and *Il Giornale* on 16 February 1991 ran a story based on his utterances that read:

Adultery, fornication, impurity, libertinism, idolatry, enmity, discord, enviousness, jealousy, drunkenness, orgies, witchcraft, sects, sex and gurus – these are the new magical and esoteric movements, communities put up by the ruthless Santoni (Big

43

Saints), all dedicated to orgiastic rituals and free love. In Italy there are about 600 such groups, about 30 in and around Turin... And the most populated in Italy is right on the hills of Valchiusella, next to Baldissero Canavese, and it is called Damanhur. There live 500 people, who are together day and night, around a temple in the style of ancient Egypt, and they hang on the words of a self-declared prophet, Oberto Airaudi.

I was in this beautiful place among the most gentle and lovely people, and this was so off-the-wall, it appeared absurd and ridiculous. More so, after 20 years of reflection. Yet this was the sort of article that filled the press-cutting files. "It was an orchestrated campaign against us," said Coboldo. Things have changed a lot since then. Stories about Damanhur are now more likely to appear in glossy magazines and be about the New Age credentials of the community and their exceptional environmental work.

Coboldo is more philosophical now and has a fondness for likening Damanhurian politics to those of ancient Greece. I can heartily recommend that anyone seeking a deeper understanding of the Damanhur way of life, get hold of a copy of Coboldo's book, *Secrets of the Damanhur Political System* (Devodama, Vidracco, 2017), a concise and accessible way into the complex social structures of the community.

Pursuing his Greek theme, Coboldo declared, "Centuries ago, the Greeks, speaking about permanence, tried with only modest results to create a new society, even if now their model of democracy continues to be the source of inspiration world-wide." They placed great importance on the agora, a central public space in ancient Greek city-states, similar in concept to the Roman forum. The literal meaning of the agora is "gathering place" or "assembly". The agora was the centre of the athletic, artistic, spiritual and political life in the city

The Greeks eventually got tired of the agora, of meetings in public spaces for political debate, and decided to elect a tyrant, put a single person in command, saving the citizens from interminable discussions and political decision-making. The cradle of democracy became an autocratic state. Coboldo thinks the analogy is an important one for Damanhur. He elucidated:

A curious fact, speaking about permanence, is that in our 44th year of life, we Damanhurians are halfway there, even though we began our journey from an opposite side, with a centralized government, to arrive at the equivalent of the Greek agora, or, better said, participatory democracy.

Some say that Roman philosophical thinking was a refined version of earlier Greek thinkers. In the years when Republican Rome's embassies and armies were dealing with Greek states, which enjoyed a genuine independence, Roman minds were not as closed to Greek ideas as they tended to be later. Philosophy was an object of interest to men of material well-being, which led in the early years of the second century to an increasing suspicion of issues like philosophy among those men of wealth who belonged to the Senate.

In other times, Galileo, Roger Bacon and Giordano Bruno, among many others, all fell afoul of the church authorities, all had their thinking declared to be heretical, and they were all persecuted for their beliefs. In modern times, several scientists have had their work condemned, implying a sort of heresy, by the scientific establishment and its associated academics.

The constitution of Damanhur is the foundation of the social aspects and has always acted as a reference point for approving laws that govern community life.

So, what sort of life do the people of Damanhur have? The idea of constitution began with the three bodies of Damanhur: the School of Meditation, the Social, and the Game of Life. To these was added Tecnarcato, thus creating the Four Pillars of Damanhur life, which have been outlined as such:

The School of Meditation – now known as **Medit-Action** – is a ritual tradition, a spiritual research pathway that is based on sharing and self-transformation, with an intention to awaken the divine aspects within each human being through the creative power of positive thinking. Medit-Action teaches those involved to not delegate their personal spiritual evolution to someone outside of themselves and meditation is seen as a way of daily life, a pathway in which the school can last a lifetime if one so wishes.

Social refers to social theory and social realization. Like all social groups, a degree of organization is necessary in order for groups to function. At Damanhur citizens choose where and with whom they want to live, according to their preferences and needs. Living together involves many moments of sharing and joy. Humour and the capacity to communicate deeply and to play together are fundamental ingredients in community life. Children live with their parents, yet every citizen feels responsibility for their well-being and has a hand in both their care and economic support. Elderly people also live in the nucleo families. Taking care of the elders is an important part of the Damanhur social system. Community life is structured, yet flexible, not subjected to an overriding dogma.

The Game of Life is about experimentation and dynamics, life as a game. The Game of Life represents the value of change, creativity and a sense of humour, all of which are an integral part of the personal and community life at Damanhur. Through the Game of Life, a foundation was laid so that the community would function by being flexible and maintaining the capacity to welcome new ways of thinking, in order to continue evolving and integrating new citizens.

Tecnarcato is about individual inner refinement. In Damanhur, a union between a person and involvement in community life, on an ideal and a practical level, is important. The individual is fundamental and is the prime valued element of each collective group. Each individual strives to make the lives of others richer and more colourful, and vice versa. Tecnarcato is a collection of techniques and tools that favours and encourages individual renewal through the use of a strategy. Falco coined a definition of Damanhur that may seem paradoxical, but only on the surface: "We are a community of individualists."

Every person formulates the principles and rubric of their own transformation and, every three months, they devise a personal programme of practical objectives and ethical values. Living in a communal way, individuals naturally receive advice and observations from others, yet they personally assess to what extent any such advice should be taken into account. In order to not be isolated in this process, everyone chooses a person with whom to dialogue, a "mirror" in which they might see their reflections more clearly.

Falco was invariably philosophical about the future. He anticipated a time of great energy and abundant change for Damanhur, a mushrooming of ideas and projects that would require the alertness of everyone and considerable attention to accomplish. "It is as if we came out of a little stream and are now in a boat on a large river," he told me. There was a silence at the end of the sentence that I sort of knew was meaningful. He was in a reflective mood: "People sometimes get used to their initiation, and they forget why they are Damanhurians, the reason why they are here." He pointed out that he was speaking of a minority and possibly putting too high a premium on it but wanted to make it clear that people should always have clearly in mind what their aims were, especially their spiritual aims. Falco had a vivid clarity, of course, about this process and what it meant in future terms:

> Being part of the Tecnarcato process entails a series of daily disciplines to ensure a high degree of personal organization, communication, introspection, care for others, reciprocal trust, active participation in the life of Damanhur.

A vital tool in this process was the idea of an "individual law", a personal rule that allowed people to decide for themselves, always with the verification from a chosen "mirror". With this help, attention could be paid to an individual's own character, so that it is not an obstacle to self-development but rather a positive stimulus towards individual goals. Falco was adamant:

> The initiated, who want to be magicians, in preparation and continuous training to extend their knowledge, can easily forget to be who they most want to be. And if they do forget, they are no longer anything, are not who they would like to become, because they don't know, they don't remember. What is important is being able to give meaning and transferring the added value from one position to another. Maybe this is one of the main reasons for our existence, to be able to transfer added value. Nothing more, nothing less.

This Tecnarcato notion was swimming round my mind. I remembered being at Damanhur when it was all new, barely spoken of, but now it is a lynchpin of the community's future. It connects directly with the idea of the superindividual, the seeds of which were sown long ago. I also remembered something that Gorilla Eucalipto had once said to me, about the union of people having to be deep and so close that it became like one individual. "At that point," he had said, "each person will be a community." Such closeness, such understanding characterizes much of the cooperative activity I have experienced among Damanhurians. He reflected further:

> Damanhur at this time is undergoing a further fundamental shift. Previously Damanhur has been rooted in the three bodies: School

of Meditation (now Medit-Action), Social, and Game of Life. Then we added a fourth body, Tecnarcato, a fast parallel path for personal evolution. We are engaged in a significant period of transformation. Damanhur's complexity in these last few years has increased tremendously. New doors are being opened in every part of our life. The Tecnarcato has opened the door towards the spiritual path of finding one's inner god.

If you are not familiar with the inner procedures of Damanhur, you may now be wondering how come I am conversing with a man named Gorilla. Safe to say, Damanhur is not the only place on Earth where people are named after personal or geographical characteristics. In Viking sagas, alive and pertinent in Shetland, where I live and where we celebrate the end of winter with the 24-hour Viking Fire Festival, people were given names that were based on personal or physical characteristics, such as Ivar the Boneless, Sigurd Snake-in-the-Eye, or King Olaf the Stout, and Icelandic Gunnlaug Ormstunga, meaning Adder Tongue. Native Americans, like Chief Black Hawk, Billy Bowlegs, or Sitting Bull, are often given names that reflect characteristics. Snooker players have for years been given an "action name" that emphasizes their playing prowess, Barry "The Hawk" Hawkins, Alex "Hurricane" Higgins, Ronnie "The Rocket" O'Sullivan. Adopting a characteristic name, even an animal name, is not as crazy as it might sound. Even the business world has its animal links with their bear markets, dragon bonds, fat cats, cash cows and so on.

Let me make it clear, however, the adoption of an active nickname by a snooker player is not at all the same as the carefully and philosophically worked out name choice of a Damanhurian individual. Though both may have a distinct air of humour about them. A name is a precious thing. Think for example how long it takes new parents to agree on a name for their offspring. Surnames often have a long-standing significance, though precise details of these may be faded and lost in the sands of time.

At Damanhur, they have a unique way of renaming, which is at the same time a reawakening. They have established a naming tradition and make the decision to assume a new name at some relevant point after becoming citizens. Taking on a new name is a tradition that occurs in many spiritual schools around the world. At Damanhur, citizens choose their own names, and with this act they define a new phase of their lives, a kind of rebirth.

Animal names are chosen to establish a connection with nature, specifically with another living species with which they can easily identify. They do say that it is fun to have an animal name. As an alternative to an animal name, citizens may choose the name of a nature spirit or mythical animal, such as the kraken, the hippogriff, or the centaur. It is said that in order to do things seriously, there is no need to take themselves too seriously. The philosophy of the Game of Life is invariably evident in such matters.

A few years after taking an animal name, each Damanhurian may also take the name of a plant, with the same kind of significance of renewing oneself, connecting oneself to nature. Everyone chooses his or her own name, and then the process is formalized by other citizens during community meetings. It may be possible that the assembly recognizes a more suitable name than the one requested; in these cases, the person can accept the name that is proposed or postpone the acquisition of the new name to another time.

Curiously, I had wondered why, for most of the time I had been visiting the community, the man who was its inspirational figurehead was known as Oberto Airaudi, the only long-standing Damanhurian not to have an animal name. It was only in the latter years he adopted the name Falco. I recently asked, at a meeting with Piovra Caffè and Anaconda Papaya, why it had taken so long. Piovra told me what he had said, that before an animal name can be taken, a person has to have an awareness of a connection with the animal and its spiritual characteristics. He set perhaps a higher threshold for himself than for others.

Anaconda shared a personal anecdote. Around 15 years ago, he had gone to Falco and asked for his plant name to be Tarassaco, which means dandelion, the symbolic flower of Damanhur. Falco thought for a while and then whispered in his ear, in a most humble, apologetic and reticent way, that he had really wanted that name for himself one day. Anaconda told us that he had not revealed that story to anyone previously. Piovra said that she knew that if anyone had asked Falco the question, he would have chosen that name. So, one year after his death, during a public meeting, Damanhurians chose to give Falco the name of Tarassaco. His name now is, therefore, Falco Tarassaco.

In the new scheme of things, people are beginning to get a third name. These are mineral names and Piovra told me that this is not connected with any level a person reaches, but with the great leap forward that the community is making. In time, everyone would have this third mineral name to acknowledge the advancements the whole community has made. However, Falco had left word that, in order to keep people incentivized, mineral names could be given in respect of individual goals reached but linked to the major objective.

Given the knowledge and information on these matters of animal and other Damanhurian names, it appears perfectly logical, and provides a situation where one can feel quite comfortable talking to Gorilla, Octopus, Ant or Warthog. After a while, it becomes second nature.

Other aspects of life at Damanhur are often the subject of questions from people outside. What of such aspects as marriage, birth and death? How are these regarded at Damanhur? Marriage works on a renewal basis, for a period of so many years before renewal. Conception is timed for auspicious birthdays of children. Death is a part of life and it touches everyone in one form or another.

At Damanhur, marriage revives the spiritual significance of walking a path together as unique souls on a shared journey of awakening. It takes into account that life changes over time and highlights the importance of free will and choice in initiating and moving forward in a relationship.

There are some unique aspects to Damanhurian marriage:

Matrimonio a rinnovo, marriage that is renewed after a specific period of time. Damanhurian "civil" marriage is chosen on this renewal basis, beginning with a period of one year. This means when someone marries a partner, a letter of love is written to acknowledge how the couple value each other and to define their intentions of shared spiritual growth and practical goals for the coming year. They specify things they wish to change in themselves through the mirror of the marriage. Then it is formalized in a ritual officiated by a monk-priest, male or female, celebrating the moment with community and family.

At the time of renewal, they evaluate the path they have travelled together as spouses, renew their marriage for another year, affirming previous intentions and launching new ones, to continue this pathway of inner refinement, or bringing the experience to a close. The intention is for relationships to grow and last, to overcome habits that can weaken them.

Matrimonio esoterico, esoteric marriage – this kind of marriage is a different kind of union than the civil Damanhurian marriage, and it is also a commitment that is periodically renewed in time. Esoteric marriage signifies soul union, moving together through the passions, joys and trials of life as a single spiritual being, even sharing each other's karma. Entering into an esoteric marriage affirms the intention of returning to a state of primordial spiritual androgyny through union of feminine and masculine principles, as we have these dual energies and qualities within all of us.

It's a choice of living in two as one, with masculine and feminine aspects integrated together. This is why Damanhurian marriages are renewable, not because it's something to take lightly and casually, but because a relationship may last a lifetime, or may be one of several phases on a pathway towards spiritual completion.

Birthing is a challenging process that can take a woman out of her physical and psychological balance. The capacity to hold her in this condition, and be her "social-spiritual uterus", is a valuable skill that communities can develop.

Capra Carruba has given birth to two children at Damanhur. I sat with her after dinner one evening as she nursed one of her young children. The abundant, powerful love between mother and child was self-evident. Earlier, at a time between the births of her two children, she had been interviewed by people from the Global Eco-village Network. She said:

My daughter was born seven years ago in our communal living room. We were six mothers pregnant at the same time, a small community of "bellies" within the larger community of Damanhur. In spite of our initial aspiration of home birth within our various core families, everyone had a very unique story. Two gave birth in the nearby hospital, one of which was a Caesarean, the other four at home. All of us were assisted by our two midwives throughout the process, starting before conception, throughout pregnancy, birth, and the first months afterwards. In the last months, they had been continuously present in our process of transformation, in spiritual and physical terms.

Midwives are part of the community and also work in the local health system, creating a continuity of safety as well as sacrality, that state or quality of being sacred, in any situation that may develop. Their preparation towards conception contains practical aspects as practised by good midwives anywhere, as well as more spiritual activities, including choosing the godparents and the child's name. There is also an important social dimension, with the education of children being a common endeavour, not only in economic terms, but also on a practical day-to-day basis. The decisions around parenthood are personal, but immediately afterwards the community is involved, taking an active role in raising the child. The process has a common thread of finding well-being, constant re-balancing and identifying the needs and desires around the birth of a child. Capra recalled her own experience of giving birth:

> Some of us preferred a more intimate surrounding in their bedroom. My experience was a rather tribal ritual, exactly as I had hoped for, a group awaiting the new baby in an atmosphere of joy, expectation, and celebration. We were dancing and some wild women friends joined me in shouting out during contractions. Drumming accompanied the entire night. While I slowly entered the state of the "birthing trance", I was aware of the energy field and concentration of my family around me, which carried me through the difficult parts of my journey. After six hours – and three days of "false" contractions – my daughter was born in our living room. I was standing, supported by the godfather and father of baby Zela, who was caught by one of the midwives.

Capra believes that the story of giving birth within a community cannot be separated from the next big chapter of education, when babies, at the age of six or seven months, enter a "community cradle". Initially for a few hours, soon for the entire day, the children enter a little "community womb" of their own, while mothers return to be more present in their social roles.

The involvement of the midwives continues, who mediate in this transition, sharing characteristics and individual needs of every baby with the caretakers in the kindergarten. In Damanhur, there is a family school from six months to fourteen years. The birthing approach in community, with over-arching spiritual aspects, takes place in various stages for the children, be it developing phases in the first years towards independence, or the initiation rite at seven or eight years, called "test of courage". Capra added: "But this is maybe another story."

For me, it was indeed another story, one that took place on the next day, when I had the special privilege of sharing the experience of a young boy, named Morgan, eight years of age and on his "rite of passage" challenge. He was to embark on a quest, a personal challenge, where he would leave a point in the Sacred Wood on top of the temple mountain and find his way, alone and without assistance, through the forest, down the hill, to arrive at Damjl, behind the Open Temple. At Damjl, a group of drummers, percussionists, conch-shell players, played, sang, shouted his name for 30 minutes before he arrived. I joined in, beating the drum with vim and vigour, if not in regular time. This helped guide him and spur him on in the latter stages, but also gave him a celebrity welcome when he finally arrived, safe and sound.

He was given a symbolic scroll, presented by the boy who had completed a previous similar challenge, along with a ceremonial totem stick, with many ribbons. It was a truly inspirational event, a lovely memory for young Morgan, and the huge smile on his face showed exactly what it meant to him. There was a safety backup, though he was not made aware that his challenge journey was being monitored from a distance by those who protected his back, ensuring his safety. That backup was discreet, yet present.

From the joyous event of a rite of passage to the further joys of childhood in Damanhur – the next day, I spoke to two young people who had grown up through the Damanhur education system. Gau Erba and Nefje, young women now in their twenties, had been born in Damanhur, were educated there, had been to state high school and university, and were now back living in Damanhur. We talked about the importance of education. No civilization or culture can exist without education. The Damanhur vision of a school places the child at the centre of the educational process; Gau and Nefje confirmed that was the case.

I asked the girls what it was like growing up in a community like this. Gau told me that, for her, it was a very good experience, to be surrounded by so many people and not just to have two parents, but an extended family within the nucleo, to grow up with a generation of children who, in many ways, are like brothers and sisters. Some grow up and go out of the community, but for Gau there were strong feelings of being part of a community.

Nefje agreed with Gau. There were so many opportunities to be with and share experiences with a group of other young people in Damanhur. "We travelled a lot," she said, "We went abroad and travelled a lot." On one of my earlier visits, I recalled a day on a Greenpeace boat. "Yes, we had a lot of interaction with Greenpeace," said Gau. "Projects, help with developing petitions, assisting with the running of the boat." For her, education was about engagement with the community and with other places in the world, a most important aspect of school life. Not simply reading about things and places but making visits and sharing experiences. "Study travel," she remarked, "Go someplace and then make some projects."

The girls had been on projects in South America, a cultural sharing, where they planted trees and helped with forestry. Children from the school now travel from the age of two or three years, and they start to learn not to be just with parents, but with other children, other adults. They start with interesting places in the mountains. When they are older, they have the opportunity to travel further, go abroad. It would be nice if there were more of this but sometimes there are money problems and so on that prevent more of such projects. There are Damanhur centres in a wide range of countries around the globe, all ready to help with such visits.

I remembered an exchange from many years ago, between young people from Damanhur and young people from Essex. Anaconda and I arranged it. It was an excellent experience for everyone involved. The Essex young people stayed in nucleos and the Damanhur people stayed with the families of the Essex young people, as well as some shared time in a large education residential centre in rural Essex. Gau recalled something more local, staying in the log cabins in the Sacred Wood. "I really liked that. We had to cook, look after ourselves, and learn to work together as a group. They said it was an experience we would remember all our lives." Nefje thought that was right. "You do remember things all your life."

To comply with Italian education authorities, the pupils take part in regular examinations and spend the last years of their schooling, after the age of 14, in a mainstream school. I asked the girls what this transition was it like. Nefje considered it strange for her, at first. At Damanhur they had been taught in small groups and those at the Italian schools were larger, so there was not so much interaction with the teachers:

But it was interesting to compare what life was like in the more "normal" situation. Very strange at first. I was a little shy and, until I made some friends, I was a little isolated. But then, things got better. I invited some of my school friends to Damanhur and they liked it very much.

Gau thought that there was always misunderstanding about Damanhur, a little prejudice, but more from parents than from the children. However, for the girls, it had not been a big problem. Things had changed over the past few years, Damanhur was better known, locally and nationally. Consequently, there was not so much prejudice. They both felt they had been academically well prepared at Damanhur for their further education, and they were able to thrive in the state system.

The Damanhur family school first opened in 1985, originally only with kindergarten and then elementary. Many community parents were active in setting up the school and its educational principles. Later, the family school extended up to middle school. A curriculum was adopted that aligned with all the programs of the Italian educational ministry. At public schools in the area of Turin, there were annual educational verifications and final exams for the students and the Damanhur schools reflected this.

Beyond the standard Italian curriculum, there was an abundance of activities that gave space for self-expression, from having contact with nature to practical experimentation in many fields – for example, in the arts and ecology. Children often worked together in classes with different age groups. This fostered skills and provided mutual support. Each group had an educator as a reference person who collaborated with all the other teachers. For Gau and Nefje, who are now both qualified as doctors, the Damanhur school policy had served them well.

I learned about a recent initiative, where a group of young people who were born and grew up in Damanhur were now running a series of education courses for young people. Capra, who is one of the parents of younger children, had encouraged the young people to set up these courses and had insisted they did it completely by their own design and delivery. The first of these courses had been, perhaps ambitiously, about sex education.

I spoke to Ariel, a confident young person currently studying education at university, and one of the course organizers. He told me that he thought the sex education course was very important:

In some schools, outside of Damanhur, if you go to a school that teaches sex education, you are likely to get more information from the other children than you do from the teacher, from the playground talk. So, we did this five-day course, one day a week for five weeks. We had a concept of starting with practical things and then we moved to the theoretical elements. For example, we started with a session about relationships. Very important. We started by having them dancing, freely. Then we asked them to dance in couples and next we gave them a pencil and they had to dance with each of them holding the pencil, not letting it go. We then gave them a football and they had to do the same thing. We finished the practical and discussed what had happened. We explained that when they danced freely, they were single, but when you are in a relationship it is normally with two people. The pencil and the ball represented the relationship. If they held on to these objects too tightly, it restricted them, if they held it too loosely, the object fell, like a relationship.

They organized more courses teaching children and they asked other people of Damanhur, those who had a specific expertise, if they would input some elements into the courses, but they had to do so according to the young people's own methodology, by doing the practical first and then following up by relating it to the theoretical. The courses were on physical education, drug addiction, a second sexual education course, identity, multi-ethnic and multi-cultural, mixed religions from different cultures, a course about Damanhur, and a practical course about making things with their hands. The Damanhur school gave them two hours a week to teach the children. "That was a big thing for us," said Ariel. They also organized an away journey for the children, fully organized and staffed by themselves, but they needed one adult, to drive the minibus. Ariel was so enthusiastic about this:

The overall theme of the trip was "identity". We found the younger ones had a quite lot of insecurities. We visited other eco-communities and met with their children, doing all sorts of activities together. We did team-building exercises and workshops. We even had a water-pistol battle, where the object was to "win" the other teams' flags.

I later spoke to three of the girls who had been on the journey, Irena Gaia, aged 12, Eva Luna, aged 12, and Zela, who was Capra's daughter, aged 11. The girls were brimming with excitement and impressed me in the way they told me about the adventure, told me in their limited English that put my total lack of Italian to shame. They had chosen to do this, rather than speak through an interpreter, and that was indeed part of the learning process.

Zela did most of the talking, I guess because she knew more English, but the other girls chipped in with excited bursts of enthusiasm. They said they had really enjoyed the devised water-pistol battle, and when I provocatively questioned the educational value of such mock fighting, they were very clear about the group processes involved, about coming together as a unit in their own teams, and how they had to make their own group flags, their symbol of group togetherness and the target for the others to take. When one team had all the others' flags, they were the "winners". Yes, the girls were abundantly clear about the educational values.

The other striking thing they said was that they much preferred the educational courses that were organized by the young people than the more formal education of the school. And that, in spite of the creative liberal education of the Damanhur school. The striking thing about most Damanhurian children and young people is their confidence in themselves, their boundless enthusiasm, and their bright-eyed approach to life. This is a community that breeds such an uplifting creative life.

Irena Gaia told me: "We made lots of friends among the other groups, we'll keep in touch." Zela showed me a fabulous book of quotes they had made, and Eva Luna said how much personal confidence she had gained.

Ariel said that the group of young educators were well pleased with their efforts and that they had learned a lot in practical and theoretical terms. They may have flagged up something very important to the future of Damanhur, the idea of identity. In all the upheaval of going through a process of opening up to the world, the work of Damanhur in developing the concept of the superindividual,

there was another thought to consider – maybe, just maybe, it was important to focus in and dwell on the idea of identity.

Elderly people are not neglected and there are not the same concerns about social care that exist in many parts of Europe. The elderly of the Damanhur community reside in settings suitable to their specific needs, so they mostly stay in the nucleo families with everyone else. Like the children, they become part of an extended family support system that ensures their safety and well-being.

And so to what happens at the end of life, to the more serious time when we "shake off this mortal coil". Death can be scary, fascinating or fretful and it calls forth some of our deepest emotions and soul questioning. I've heard it said at Damanhur that death is a moment of contact between our dimension and the beyond. When people think about their own death or the death of a loved one, they are often overcome by fear or a sense of helplessness and loss. Establishing a connection with the realm of the beyond can help give understanding, creating a peaceful relationship with this important passage, rather than fearing it.

I had a very dear friend at Damanhur many, many years ago. She was also called Gau, like the young woman I had interviewed previously, and she was one of the most serene and placid people I have ever met. An elderly lady with a calming radiance and a beatific smile, Gau was one of the original founders of Damanhur, one of the first group of pioneers who established the community. She spoke no English and my grasp of Italian was less than minimal. Yet we established ways to communicate instinctively, almost like telepathy. There was much smiling involved. When she passed away, at a ripe old age, I was heartbroken, as if there was a big, empty hole in my soul. I was pleased to discover on a later visit that her ashes had a dedicated space, inside the Temples of Humankind, with a stained-glass portrait of her behind. I was also delighted to find that Falco's ashes were also in a dedicated space inside the temple, together with a striking stained-glass portrait.

The community have a group of people who specialize in caring for those who are dying and those who have passed away. This function is not unique and has been an important and honourable function in many ancient civilizations and among indigenous peoples. They help the people to prepare the passage to the other side and guide them through the process. The ancient Egyptians are fabled for revering the passage from this life to the next world and the Tibetans had their renowned *Book of the Dead* to guide them. Recent archaeological researches, in places like Stonehenge and the Tombs of the Eagles site on Orkney, have shown that they were probably places of celebration and procession dedicated to the dead, associated with rituals of burial.

Between spirit and matter, we find highly original features, such as the game of "Damanhurian Risk", known for its fun and useful nature capable of developing multiple levels of logic, as well as possible proposals for an alternative economy destined for a more expansive territory. Not just a game where the risk of any interaction between nations is examined, in this version there is an intergalactic dimension. There is an ongoing game that has been played every Thursday evening for the last 30 years or more, usually with around 20 players, always accompanied by a pizza supper.

Great changes are taking place at Damanhur during these times and some of the impressions formed on previous visits required revision and rethinking. I went to see Caimano Salice, who I have known since my earliest times visiting Damanhur, a man who knows almost everything you need to know about the community. "New book…?" he said, a big smile on his face. "Magic book," I replied. We shared that moment. "Now, tell me, the main community structure, when I came here years ago, was the nucleo. Is that still the same or changed?"

He told me that the favoured social structure is still the nucleo, because the human way is the modality of living together, but it is not the only way. The Vajne citizenship has opened up different ways of social living, not all based on the extended family. For Caimano though, being together in a community means living together and having things that you share. "This is a social and spiritual experience," he added.

The nucleo has nearly always been the living choice for members of the community. There are large houses, many and varied beautiful houses, and a number of people, usually around ten or 20, live together and share the house as their home. Each individual or couple has their own living space, for much needed personal relaxation time, and the rest of the facilities of the house are shared, with meeting and social areas, communal dining areas and kitchens.

Couples, or couples with children, singles, youth and the elderly live in the same dwelling to allow for the exchange of experiences among various age groups. Each Damanhur citizen chooses where and with whom they want to live, according to their preferences and goals, and the possibilities offered by the community houses. Children live with their parents, yet every citizen feels a responsibility for their nurturing and has a hand in both their care and economic support. The elderly people of the community mainly live in nucleos that are suitable to their specific needs, and they are particularly cared for as if they were a member of a family, which in a profound way they are.

"Politically and socially," explained Caimano, "the nucleo can organize itself in broader terms as a region or territory, a process that has gone through cycles in Damanhur. Now, we have nucleos that are part of

a bigger region." They have common identities and objectives that
nucleo communities share and because in administrative terms there
is a connection between the nucleos. "This social structure gives us the
possibility of having a governance on a regional level," he elaborated.
"In this, we have new job titles, but the roles are more or less the same,
'captains' or 'governors', which have a role of leading the community. The
title depends, but the role is the same. Depends on how the community
wants to name it."

The political system of Damanhur is structured year-by-year on a
foundation of shared ideals and common needs and expectations, with
relationships being the glue holding everything together. The individual
is the first instrument of change or can be a temporary weight that others
support with the best possible solidarity. Groups are important, because
they are fertile ground for debate, analysis and a constant stream of ideas.
Action is the philosophical principle, demonstrating a desire to create,
perform and evolve.

The maximum expression of participatory politics in Damanhur is
posited in various management roles. *Caponucleo* (head of household)
is the elected representative of a small nucleo, while the *Reggente*
(regent) is the head of household for a larger community nucleo; there
are the *Responsabili* (managers) for the Ways and *Capitani* (captains)
or *Governatori* (governors) for the regions that group together nucleos
with adjacent territories or similar projects. The nucleo family that lives
together in one house has been the main focal point of the Damanhurian
social life.

Then there is the governance on a higher level, which seems to have
changed over the years. Or, rather, some things have changed while others
have remained the same. "We have now adopted the term 'governance',"
Caimano told me, "which comes from the English language, to distinguish
it from the Italian word which means 'government' (*governo*)." By
governance, he explained, they mean the whole decision-making apparatus
of Damanhur and all the heads of different aspects of bodies and
organizations that are connected to the governance.

The physical departure of Falco meant they did not have his role of
spiritual guide and giver of inspiration any more. Falco had planned a
structure that would ensure the continuation of Damanhur without his
physical presence. This structure began with the nomination of two triads
of sages. The first triad of three *Saggi* (sages) was where his own functions
as muse and guarantor of core values was entrusted. They are assisted by
three other *Saggi* with analogous roles of council and support. They were

to have the responsibility of guiding the continuity and to be the general inspiration of Damanhur.

He chose the triadic system, Piovra Caffè told me, because it was the most functional and, with the nominations, they passed to a higher grade of initiation in the School of Meditation while he was still alive. The first of the triads, the sages, were Cicogna Giunco, Sirena Ninfea and Condor Girasole. In his dying moments, Falco entrusted them with this weighty responsibility, which he carried out himself until the last days. As a support to the first three sages, a second triad was chosen a couple of weeks after his death: Cormorano Sicomoro, Orango Riso and Caimano Salice.

In a message he left behind, Falco explained that he had no real desire to leave the ominous responsibility of guiding Damanhur to one person. That's why he chose a triad of people, each of whom holds one element essential to being in that role, while the element common to all is being completely Damanhur. This means having a great deal of knowledge about Damanhur, the basics and talent for the role, and experiences working directly with him, so they possess the coded data awareness to be able to decipher the necessary aspects and so be able to guide the community.

The second triad were chosen according to instructions and letters he had left. "The triadic system takes into account that they have already merged these talents into one," said Piovra, "that they are interconnected. This is a teaching we are all now trying to comprehend. We are doing our best." She pointed out that Cicogna Giunco knew more than the rest as she had more involvement with triad thinking. She asked Cicogna to explain:

At the beginning, when Falco asked each one of us if we were willing to adhere to his request, each one had to individually respond. And after the new initiations were completed, which happened in different stages, at the time when all three of us were initiated this was communicated to all of us. Even before the starting of the letters, what the role would consist of was actually guaranteeing the spiritual aims and values of Damanhur. We needed to guarantee the dream of Damanhur and not just Falco's thoughts and philosophy.

Cicogna considered this to be very important because Falco taught this principle during his life. She also confirmed that the second triad was formed in order to offer support to the first one. The sages represent the coherence of Damanhur with all its objectives and teachings. When necessary, they consult with the king guides on issues related to the general direction and management of Damanhur, and they also speak directly with citizens regarding specific situations. The *Re Guida* (king guides) had traditionally been the elected representatives of the people, subject to regular election and with responsibility for the overall administration of Damanhur. Falco had left instructions in the form of letters, but he also made "gifts" of roles and tasks to be given to different people. This structure is the turning point, which was represented in his role; today, the role he previously held can only be undertaken, in a primary or secondary way, by an administrative body that has elected representatives. Caimano added:

> We no longer have anyone with such a charismatic characteristic as Falco, who was a glue and a catalyst for change and for connections between the people. This is an obvious disadvantage, but it also opens up all sorts of opportunities, because we now have this necessity to fully cooperate with each other.

From the time of him making the nominations until the time of his passing, those chosen were dedicated to Falco's everyday needs, as it was a very tough period. The period following his passing was also strange and perhaps even tougher. Cicogna Giunco explained:

> We were filled with a sense of foreboding, even a bit of terror, because we saw the enormity of the responsibility that he had placed in us, the ensuring of the politico-magical and philosophical aspects of Damanhur. At first, we were holding lots of meetings, trying to understand and comprehend what our role was to be. Then, after the first 70 days of his passing, we started to get the letters and we understood that he had thought-through everything.

The first transformation recommended by Falco was by way of establishing the respective roles of the sages and the king guides. Previously there were two king guides and at some latter stages three, who were managing the whole of Damanhur from the social and economic points of view, as well as the financial and spiritual needs of the community.

"Phew!" said Caimano. "We came to the awareness that it was impossible to manage in this way anymore. Everything that was contained in the guiding role we have opened up and assigned to new roles." In response there was a new structure of governance implemented which had in it two king guides, responsible for all the social aspects and all the projects. Further roles assigned were: one head, at the same level as the king guides, as the head of economy; one nominated person for the head of economic development, again at the same level as the king guides; then they assigned a head of all external affairs for Damanhur in the world. "So, you see," said Caimano, "we already have five people doing the work that was previously done by two."

The king guides serve fixed terms and present a report at the end of their incumbency. They can be elected no more than six consecutive times for a total of three years. The evaluation by the voters is implicit in their re-election, even if the change can simply derive from the need to have a specific experience in the highest role in the Damanhurian governance. Caimano summarized:

> This is today's governance of Damanhur, but it is still not enough to carry out overall governance, because we want to connect with all the other aspects of Damanhur, including the College of Justice, which has almost the same body and responsibilities as before, and also connected within the governance is the role of the sages, the Game of Life and the path of Medit-Action.

All these bodies meet periodically in a summit and decide on the direction that Damanhur needs to take and refine the vision of how it will progress in the future. In the time when they are outside the summits, the heads work on the aspects of their own role and its responsibilities. "This gives a guarantee, more or less," explained Caimano, "that we can provide surety for all the bodies of the people and that all have the same idea of what it is to be a citizen of Damanhur today. This is our vision of the governance." I asked him if it was working. He replied emphatically:

> Yes. When we hold the periodic summits, we set out beforehand what we will discuss. We also prepare ourselves before the meeting. After a few days of working together, we conclude. The results of the summit are then metabolized and adjusted by each of the individual bodies and responded to via practical action. For some of the bigger decisions, and those that call for ethical transformations, this process works in a most efficient way.

I spoke with Rinoceronte Giuggiolo, the elected king guide with responsibility for the growth and development of Damanhur. I asked about the current process of governing the communities. His response:

The project of really becoming a federation is what we are doing now. This was not there last year at all. One community region has signed a pact with the central Government of Damanhur already, the other three community groups are preparing their pacts, their agreements. This means that these community groupings will become completely independent from the central administration of Damanhur. Each of them has the purpose of growing until they reach 200 or 220 people and then they will split and form another community. This is essential for the survival of Damanhur.

Falco always said that when a community becomes more than 220 people, we cannot manage in a correct "brother and sister" kind of way. In larger groups you need more bureaucracy and you lose the direct contact with your citizens. So we reach the breaking point and we really become a federation, where autonomous community groupings relate to the central government, in a similar way to the Swiss system. The central government can then concentrate and carry on the great projects of Damanhur, the temples, the new Parliament of Peoples and the Temple of Concordance.

The central administration will still help all of the citizens in the areas of health, pensions and the schools, and supporting people who have difficulties for whatever reason. The communities will be completely independent and can grow in whatever way they want. "Here is Damanhur first," said Rinoceronte, "then hopefully around the world."

All the citizens of Damanhur are now considered to be Vajne citizens and this, too, will spread to everyone in the world connected to Damanhur. The whole body of the king guides is a different body from previous. There are four now, each them with a specific task and within the group they have chosen a head of the government. "We have connected", said Rinoceronte, "with all the councils of the bodies of Damanhur, School of Meditation, Game of Life, Tecnarcato, and College of Justice, together with the new governors of the four communities. We feel that for the next few years this set up is going to work."

There is another important aspect of Damanhur, Coboldo reminded me, which is subject to frequent reflection: that the social and management roles are often entrusted to women, though this does not merely correspond to a slightly higher numerical percentage of female citizens. Gender quotas have not been thought necessary:

It seems that women are more adept at taking care of the common good, something that has manifested itself since the beginning and is confirmed year after year. At Damanhur, capable individuals do distinguish themselves from those who are all talk, and no one looks at skin colour, educational degree, personal fortune, age, gender or any questions of the type.

Damanhur has devised its own economic system, which involves the use of the Credito, a complementary currency that has been in use for over 40 years.

The objective in creating this coinage was to develop a new form of economy based on the ethical values of cooperation and solidarity. This is a return to use of money in its original sense, a means to facilitate exchange, based on an agreement between those involved.

The word "Credito" (credit) is a reminder that money is a tool through which we grant trust. This currency system raises the concept of money to a noble status. It is not considered a goal in itself, but as a functional tool for exchange between people who share ideals and values. In technical terms, the Credito is a functional account unit that, according to monetary experts visiting Damanhur in order to study the idea, is "active in a predetermined and predefined circuit". Today, the Credito has the same value as the euro. In compliance with Italian law and administrative obligations, the circulation of Credito is a system of internal exchange in Damanhur.

Upon arrival at Damanhur, it is possible for guests and friends to convert euro currency at the Welcome Office or in the designated change machines located around the main areas. Crediti that are unused may be reconverted into euros at any time. The 50 Credito silver coin, equivalent to 50 euros, was given the Bulino d'Oro 2006 award by Red Exhibitions Italy and *Graph Creative Magazine* for the creation of the exquisite design of a coin.

Damanhur now has many ambassadors who travel far and wide. Ambassadors have been described as "Damanhurians with a suitcase". These individuals share the experiences of Damanhur and teachings of Falco. They establish relationships with other holistic organizations that regularly host conferences, courses and activities related to Damanhur. They do not proselytize but engage in promoting a different vision of how humanity can live together through the creation of diverse communities and valuing the identity of diverse cultures.

Each ambassador concentrates on a specific geographic location, where they visit regularly and gradually create a network of friends. Some of the most successful initiatives that the ambassadors have organized in recent years are projects of connection with nature and trees, and the building of stone spirals all over the world. Ambassadors are currently active in several countries around the world. One of their objectives is to assist in creating Damanhur centres where there are events and activities with the participation of other Damanhurians, to offer a more complete experience and teaching in all fields.

CHAPTER 5

ENERGY FLOWS AND SPIRITUAL CHALLENGES

For a deeper historical context that had previously been beyond my ken, I went to see Coboldo again. As the governor responsible for the College of Justice and a former press officer, he had a firm grasp and clear perspective on Damanhur's origins. "It was 1979 when the inauguration of Damanhur took place," he told me, "and it took several years to clean the territory and start constructing buildings. It wasn't as if it were 1979 – boom! – it was there."

Falco started meeting, several years previously, with a group of people in the Horus Centre. It began in a small village just outside Turin but moved into the city and was situated in two different buildings at separate times. They mounted conferences, seminars, experimented, and ran courses and workshops.

There were around 100 people attending these events. Falco had the idea of forming a community, not the same as it has become now, but a holistic idea of a community. Many people followed him in researching, but when it came to the point of really doing something, some faded away and numbers decreased to around 15 people. The main group included Falco, Condor, Fenice, Canguro, Gau, Puma, Salamandra, Vongola, twelve in all, then other people came in quite soon afterwards, like Orango and Caimano, not among the first but immediately following. These were the ones who actually engaged in finding a territory suitable to base the project. From that time, also, there was the search for the synchronic lines. Members of this group travelled round the planet, celebrating solstices, researching synchronic energies.

Condor was with Falco and others on a trip to the ancient Inca site of Machu Picchu, where they travelled on an airline called Air Condor.

67

This group travelled all round the world searching for the energy points. They were also searching for the places on the planet where these energy points were most powerful because of synchronic lines crossing, a phenomenon termed a "synchronic knot" (See Plate 7). Such a synchronic energy point was situated in Tibet, but there were problems reaching it physically and politically, especially with complications regarding the Chinese.

They discovered that there was a synchronic knot in a subalpine geographical and historical area of north-west Italy, Canavese in Piedmont, with currents above and below the ground, enhancing its flow potency. They were a little disappointed to find that the place was rough, muddy and difficult to maintain, but it was acceptable in the sense that it could

actually be purchased and developed. Coboldo pointed me towards some text by Falco that laid out his interest in the topic of synchronicity:

> But looking more closely at chance events, events that happen apparently without rhyme nor reason, one can see that they recur constantly. Which brings us to the question of probability, and consequently, the theory of probability. This theory is able to predict, with inexplicable precision, the total result of processes involving a large number of individual events, each one of which on its own is unpredictable. In other words, a large number of uncertain events produce a certain event, a large number of chance events lead to a very definite result. As such, this is a paradox, yet it seems that it happens that way in practice.

In scientific circles, synchronicity is rarely the term used to describe things happening by chance. More often, the term used is "serendipity", to describe a pleasing and unexpected event that occurs by chance and often appears when searching for something else. Serendipity can be a delight when it happens in daily life and has been responsible for many innovations and important advances in science and technology. It may seem odd to refer to chance when discussing science. Scientific research supposedly operates in a methodical, precise and controlled way, with little or no room for chance in areas of investigation. In fact, chance plays an important role in science and has been responsible for some of the most significant discoveries in the past. Gnomo Orzo is one of the Damanhurian researchers into esoteric physics and told me a funny story about synchronicity:

> There's story about a Damanhurian and synchronicity. I think it was a client of Orango Riso who was using the book of synchronicity, the one with the dice in it. A divination system devised by Falco. So, this person did not like the answer the book gave him and put the book on the fire. The book was destroyed by the fire and the day after, when cleaning the ashes from the grate, he found a little piece of paper that had not burned with the phrase, "what a stupid way to use me" (laughter). So, he bought another book the day after.

According to Carl Gustav Jung, synchronicity is the simultaneous happening of two events linked by meaning, but not by causality, or a coincidence in time of two or more events that are not in a causal relationship to each other. Jung theorized that meaningful coincidences, which he termed synchronistic events, indicated a "self-existent meaning" based on an order of the macrocosm and microcosm, independent of our will, and, furthermore, that synchronicity is a phenomenon linked in the first place to psychic conditions, or the processes of the unconscious. According to Jung, the deepest strata of the latter are those of the "collective unconscious", potentially common to all those who are part of the human race. The decisive factors in the collective unconscious are archetypes that make up its structure, a distilled memory of the human race, not to be represented with the words of a language but by elusive symbols common to all mythologies. Jung's book, *Man and His Symbols* (Dell Publishing, New York 1964), is a glorious exposition of this subject. The last work undertaken by Carl Jung before his death in 1961, the book, full of glorious illustrations, seeks to provide a clear explanation of Jung's complex theories in an unpretentious way.

The search and discovery of the synchronic lines sounds like the beginning of a science fiction story, set some 75,000 years in the past. This was the way Falco chose to explain this mission, by supposing, as elucidated in his book *The Synchronic Lines: The Energy Streams of Planet Earth* (Devodama, 2015):

> The beginning of the science fiction story we are telling, lies some 75,000 years in the past. The Lines were formed at a moment in time owing to their being inhabitable within the concept of the developing complexity of life. Their discovery on the Earth at first marked a very important event, as it happened while exploring the significance of death. By observing the path of the dead, it was noticed that all the deceased went in the same direction. It was then understood that there must be something special here.

Falco's group travelled the world and their major question was: how can they see whether there is an energy focal point there? Falco was clear about this: "First, there is a need to know how to 'read' the territory, how to read everything, the rock, the disposition of the rock, the rivers, water, and then there is the classic system of connection to sensitive perceptions." In this way the synchronic lines of the Earth were annotated.

Falco stated that it was not the time any more to meet in small groups but that there was a need to work on the consciousness of people and the level of their memories. He said that there needed to be a completely different strategy and that this was also happening at different points in the world, that he was not the only one leading such thinking. Other people in the world embraced similar concepts, because the basis of esotericism is equal to everyone.

I wanted to know if Falco had ever been in contact with these other beings. Coboldo gave an enigmatic look. "Yes, and no," he said. "Contact was more on a telepathic level than physical or spiritual ones. Because they have to cover their own territory or areas of importance and they were not all even on the same level." Coboldo pointed out that the ambiance of their surroundings were all quite different. "You can imagine the dissimilarity between Petra Meyer, the guardian of the European branch of Theosophy, Madame Helena Blavatsky, the Russian founder of Theosophy, the magus Aleister Crowley, and Falco Tarassaco, each in their respective surroundings and times, the peculiarities of each in their historical periods."

This linking to Theosophy intrigued me. I had come across it many years ago, when Fenice Felce was still in the region, before he moved to Japan and placed his Damanhurian efforts there. We had talked of Theosophy and its philosophy. I asked Coboldo if there was a strong connection with Theosophy. "There are contact points," he said. "But all the schools have contact points. If you pay attention, what is different is the way you reach the goal. This is the reason we amplify the possibilities of recall."

If this were common knowledge, it could be accessed from different points. If there was only one road, it would be highly selective. Different spiritual guides offer different parts, they offer the parts within their own line of branding and traditions. Coboldo talked of the journey taken by Osho, who started out from India in the guise of Bhagwan Shree Rajneesh, and a philosophical movement, which had an esoteric background that he did not openly reveal, save to a very close circle of confidants. Rajneesh emphasized the importance of meditation, mindfulness, love, celebration, courage, creativity and humour, all qualities that he regarded as being suppressed by adherence to static belief systems, religious tradition and socialization. In advocating a more open and relaxed attitude to human sexuality, much misunderstood, he caused controversy, particularly in India during the late 1960s and became notoriously known as "the sex guru".

I recalled the alarming, often exaggerated, news stories from those times. Rajneesh spent time in Mumbai initiating followers, who were known as "neo-sannyasins" or more popularly as "the orange people". Later, he set up an ashram at Poona. He expanded his spiritual teachings, commented extensively in discourses on the writings of religious traditions, mystics and philosophers from around the world. However, moving from India to the United States, where he was caught up in a series of scandals related to activities of his followers, he left the US a rather sad and broken figure and returned to Poona, where he lived holding down his illnesses. When he died in 1990, the official cause of death was heart failure, but a statement released by his commune claimed that he had died because "living in the body had become a hell" following alleged poisoning in US jails. His ashes were placed in his newly built bedroom at the Poona ashram. The epitaph reads:

Never Born – Never Died – Only visited this planet Earth between 11 December 1931 and 19 January 1990

I also recalled asking Falco, when he was still called Oberto, what he thought about Osho. He spoke highly of the man's spirituality and philosophy but thought that he had allowed himself to be manipulated by people who were not as honourable or honest as he was. Coboldo thought

Osho had taken too much on his own shoulders and apparently chose to do things on his own and in his own way:

> I would say there were security reasons behind it. Not only are different roads chosen to reach the same point. There is more possibility of choice, but there is also more possibility of accidents. Osho suffered a huge accident when he was poisoned. Because he worked alone, he was killed.

However, there are deeper thoughts about this approach. If all the spiritual people were working closely with each other, there would be greater chance of accidents and outside interference. The reason for keeping groups apart is that some will go wrong, but others have a greater chance of success. "These are the reasons for keeping a smaller circle alive," summarized Coboldo. An important consideration as Damanhur is about to link up in an open way with the rest of the world.

What effect would the opening up have on the Medit-Action and its initiate body? Coboldo told me that, over time, the very meaning of esotericism has gradually assumed a different connotation in the language of Damanhur. Esoterica is more experience than knowledge and such experiences can be shared but never trivialized, as it is the key to self-transformation for those desiring to pursue a spiritual goal. Falco continued to follow closely the groups in the School of Meditation, then he stopped. "I had Falco as a teacher for more or less a year. That was in 1985. After that, he no longer followed the groups." He had sown the seeds and could see groups were growing under their own energies. He continued overseeing the groups from a distance, but without giving any direct lessons. He directed others to teach others, then they would teach others. This was quite different from other spiritual schools and their guides, who mostly took the lead in teaching.

For all this time, I had assumed, to all intents and purposes, Damanhur's Path of Initiation had been a closed school, an esoteric school, a secret school. Coboldo corrected me slightly. "It's an esoteric school that chooses to talk about many things in a very open way but leaves the indepth research to only a few."

I had grasped, from Coboldo, that you no longer had to be an initiate in order to access the knowledge, but if you wanted to understand at the deepest level, you could still become an initiate, but the difference is, it is possible to "know" things without necessarily knowing how to use them.

Initiates are shown how to use them.

Now the whole world will gradually have access to Medit-Action material, its spiritual principles, its esoteric teachings, its philosophy, everything. "We are now engaged in a huge body of writing, including mine," Coboldo stated, "which is not usually done in classical esotericism. None of the esoteric circles have done this and it should not be done, by definition."

The situation at Damanhur allows for a new open approach, with all the risks that involves. To be open means being open to attack, as well, from those who might think it all stupid, or call it lunatic behaviour, remarking that "they take money from vulnerable people". Falco recommended the taking of such risks. He was an advocate of risk, including his game of intergalactic "Risk" that has continued meeting for over 40 years.

The evening before my visit to Coboldo, I took part in a rather special ritual, one recently added to the Damanhurian canon of rituals. Called the Ritual of Form, I was told it was connected to the Damanhurians who had passed on, and food. Indeed, it was, because a very special meal had been made for us, consisting of many courses. The dining room was immaculately set out, the lighting atmospherically adjusted. Dining tables were set out in a circle, with an additional table in the centre, which I was informed was "for Falco". The usual purification of food, ritually undertaken, then there was 15 minutes allocated for meditation, to be in silence, with time and space for ideas, questions, notions, maybe even thoughts from Falco or the other Damanhurians on the other plane. We were to write these down and this is what I wrote:

Was it a dream that brought me here at this time? That was my first thought. Is that why I am here at such an important time? The form. What form should my book take? Are my thoughts in a positive direction? Am I thinking along the right lines? Will those who help me in this project be guided in the most appropriate way? Have they already? How can we all come together to influence the man who might best bring this project together? [I was thinking here of Etan Ilfeld, owner of Watkins Books, approached as possible publisher.]

Philosophical strength. Sincere dedication. Appreciating supposing. Observing the magical. Knowledge from knowledge. The confluence of time.

These were just some of my thoughts in the 15 minutes of deep meditation, obviously reflecting my concerns at that time. The dream I wrote about was an incident I recalled some months ago, waking up in the morning and, in that moment between sleep and waking, I became aware of a shaft of very bright light that hit me somewhere in the middle of my forehead. And Damanhur came into my thoughts, even though I had not been there for almost two years. I contemplated on the fact that it was some 20 years since I wrote my book on the community, and at that time Damanhur itself was 20 years old. In the idea of the ripples of time, maybe I should be writing another book? And then I went back to sleep.

Months passed, and then came the tragic news that my very good friend Irving Rappaport had died. Irving was like a brother. We had shared many happy adventures together over a large number of years. These included several trips to Damanhur, where we had many friends. His death hit me hard. I left my Shetland home to attend his funeral in Epping Forest. Betsy Pool and Formica Coriandolo, two of our mutual friends, had come from Damanhur. Later, at his wake, I told them about my waking-moment dream-thought. The notion solidified in my mind that I should set about the process of writing another book about Damanhur 20 years after the first one.

It was only when I got to Damanhur that I realized I was visiting at a crucial time in their development. I had not realized, at first, what a significant moment it was. Then, it occurred to me that some deep synchronicity might be at play here. When I first visited the community, in 1997, it was at a most crucial time, when the world had only recently become aware of the secret subterranean chambers of the Temples of Humankind and their future was uncertain. Now, here was another crucial time when, following the demise of their founder and spiritual guide, they had been left his legacy statement of opening up their work to the whole wide world and continuing in this open way. Maybe the shaft of light coming through my bedroom window in my semi-conscious waking state had more significance than I realized at the time.

Back in the dining room, experiencing the Ritual of Form, it was my turn to read out my thoughts from the meditation exercise, as described above. After I had finished my reporting, Cobra referred to me as a "priest of the change". That came as a surprise, right from left field. Cobra Alloro is a long-standing member of the community, whose acquaintance I first made during my earliest visits. He has a sculptor's studio in Damanhur Crea, the superb multi-functioning cultural centre built from the ruins of an old Olivetti typewriter factory in Vidracco, from where he makes, for the temples and for projects outside of Damanhur, exquisite and monumental sculptures, statues, columns, fountains and artistic architectural adornments, as well as giving stone restoration and sculpture courses. Cobra is an artist for whom I hold a profound respect, and his words filled me with a humble kind of pride. I do cherish change.

During the ritual, as each course was eaten, a sample of the dish was placed on the table laid for Falco. We ate all our dishes, which included a most delicious "oracle salad", created by Toro, one of the most enchanting food dishes I have ever tasted, as well as mountains of lasagne, which defeated me. As the ritual ended, the food laid out for Falco was ritually put to the flames. It had been an interesting evening.

Deep in thought about what I had experienced in the Ritual of Form, I was intrigued by what Coboldo said next:

> You can open this content to what we have been used to. We are used to doing everything because we are alive, right? We can communicate. We do everything and, for a while, we did everything like that in the great rituals. The others come, make a circle, participate. In this moment, in this ritual, they come, they prepare, and they manage the ritual. In order to perform this ritual, participants are required to fundamentally use their emotions. To feel.

In that instant, I recalled the deliciousness of oracle salad, conceived and made by Toro, and I realized just how deep I had participated in this ritual, emotionally, spiritually and gastronomically. This had brought about a very clear vision for me of why I was here at this moment in time in a curious continuum, the purpose of where I had come from, why I now found myself in this place and where my project mission was leading. I felt fulfilled.

CHAPTER 6
SUPERINDIVIDUAL!

It was Facocero Radicchio who first alerted me to the intriguing concept of the superindividual. My initial thoughts were that it suggested elitist overtones, a notion of some sort of superiority of person. How wrong I was. It took more explanation for me to realize the true nature of the concept. The superindividual has been defined to me as a group of people capable of moving together as a single entity, coherent with each other and animated by reciprocal love. In a superindividual, every individual contributes to the realization of a collective identity and is exalted by it. People relate to each other with respect, love, acceptance and the ability to help each other improve.

Facocero told me that love was the most important goal, to love one another, to love oneself. "The superindividual is our aim, our goal..." he said. However, he pointed out that he felt things were at something of an impasse. Things were preventing the achievement of their ultimate goal. The economy, the pressures of life, the demands made on an individual from one direction or another. Like most other aspects of Damanhurian

philosophy, it required a considerable effort to bring it about. What was needed to overcome obstacles, as far as Facocero was concerned, was more trust. "Love needs trust," he said, "and trust is sometimes lacking in some of our social interaction. Love, trust, and our aim to become a superindividual."

The Damanhur spiritual vision embraces the deeper understanding that you can achieve enlightenment only in connection with others.

Moving closer to this goal can deeply transform each individual. Recognizing ourselves in others, to think together without losing our own individuality, contrarily valuing it even more, are the steps to accomplish the superindividual. Just as in group theory, gestalt is a concept where the whole is far more than the sum of its parts. The term superindividual indicates the capacity to unite together with love and mutual respect, obtaining a result that is greater than the simple sum of individual characteristics, achieving dreams that would otherwise be impossible.

This shared path of enrichment is in full swing at Damanhur at this time, and it is currently the most important collective spiritual goal. Each Damanhurian is committed to offering the best parts of themselves in this process, with the idea that such a fusion is possible even among hundreds of people, as many as there are Damanhurians.

Within a superindividual group, paratelepathy is evident, which is the possibility of diffusing talents and abilities from one person to another. It operates in micro and macro ways. Thus, the superindividual is an objective of every Damanhurian social or spiritual grouping; every spiritual way, every company, community, every nucleo and so on should reach the state of superindividuality. So, this is an example of research that is not only theoretical, it is typically practical. It is, perhaps, the rebirth of the consciousness of the divine spark, as a developing group, rather than as an individual aspect.

Such an approach is not without its pitfalls, and I had discussions with some long-term members of the community who reflected on some of these. For this idea of the superindividual to reach fruition, it will be necessary to foster levels of trust and mutual understanding at a very deep level. A very important part of building trust is to know yourself well and to be transparent. This takes time and considerable effort. There is a need to foster love and friendship at a deep level. This takes time and effort. There is a concern that the people of Damanhur, living in a "busy bubble" as they do, will not have the extra wherewithal above and beyond the multitude of tasks and responsibilities already evident. Still, a community that constructed the Temples of Humankind and built a stable community that has lasted over 40 years would seem to be capable of anything.

I spoke with Anaconda Papaya about this idea of the superindividual, how an individual needed to be able to utilize the most effective communication. We spoke of the way bees acted as a potent group as they served the queen bee and functioned within her hive. A great deal of effective communication in the bee group was necessary to accomplish a plentiful supply of luscious honey.

A more dramatic example is the coordinated movement of a flock of starlings when they are in swarm mode. It's called a murmuration, possibly because of the delicate murmuring sounds they make. Starlings are the most likely birds you would see swarm. They create beautiful formations as they fly as a group before settling down for the evening. The small birds engaged in a murmuration exhibit strong spatial coherence and show extremely synchronized manoeuvres, which seem to occur spontaneously, or in response to an approaching threat, like hawks or peregrine falcons. The skilled pilots of a flying display team don't come anywhere near the clear communication skills of these tiny birds, which have also adopted the practice of regularly changing the leadership of the swarm from one bird to another. Effective communication among a group of individuals is crucial for their transformation into a superindividual.

One of the fundamental concepts in the philosophy of the ancient history of humans, according to Damanhurians, is that of the temporal empire, with a fine balance of sacred and profane required to keep them viable. When they talk about their hidden history, about the roots of "that great tree of humanity", Damanhurians proudly refer above all to Atlantis, the lost continent sunk into the Atlantic Ocean about 12,000 years ago, as the story was told by Falco.

Of course, Atlantis is not the only disappeared civilization that history fails to take into account. Names like Lemuria, better known as Mu, an island civilization of the Far East, or Hyperborea at the gates of the Arctic, or Agarthi in the subsoil of Central Asia, the mythical complex of caves underneath Tibet inhabited by evil demons that the Theosophists spoke of and wrote about, the famous *Terra cava* (hollow Earth) known to lovers of historical mysteries. They have given life to the many literary sagas that spawned those legends and rumours circulating around them.

The mythologies and mysteries of history are many, and that of Atlantis is one of the most enthralling and enduring. It is commonly thought of as a continent of several islands in the Atlantic Ocean, east of the North

American coast, which collapsed due to some terrible cataclysm, after a period of extraordinary spiritual and technological development. Falco said that by the time of its demise, the inhabitants of Atlantis had "dried up and no longer represented the lighthouse of civilizations" that it had once been. He felt that signs of the Atlantean culture are to be found in ancient Egypt, in Crete, and in some Greek islands, where Atlantis had found time to fund some colonial bases.

Atlantis is mentioned within an allegory on the hubris of nations in Plato's works *Timaeus* and *Critias*, where it represented the antagonist naval power blockading ancient Athens. In the story, Athens repels the Atlantean attack unlike other nations of the known world, supposedly giving testament to the superiority of Plato's concept of a state. The story concludes with Atlantis falling out of favour with the deities and being submerged into the Atlantic Ocean. Their fate had been determined because they ignored the will of the gods.

Notwithstanding its relatively minor importance in Plato's work, the Atlantis story has had considerable impact on literature. The allegorical aspect of Atlantis was taken up in works of several Renaissance writers, such as Francis Bacon's *New Atlantis*, thought to have been inspired by Thomas More's *Utopia*. Such works blurred the lines between reality and fantasy. Atlantis, for the moment, hangs like an image of what many "would be ready to set their hands on fire for" while others believe it to be a beautiful invention of fantasy. It is a truth in the balance between imagination, legend and clues that are not enough to make it part of what is accurately studied in academic texts.

Falco said that recent history is the result of a much longer history than is told in books. In this wider historical context, besides Atlantis, are similar legends like Tuatha Dé Danann, a race inhabiting Ireland before the arrival of the Milesians, the ancestors of the modern Irish; and Mu, the lost island of Lemuria, most recently commandeered by the band KLF as their inspiration for their *Justified Ancients of Mu Mu* song; and still many others.

Back in the mid-1800s, a few scientists working from scant evidence decided there must have been a lost continent in the Pacific Ocean, and they called it Lemuria. On this lost continent, some thought, there once lived a race of now-extinct humans who were called Lemurians, and who had four arms and huge hermaphroditic bodies, but nevertheless are ancestors of modern-day humans. And as absurd as this all sounds, the idea flourished for a time both in popular culture and some corners of the scientific community.

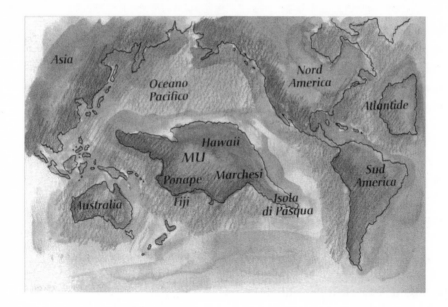

Of course, modern science has long considered that they debunked the idea of Lemuria altogether. But then, in 2013, geologists discovered evidence of a lost continent precisely where Lemuria was said to have existed and the old theories started cropping up once again. Today we do not know if these civilizations really existed, if they are simply narrative myths or if one day the signs of existence will finally be discovered. In a way it does not matter. Falco teaches that we should wonder how glorious civilizations such as these could develop and just disappear into thin air. This is an important meditation on the origins of Damanhur that can lead to significant reflections.

There are many cases of human civilizations that have disappeared over hundreds of thousands of years, beginning their history time and time again, glaciation after glaciation, so much so that the prehistory that we know is only the most recent. Atlantis, in its vision, is the seed from which so many successive civilizations have developed.

Geologists are developing and defining a new geophysical age in the timeline of planet Earth. The era, or age, we have just moved into is a geological period identified as the Anthropocene epoch or the age of humankind. A group of creative students and tutors from Edge Hill University, near Liverpool, put up a pertinent welcome sign, though they got it slightly wrong. We are entering the Anthropocene *epoch*, sometimes referred to as an "age". A specific "age", though, is a sub-division from a larger geological period. And a period is one of several sub-divisions of geologic time, enabling cross-referencing of rocks and geological events

from place to place and time to time. These periods form elements of a hierarchy of divisions which geologists use to define Earth's history. Eons and eras are larger sub-divisions than periods, while periods are further sub-divided into epochs and ages.

A phone call from a close friend, the late lamented Irving Rappaport, first alerted me to the notion of the Anthropocene epoch and its importance in regard to a period when humankind has made such a mess of managing our planet.

EONS OF GEOLOGICAL TIME

Chart shows the names scientists use to refer to various periods in the distant past.

EON	ERA	PERIOD		EPOCH		MILLIONS OF YEARS AGO
						NOW
Phanerozoic	Cenozoic	Quaternary		Holocene	(Into Anthropocene)	
				Pleistocene	Late	0.1
					Early	0.8
						1.8
		Tertiary	Neogene	Pliocene	Late	
					Early	3.6
						5.3
				Miocene	Late	11.2
					Middle	16.4
					Early	23.7
			Paleogene	Oligocene	Late	28.5
					Early	33.7
				Eocene	Late	41.3
					Middle	49.0
					Early	54.8
				Paleocene	Late	61.0
					Early	65.0
	Mesozoic	Cretaceous		Late		99.0
				Early		144
		Jurassic		Late		159
				Middle		180
				Early		206
		Triassic		Late		227
				Middle		242
				Early		

The Anthropocene epoch will define the slice of Earth's history during which people have become a major geological force. This will be the age of people, for such is the impact that humankind has made on this planet. Through mining activities alone, humans move more sediment than all of the world's rivers combined. *Homo sapiens* have also warmed the planet, raised sea levels, eroded the ozone layer and acidified the oceans. Given the magnitude of these changes, most researchers propose that the Anthropocene must represent the new division of geological time.

Recent research into the enigmatic cave paintings left by our ancestors has had to be somewhat adjusted in estimated timescales of origination. It has been a commonly and long-held academic view that the art of the Upper Palaeolithic period was the earliest form of cave art, being dated at some 40,000 years agao, with stencilled hands and various figurative animals.

There is little doubt that this was the work of *Homo sapiens*.

However, recent discoveries of stencilled hand pictures, as well as pictures of ladders and dots, have been dated to 73,000 yers ago. One must assume, therefore, that this burning desire to make our mark, leave our imprint, during the brief time we are allotted on Earth, is as evolutionary as our toenails and ears. It is a precious inheritance we must preserve with our lives and make attempts to add something of equal or greater significance.

At Damanhur, preparations for dealing with life in the Anthropocene epoch are probably more advanced than anywhere else on the planet. We all need to be prepared for such a newly defined geological age.

Atlantis is not the fruit of the imagination of ancient men, who gradually nourished it and enriched it with details. It represents instead a precise page of the history of humanity. An important page, rich in content and values. From the past to today, from generation to generation, the genetic, cultural and philosophical legacy of Atlantis has come down to us and in some way we are all descendants, as well as classical civilizations, of the Atlantean. It is a significant part of our collective unconscious, as Carl Jung termed it. Therefore, studying our ancient and mysterious history is, in many ways, like reliving the film of our lives. Have you never dreamed of living in an ancient civilization? Have you ever had the feeling of coming from a long way away?

Falco asked: is it possible to study the life of a tree without analyzing its roots? Can we really understand someone without knowing his childhood? The answer in both cases is "No". So how can we think of knowing our world, if we ignore its origins? Especially those we have not yet fully discovered, because they represent a kind of great unconsciousness of history.

For all these reasons the exploration of Atlantis and the ancient history of humanity is such an important field and it fascinates us, because we feel that from there can come the many answers that we seek. In Damanhur it is so important that the Mystery School of Damanhur Independent

University includes two courses, in two successive levels, dedicated to this theme. As for history and historians, Falco said that, little by little, the evidence of the actual existence of Atlantis will become so obvious that no one will be able to ignore it. "Just be patient!" In his own words:

The theme of temporal empires is linked to these conversations. We are used to considering the term "empire" as the conquest of territories. When we talk about temporal empires, we have to change logic. First of all, the idea of an empire is that of controlling various points of time. Imagine that a civilization, such as Atlantis for example, develops a revolutionary technology that allows you to move in time and control it.

Nature is a treasure chest full of secrets, which zoologists, botanists and geologists explore relentlessly. Even history is a book that is still largely unknown: our ancient ancestors wrote it with alphabets and codes that we do not yet understand. But the story belongs to everyone, and we can all ask ourselves through a course or through a personal reflection: to which of the great, ancient human families do I belong? In which periods of history, known or not, did I live?

Today, quantum physics affirms that time is a territory within which it is possible to travel; the problem is that we have not yet understood how! Let's instead suppose that the Atlantean researchers understood it very well.

They started missions of exploration of the past and of the future. These missions, once they have verified the conditions present in past and future, are transformed into missions of the conquest of "parts of time". In this way, eliminating enemies in the past makes Atlantis stronger in its present, while building colonies in the future certainly makes its development favourable. Not only that, but knowing the epochs of earthquakes, volcanic eruptions and tsunamis, may suggest in what era of time to be present and when to stay away.

In this idea of the ancient history of humankind, Falco advised us to consider Atlantis and other civilizations, not so much as physical empires, measurable on the basis of owned square miles, but as temporal empires that are able to exist simultaneously in different points of time and to keep their power because of it. Here is the point: Atlantis, Lemuria, Hyperborea, Agarthi, and who knows what other civilization that we do not yet know about, may have planned not to exist in this era, say in the past 3,000–4,000 years, because it is not so hospitable or even uninteresting to them, and then perhaps eventually they will reappear in the future. In this way, their signs will be evident and not just legendary.

All of this might be science fiction, of course, speculative supposing. Falco himself said to reflect on these things, taking them seriously, but also leaving space for doubt. The concept of a temporal empire, however, allows us to explain many mysteries, including those of civilizations that suddenly appeared and then inexplicably disappeared.

In his book *The Divine Blueprint* (Invisible Temple Books, 2010), Freddy Silva, an established researcher of ancient knowledge, talks about the concept of gods or sages emerging from sea-going vessels and other safe havens, after a global catastrophe, as a recurring theme in traditional myths that are maintained by supposedly unconnected cultures. However, Silva points out that there are connections and they are interwoven like the finest Persian carpets. Groups of builder gods, referred to as the "seven sages", set about locating other mounds at "carefully chosen locations" that would act as foundations for future temples, the development of which was intended to bring about "the resurrection of the former world of the gods" following its destruction by a world-wide flood. He quotes the philosopher Homer, from *The Illiad*, Book 18:

> And the elders sat on rough-hewn stones within a sacred circle and held in their hands the spectral rods of the loud, proclaiming heralds, on receiving which they then rose from their seats, and in alternate order gave good judgement.

Anaconda Papaya is one of my closest friends at Damanhur. When I first went there, he was heavily involved in the school programme for the community and we were involved in a number of exchange projects for young people between Damanhur and Essex, where I was a youth-work adviser at the time. As one of the designated king guides, he now has an important specific role in opening up the work of Damanhur to  the wider world. We talked about the legacy of Falco and its impact on the members of the community:

When Falco died, he left many, many letters for specific purposes, for specific people, we don't know how many. Piovra is putting them all together in a book. He also left "gifts" for people. Like, for the sages he gave them this and he gave them that. Gifts like assignments, like responsibilities, like potential. Sometimes the gift of quite specific powers. Much to my surprise, me being a bit outspoken and all that, Piovra came out at a meeting and she gave me this gift from Falco.

He reminded me in the rubric for this gift that he had once discussed with me Damanhurian hypnosis and asked me to consider how it converges with the method that I had used in groups before I came to Damanhur. I will leave you, he said, some of my wittiness to find out how they meet. That was his first assignment for me. Let me know the progress when you have done some work.

Anaconda told me that he wasn't totally aware that Falco actually knew all that much about his use of hypnosis. Anaconda had studied as a therapist when he was in his twenties, and got seriously involved in transpersonal psychology, studying NLP (neuro-linguistic programming), travelling round the world discovering techniques of hypnosis, theories of groups and interpersonal communication.

That was my thing, I was passionate about it, but when I came to Damanhur, I sort of shut it down, gave all that up. Falco implied that he wouldn't mind if, for example, I helped the school, helped with the education of the young people. So, I completely quit my centre in Milan, where I had my practices, my studio, my yoga, and other stuff, and in a 20-minute decision moved from that life, where people gave me money for doing what I really liked doing, and came to Damanhur.

He recalled a conversation about the way he used hypnosis to help with past-life researches. Falco had completely ignored his question and told him he had mentioned his name to Antilope and others in relation to plans for a new wave of tutors for the Damanhur school. Anaconda went to a meeting where there was much talk about old ways of teaching and how these needed to be changed. It was decided that the school should have a dedicated tutor staying with the kids and guiding them through their education, not just teachers coming, teaching their subject for an hour or so, and then leaving and another one comes in. Anaconda continued:

We needed someone to create a group and to follow the kids as they grow. I asked how much time was expected that this stuff would be taking and Antilope said that she anticipated, say, about nine hours a day for six days a week. I thought wow, this is a complete life changer. I was in. I saw this as an opportunity to do some really revolutionary teaching, something positive. I was a tutor for the next 16 years. We made it more international, made exchanges with other countries, we made a lot of progress in teaching English to the students, and we carried out a great deal of teaching outside of the classroom.

Then I get this gift by Falco in a letter, asking me to compare the way that I had used hypnosis in the past and how it is used in Damanhur. His gift was the wisdom to understand this and he asked that I review the process. I thought about communication and how this related to the various groupings here. I started groups that would meet and take part in something that I called "harmony circles", where people learned about communication in a spiritual way.

After about six months, he had a meeting with Piovra and told her about their experiences in these groups, how positive they had been. He said that she had then started acting in a strange way. When he asked her about this, she said there was no problem, but advised him speak to Orango about this, about how he had had a conversation with Falco many years ago about including communication in the School of Meditation. He wondered why she had raised that point. In order to clarify, he confirmed that after becoming a citizen of Damanhur all those years ago, he did have a conversation with Falco when he asked him how things were going.

I had told him that I was doing fine, but if I had to look around, things seemed a bit risky from the idea of relationships and communication skills, which seems really low here. He went all serious and said that he totally agreed with me. He thought that the basics of communication that I was talking about should be taught at all levels of meditation. He said that to me.

The next day, Anaconda was asked by the Medit-Action secretariat whether he could run a course about communication. He told them about a course he had run 25 years ago. He had trained in all manner of group techniques at Esalen Institute in Big Sur, California. The course he ran was termed "evolutionary communication". He explained that this was akin to the three laws of magic in the Hermetic tradition – the Law of Contagion, "once together always together"; the Law of Sympathy, "that which looks alike is alike" and "as above so below"; and the Law of Names, "names have power". He concentrated on internal communication, between the personalities, interpersonal relationships, then the dynamics of the group. Anaconda ran the course for Damanhurians, and most people loved it. They said that if they had these things included in the nucleo meetings it would be great. He wrote a letter to the king guides about the success of the course and how it might be more widely rolled out.

> I also suggested, and don't forget this was 25 years ago, that everyone in Damanhur should learn English, how useful that would be in widening things out and communication with the world. I thought it was crucial that we all speak English.

He also put forward that the communications course ought to be set up for managers and leaders. He was quite fired up and full of anticipation. However, Anaconda got no response and simply put it down to the fact that he was very young in Damanhur, a bit of a put-down, how he had maybe overstepped the mark.

> Then, years and years later, following Falco's demise, I find that he has left me a letter and a gift. In the letter, he reminded me of the conversation we had back then, about my way of using hypnosis and the accepted Damanhur way. I was very pleased. Then I had this light-bulb moment. I remembered how I had used hypnosis as a tool to help people awaken and sharpen awareness. Using hypnosis to protect the mind, to free yourself from your mind.

Anaconda had studied with a Buddhist practitioner who ran the NLP courses at Esalen. Having been a yogi-monk for ten years of his life, in his practice as a hypnotherapist his whole approach had been to promote spiritual insight and enlightenment. Several months went by and Anaconda inaugurated a series of "harmonic circle" groups, using techniques he was well versed in, and once again people really liked them.

At a meeting, Piovra made a very public statement that he was to receive a second gift, as he had made such active use of the first one. Piovra spoke to the meeting and said that, though they may be wondering what this had to do with the first gift, that Anaconda did not know himself that the first gift had actually been an "introduction" to the second gift. Falco's new letter said that Anaconda should "teach the basis of communication to all my people". He had been given the gift as a task, to create a container, a common container, which would hold everything together. Everyone was to have the same information, a "minimal common denominator", and that this was to be done in the School of Meditation, so that everyone has it, even the ones who may not like it. "He went on to say why he had given this to me, two or three paragraphs of clear, precise instructions." Anaconda told me:

> Since then, I've been working with groups of 12, 25, 70, or 100 people. We've been meeting every week, doing things in an unofficial way, by word of mouth, inviting people to come to my course if they wanted to. We had meetings on Sundays, Wednesdays and Saturdays, each of two hours and a half. Also, you had to be on time, or you could not come in.

The workshops covered communication, self-awareness and interpersonal relationships. Between sessions, people were expected to do some work every day on mindfulness, self-observation practice, and breathing exercises designed to separate parts of the self, the body, the emotional body, the mental body and the total self.

> And then they had to study, read something, every day, five days a week. People said it was changing their lives, into a place of more awareness. They told me this path was leading to a place of spiritual consciousness, and was one of the most profound introspective experiences they had had in Damanhur. When you think about the journeys of Falco and the plethora of courses, to have them acknowledge how mind-blowing this had been was humbling.

When Orango occasionally visited the group, he was complimentary and reiterated that Falco had said in his letter that this should be done within the Initiation School. Soon after that, Anaconda organized a course for every single initiate in Damanhur, 400 people, four groups each of 100. Each group came four times for the full two and a half hours, during the following two or three months, so that everyone had the full course.

For Anaconda, the opportunity to carry out this work had been an inspirational experience:

We realized that every person you meet is part of the divine fulfilment, if only you are able to see it that way. It is good to remind ourselves of a very simple fact, that we are all here to die and we have to value the time we have been given, to value the space, to make the fullest use of life.

To bring things back to the concept of the superindividual, I met with the person responsible for the Game of Life element of the Damanhur project, Bruco Tartufo, who I was told had a particular take on the concept of superindividualism. He related something that Falco had told him, as a declaration: "I, the Damanhurian, will get a level of integration, all united in understanding, or there will be no future for Damanhur." He had used it as a guiding principle ever since.

Bruco told me that he considered the superindividual was directly connected to social alchemy. He had become attracted to Damanhur as a 17-year-old by the aspect of the social dimension, by the idea of a community that was directed towards a common task, but that allows an individual full expression of their own sentiments. Relationships between people are the most important thing. The idea of the superindividual in Damanhur corresponds to a specific moment in Falco's own thinking, and he spoke of that moment. It was when he first became aware of the seriousness of his illness, that he did not have much time left. He started accelerating all his projects into overdrive. He spoke about love among the people of Damanhur and about union. Bruco was mightily impressed: "For me, he spoke of this in a way that was completely new. He has said that even more important than the temples were the people. This is the practical application of the superindividual in my personal story."

Falco left Bruco an invitation, saying that he could be of great help in the work of the superindividual. He said: "You can help the Popolo, become a connecting thread between people." Bruco had a mission and he has embraced the idea with all his energy and effort:

In this crisis, after Falco, for me there was an opportunity to make a new turn within the community, to create a new community without contradiction, with attention on the other person. My mission is the opening of the world to this concept of the superindividual as a way to diminish selfishness and be more open to mutual cooperation. Life at Damanhur is more focused now, more simplicity in organization, more clarity of purpose. We must grow with respect to people. And we have a duty to take this mission to the whole world.

Damanhur grew out of the need for Falco to set in motion the results of his research and discoveries about awakening memories, ancient knowledge, and artistic and healing abilities. The path he proposed is leading to the awakening of the inner master in each person through study, experimentation, the elimination of dogmatic attitudes and a full expression of individual potential. Damanhur is a society in constant evolution and transformation.

Since the demise of Falco, a major community change was the creation of a council for food sovereignty, facilitating the various elements of food production within Damanhur, such as the organic food store, the nucleo families of the community with their family gardens, and the agricultural cooperative. Damanhur has always shown interest in the exchange of experiences with other eco-villages and communities, because their agriculture is partly internal (the family gardens), and partly official (the agricultural cooperative), and yet all is run within community structures.

In their jargon, the Damanhurians called this connection of different entities with a common theme "Astronave", a word that can also be interpreted as "Spaceship", revealing another secret of the Damanhurian political philosophy: act with playfulness, while at the same time, seriously move events. This not only created synergy, but it removed a leadership vacuum: not a business run from the top down, but a community with its own organically grown complexity and, sometimes, also contradictions.

Such contradictions were beautifully "fixed" by the "Captain", defined as a person with prestige, knowledge in the field, and social skills to mediate amongst all. Community discussions are leading to new and innovative forms of management with more autonomy for regions, often grouped into Astronavi.

Not long after the community had purchased the derelict ex-Olivetti typewriter factory in Vidracco, and transformed it into Damanhur Crea, the proposal of business activities based there to refer to themselves as divisions of a spaceship was approved. This focus has become an effective starting point to change the balance of some internal policies and is characterized by shared play and direction, responsibility and actions that produce reciprocal advantages. Following this lead, community regions re-evaluated their goals and projects, which subsequently caused some to conquer new identities more characteristic of where they are today, with dedicated Captains at the helm.

Bruco took on the mantle of Captain of the Astronave Tempio, the hillside region that encompasses the nucleos in and around the Temples of

Humankind and the Sacred Wood. In one of his reports towards the end of one phase of the community development, he ponders:

> I feel I can say that it was an important phase, a birth that gave birth to a new social organism, where now, after a year of work, we can begin to understand the potential and advantages given by the new connections that the community path develops.
>
> The production of energy needed to move the engine of this great machine, comes from the most diverse containers, from the ability that each person has to express the love for this project. All members now have a political structure capable of developing our projects through a broader vision, creating collaboration and new synergies between us.
>
> The most challenging part I experienced was to perceive the many important projects we have and to accord it with the desire to want to do them all at their best. Difficult to prioritize as everything that is Temple must be thought and developed giving precise meanings to things. I have spent energy in trying to develop every stimulus brought by people by collecting requests and opinions from everyone.

As befitting a person with responsibility for integrating the Game of Life into the Damanhur scheme of things, all this was accomplished with joy and happiness. The Game of Life, life as a game. On this topic, on the occasion of the International Day of Happiness organized by the United Nations on 20 March 2016, Crotalo Sesamo, who was present in New York at the "I Do Happiness" event as a Damanhurian ambassador, read out this message from the sages of Damanhur, from a paper titled "Community, Vision, Action, and the Responsibility for Happiness":

> Esteemed audience and dear friends, we are aware that reflecting on happiness means that we are part of the lucky ones who are not facing problems of survival, violence and war, forced immigration, health emergencies or hunger. We say this with the full spiritual awareness that no-one in the world will ever be able to achieve happiness, as long as there are people suffering. Just as a wise saying goes, "A mother can only be as happy as the most unhappy of her children", one day we will comprehend and feel inside our hearts and bodies that no human being can be truly content as long as there are other beings who suffer. This includes our whole

Earth family: all the animals, plants, and other forms of life – both visible and invisible – whom we share our beautiful planet with. We will start to experience happiness, as a species, only when we learn to perceive the world and the universe as an integrated and intelligent whole, where we humans have responsibilities and duties, even before having rights. A fundamental element for the respect of the whole of life is the protection of the identities and traditions of each people – especially indigenous peoples, who are the spiritual elders of humanity – because it is through a sense of belonging to a larger community that we can participate in Earth's greater rhythms.

The address went on to state that Damanhur hoped that concrete initiatives can start from here. Projects based on the sincere intention of individuals and nations, so that the happiness we are talking about, happiness that comes from awareness and participation, may become the natural condition for every human being. The quest for happiness is the answer to any risk of extinction of the human race. Crotalo later said: "Damanhur was born to express new ideas, to go beyond what is apparent." He further elaborated:

Damanhur is something that you choose. Not what someone else chooses for you. What we do is because it is our pleasure, because it is what we have inside ourselves. If we didn't like Damanhur the way it was, we would change it! We couldn't live in a place that was different from what we feel is our vision. In fact, our guests come from all over the world and if, after a few months, they come back to visit again, they find a different Damanhur. Transformation is a fundamental element. We believe that each time you stop changing, you go backwards.

Esperide feels that the concept of the superindividual is inextricably linked to the concept of Vajne. Throughout human history stories have been created to make sense of the world, giving meaning to life, to inspire dreams. Mystical traditions say that in every epoch there is always a group of people, protecting the ageless wisdom and the alliance between humanity and the gods, holding the vision for the future of humanity. Humanity evolves spiritually according to the Vajne programme. Esperide thinks this is very important:

Vajne is based on love and divine intelligence, supported by extra-planetary intelligences and forces. Each one of us participates and evolves within Vajne through many lifetimes. There is a spiritual dimension, where time does not exist. It is a global consciousness that is oneness.

On our planet there are many other species connected within Vajne. Many more are in the universe. Vajne is the reconnection of humans, plants, animals and minerals, as well as beings and intelligences of other worlds, divine forces at all levels, so that we can all reach a higher stage of consciousness together.

We human beings are aware of the presence of the divine spark in them. We are a bridge between the material and the spiritual planes. Like us, other species are aware of the divine spark in them, such as dolphins, whales and elephants. They are still in touch with their counterparts across the universe.

For Esperide, we human beings have a long and glorious past. Human history is very different from the one we are taught in school. The same soul that lives in humans, is present in many forms all over the universe, but it belongs to a galactic alliance, fighting for the expansion of life against the forces of entropy. The enemy.

In this epic and millennia-long battle, we have lost the memory of our history and many of our higher spiritual powers and abilities. We have lost our sense of connection with all life and, often, the brilliance of the divine spark within. In all of us there is a divine spark. But there is also a principle that is opposed to evolution. This anti-life principle, if followed, leads to separation and pain, possibly the annihilation of all life. We are also witnessing extreme negative events. They are an effect of the old system that is opposing the new. The choices of each one of us are indispensable to make the scales tip in the direction of Vajne.

The second Damanhur Oracle of January 2018, stated:

We dedicate the second Oracle of January to the separation of planes for the salvation of humanity and the Vajne project. Message: Money, value, work. Fair exchanges, ethics. Investigate, invent, propose. Act with verve. Time urges. Currency in international evolution in the Popolo (People) first then with others.

In a superindividual, every individual contributes to the realization of a collective identity and is exalted by it. The people relate to each other with respect, love, trust, acceptance and the ability to help each other improve.

A superindividual group is a Gestalt thing, an individual thing, a superindividual thing. Investigate, invent, propose. The superindividual is the goal of all Damanhurian social and spiritual groupings. Every spiritual way, every company, community, nucleo, every action, all links with indigenous peoples, everything associated with Damanhur. Sueprindividuality is research that is not only theoretical, but naturally practical.

CHAPTER 7
ESOTERIC PHYSICS

When I first visited Damanhur, back in 1997, I was intrigued by
the way, every Thursday evening, the good people of Damanhur
went in large numbers from their homes to their community centre
in Vidracco. The whole community used to trot down the road to
the venue, just like the villagers in Giancaldo, Sicily, so memorably
portrayed in *Cinema Paradiso*, might be going to see a film, or the
townsfolk of Burnley, where I was born, might be off to play bingo.
But the Damanhur residents were strolling to their community centre
in order to discuss "esoteric physics" and similar rarefied subjects.
That, in itself, appeared to me astonishing! With the recollections
of the way that nonconformist scientists had been treated by the
establishment in our Western tradition, and the general lack of interest
in such matters shown by the UK populace, this activity at Damanhur
appeared magical.

The man who, during those first visits, taught me most of what little
I learned about esoteric physics, was a smiley man named Gattopardo
Tek, no longer at Damanhur, having departed to pursue his own spiritual
researches, but at that time he was a regular speaker in the community
meetings. I wrote about him in my previous book. He told me: "Esoteric
physics is within the sphere we more generally call magic. That is to say,
in my opinion, the sum of the total sciences of mankind: the spiritual, the
ethical and the technical."

Since then, I've met and talked with the other main guardians of the
esoteric vision, Falco Tarassaco, Gnomo Orzo and Coyote Cardo. Esoteric
physics has now transmogrified and is better known as "spiritual physics".
Having watched and discussed, I'm a little clearer now. And for me,
this is beautiful science. I discovered that it is accepted in Damanhurian

philosophy that there are eight aspects, eight esoteric laws, relating to the existence of the universe, and they are:

1. Synchronicity
2. The sole atom
3. Divinity
4. Geometric essence
5. Time matrix
6. The fall of neutral events
7. Chaos
8. Complexity

Collectively, they are known as the "primeval laws", and then later as "derivative laws" once they precipitate inside time. With the ideas explored in these laws, Damanhurians reckon that an initial explanation of the phenomena that manifest within matter can be defined.

The seekers of Damanhur believe they provide an initial explanation of the phenomena that manifest within matter – divine Oneness and therefore the divine origin of human beings, and everything there is. Oneness has entered the universe of forms at different epochs and through different expressions, that the Damanhurian call "primeval divinity". This is the time in which our species is called to have an active role in bringing full consciousness – that is, an aware divine presence – into matter. The descent into matter and form took place some 30 million years ago.

Just like regular physics, spiritual physics has laws that need to be heeded. Synchronicity is the first of the eight laws of spiritual physics. Before going any further, dear reader, some advice. Empty your mind of any laws of physics you may have already learned at school or elsewhere. We are dealing here not with laws to explain and work within the physical world, but with the laws that would bring our world, our universe, into existence. These laws originate in the realm of "the Real", which predates the material universe. This is true reality, the source of everything, the seat of the Absolute, as opposed to matter which actually represents an illusory reality or, to use a more modern term, a virtual reality. In the Real, the laws are always pure, each law expresses its pure potential, without combining with the others.

This is such an important, if somewhat mystifying, concept, that it is perhaps worth looking at the thinking behind spiritual physics in some depth. It is the meeting of the laws, and the potential that is in the meeting, that creates our universe, the universe of forms. The characteristic of our universe is that these eight primeval laws meet at an equal potential, and this is a rule to which they are inextricably bound: every form in our universe contains all of these eight energies/codes.

All the laws of our physical world, such as the law of gravity, are derived from that original meeting of the primeval laws, which become derivative laws as soon as they are considered in their varying functions inside our universe.

Falco was an inexhaustible teller of stories and many of his own philosophical thoughts were conveyed in this way. With regard to the eight primeval laws at the core of the spiritual physics thinking, he once recounted this first meeting of the laws as a superbly told allegorical story, one that fired my level of supposing into overdrive. I originally told this story in the first edition of *Damanhur: The Real Dream*:

> Let's imagine that these eight laws all go to a bar and meet there. This is what we would consider the beginning of the universe. From now on, when we refer to that moment, we can call it the "Four Seconds Bar", as four seconds is the time it takes for a human being to have a perception, on a conscious level. Of course, on a subconscious level it takes much less time. But to bring something to consciousness takes four seconds. So, when we talk about an instant, by definition, we are talking about four seconds in our time. Therefore, the Four Seconds Bar. So, the eight laws meet. Let's see what they do. Just to make things easier to understand, let's suppose that synchronicity is the first to arrive. Synchronicity just has to be first, because that is what makes the event possible. Without it, nothing happens. Synchronicity creates the opportunity for all the other laws to meet.

Back at the bar, the second law to arrive is the sole atom. This is the basic atom, an infinitesimally small particle, which constantly emanates and thereby manifests forms. The sole atom should not be thought of as a physical atom, rather an atom of potentiality for it existed before time, before matter. It is the matrix for everything, a law, a function, the vehicle through which all the laws reproduce themselves in all the forms.

Suppose the universe has a constant need to conserve energies, to be used sparingly. Consequently, the sole atom does not create all of a form but does the minimum for form to finish itself by itself. Each form, in order to fit into our universe, must contain within itself armistice, the relationship of laws which permits it to stay within the universe of forms. Imagine then a form split into mass and energy. A line that cuts through is the symmetry of form and inside this line all the laws flow. Every line has the same diameter because, on account of the armistice, all the laws come together with perfect equilibrium.

Within every form, the armistice reproduces itself.

The sole atom itself contains within itself all the forms of the armistice. It could be imagined as the locomotive of a long train, linking at infinite velocity all the lines of all the forms. It could be thought of as being like a television set, where there is one dot, but it very rapidly scans all over all the lines from top to bottom of the screen, before you or I can blink our eyes, and makes a picture.

Let us imagine that the different laws flow at different velocities. Then, it is the different combinations of these laws that differentiates one form from another. The only law that flows at the same speed through all forms is sole atom, because it is at infinite speed and it carries all the different laws within itself. It is outside time and distance does not exist. Every form is noted by its own frequency which is called the rhythm-number. The way to intervene in forms is through laws. This is what the magician and the alchemist do.

Like all other laws we are talking about, the law of the sole atom exists as primeval law, representing the possibility of manifesting the universe. As a derived law, it becomes a creator of form. Certainly it is energy, but more than anything it is a function. If those physicists experimenting with a particle accelerator at CERN, just over the Swiss border, were to spin all the particles round from now until kingdom come, they would never discover it, because it's not a physical particle, not form. The laws are outside form.

In the Four Seconds Bar, we have the bold synchronicity creating the meeting, then the sole atom arriving and starting to create the universe of forms. There are still just the two of them there, sitting staring at each other, but already the universe is being formed. Then divinity arrives. In this case, the primeval divinity. "Okay, I am bringing into this form a divine spark, so that this matter has the potential for growth. And pour me a glass of red wine."

In every form, even in the digital recorder I am transcribing this from, there is a little bit of divine spark, of free will. The law of divinity is present in all forms. Some express this in complex ways – plants, animals, the connection of physical and spiritual in humans, for example – whereas in others it is a potential only – the microphone of my recorder, for instance. This reminds me of something that Ken Campbell used to say: that you can develop a machine that can beat you at chess, but does it know that it has won? Does it have any sense of really "winning"? Nevertheless, a microphone has the potential to become alive.

But I digress. Into the bar comes geometric essence, continuing Falco's account:

"Hey," says the essence, "let's create relationships among them." Geometric essence is what gives the possibility of measuring things, of comparing them, of creating structures in the universe. It is what makes any structure reproducible. The law of geometric essence is like a map, a territory measured within which the sole atom moves, where various forms find their positioning. It is a spatial map of form. If the sole atom is the pencil, then geometric essence is the ruler. There is a map for every form and geometric essence is present in every form, because it is a law. Naturally, because solids are more basically measurable, there would be more present within a solid form than within a gas, for example, and it would have a different flow. These aspects of form are a part of a particular alchemical knowledge not spoken of in thousands of years. So that is the law of geometric essence, the geometric matrix, the spatial map of form.

Not before long, into the bar strolls time matrix, looking mean. Now that the forms are created, now that they have spatial relationships, it is time for time to be created. Time is a way of relating forms to each other. If we do not leave in relation to the same time, we will never meet. The law of time matrix is one law for everything, form and beyond form, but also each of the other laws has its own time matrix, in order for it to relate to time, because this is a universe made of time. The law of the time matrix deals with this very complex aspect of the laws. He's like the sheriff of the group.

Form has three fundamental parameters: rhythm-number, colour and time. The first, rhythm-number, is a frequency, the DNA of form, if you will; the second, colour, is the direction given to form by divinities that control the time territories; the third, time, is an actual quality of form. Three-dimensional space is not enough to understand where a form is. It is necessary to indicate *when* this form is. Every substance will have been created at a different time. So no two things are ever the same. The time of form indicates its participation in the time flow and measures its capacity to evolve in the direction of complexity to transform itself.

However, we should consider that all forms in the universe must be in equilibrium. Therefore, if we imagine the universe as a division of a single mass, the total of the mass must always add up to one. If we have only two forms in the universe and the mass is increased of one form, then the mass has to be decreased of the other.

Equilibrium must always be constant.

Equilibrium is always constant. This is true for all the worlds of the universe. You can have compensations between one world and another. In the spheres of magic, there is a principle that pronounces: similar corresponds to similar, like responds to like. All the forms in the universe are linked to each other, because the universe must always be in a state of equilibrium. Therefore, transformation inside a form produces a compensatory effect in the rest of the universe. It does not happen in a uniform manner, but like responds to like. One form is like another not because they are alike, but because they have the same time, a time that is alike, not the same, but similar. So that forms which have the same speed of evolution respond one to the other.

The time matrix, as a law, measures all the times of all the forms. This is why it is called "temporal", in order to create compensations, moment by moment, though some people at Damanhur would insist that this is really simplifying it. Some of us need it to be simple!

After a while, the five laws gathered at the bar are joined by the fall of events, also known as the fall of neutral events. This brings the opportunity for new events and also the chance to put into operation everything the others have been planning. Things get much livelier in the Four Seconds Bar from now on. The piano player strikes up and there is a much happier mood. What are events? They are forms. My tape recorder is an event and my microphone is an event. The energy that flows within the microphone is an event. The pen on my desk is an event. The paper is an event. The ink that transfers from pen to paper is an event. My computer is an event.

We can suppose that the law of the fall of events wants to represent a series of possible events which fall, or happen, within the flow of time. Time is a container of forms. For us it is also a container of the events of history. As we increase complexity the significance of the event changes. In the more complex forms, leading right up to the divinities, who are so complex they no longer need any form to manifest themselves, events do not have to do with a form, but to do with a direction.

The swing doors of the bar are thrown open and chaos is standing there. Chaos is like the stranger from out of town. This law has not been explored very well yet, but it is one that needs to be concentrated on. Chaos here is not to be confused with confusion. It is more to do with forces that do not have a direction yet. When we are talking about chaos from a scientific point of view we are talking about the primordial soup. From a religious or philosophical point of view, it is regarded as the time before God separated the elements, separated Earth from the heavens and gave an order to things.

Esoterically, chaos is the law that allows transformation, which permits the system to collapse, to put itself in a state of disorder, in order to achieve a higher state of order. This relates to being able to question one's own state in order to encourage an evolution. All forms are ever evolving. The universe itself is not fixed. The laws themselves may change. There are not necessarily eight of them. This is why in the Damanhurian esoteric school, the School of Meditation, nothing can be based on dogma. The truths that we find inside ourselves are always partial truths, not absolute ones. Mathematicians have discovered that what seems to be chaos often turns out to be a very high level of formation, so complex that it had appeared chaotic. Fractal theory is one example. In fact, at this level chaos and order have come together.

"Make room for the big one." The voice boomed outside the Four Seconds Bar and everyone got ready to greet their old friend. Big in size and big in personality, in came complexity. The law of complexity, sometimes known as the arrow of complexity, is the only law that comes out of our universe as a product. Suppose that there are many, many different universes. Each universe produces something that nourishes another universe. These are all physical universes, but by "physical" something different is meant from the multiverse or parallel universe theory of the physicists. Still, there are infinitely different universes in the universe of forms. And our universe has to produce complexity. This is its whole purpose.

We might examine how our universe creates complexity by having more information in less matter. Once upon a time, for instance, we used huge computers to do quite simple calculations and now we have exceptionally tiny microchips that can handle millions of calculations. Could it be that computers are spiritual things, and technological advancement derives from complexity? Two things not to be confused are complexity and what we call "progress". In many ways, the age in which we live is much less complex than the citadels of study and the cathedrals of the Middle Ages. Scholars there were more actually aware of the natural processes of the planet and there were people who were able to use a wider range of senses, a sense of dream, for example, an ability to manipulate other forces.

It has been said that we have over 40 senses, yet we use only five of them, and we use those very poorly. Some places on Atlantis, apparently, also had a complexity that was at least equal to ours, if not higher. However, when talking of complexity, it must be understood that not everywhere is the same. It could be thought of as being like a leopard, with dots here and there, but in no way uniformly spread. You can have a place where the complexity is low, then you have a citadel, or an oasis, like an old style university or like Damanhur, in fact, where complexity is higher, and which as a consequence works for the whole of the world.

Complexity increases in leaps and bounds, which are known as "levels of justice". An example would be the evolutionary leap of cells organizing themselves and developing thought. It was only when forms on Earth had developed far enough that the divine human form chose to inhabit them. The physical bodies had then reached a point where they had all the organs that were needed.

Another leap forward came when human beings were able to transcend their mere survival needs and start creating something that was not just for their immediate satisfaction, art for example. So, where is this complexity taking us? It could lead us to become totally spiritual and leave the universe. We have a limited time in which to grow, according to people in Damanhur. We have to go on, conquering new levels of justice. If we do not do that in the right time, bye-bye. We will all have failed.

I was at first rather taken aback by this, but it was explained to me that at each leap, something major happens. If we reach a new level of justice everything will be affected, not just the spiritual. The physical will have to change in order to support it. New organs will develop in the body, new connections. It might even be that we will be able to communicate telepathically or develop teleportation, or something else we cannot even imagine. But it will be something that will be crucial to the future of the universe. It's a thought-provoking philosophical concept.

I loved that story, as a way of telling complex concepts simply. However, it does have its drawbacks. Esperide told me that the concept of the Four Seconds Bar should be read as the Four Seconds Café, where coffee is partaken of, not alcohol. But, when you are supposing, I guess an individual interpretation is a bit like the Wild West. That's what had stuck in my mind. To add a bit of clarity, Esperide took me to see Coyote in order that he explain a few concepts in a more accurate way.

Coyote made a few amendments and explained:

The primeval laws will not change. Our understanding of them

does, and as a consequence, the way we interact with them changes. Damanhurians hypothesize that there might be other primeval laws, which, at the state of evolution of our universe, do not yet participate in it. As everything, and the universe itself, evolve, the intertwining and the number of these functions may change.

Complexity is actually the smallest, if you wanted to use a space metaphor. The less the form, the more the complexity, as you explain later.

The decrease in mass is a phenomenon that is only observable from a general point of view and not singularly in each form, although in each case there is an increase in the information contained within the form itself.

To take an example we can say that human beings will almost certainly increase their level of knowledge over the course of their lives, while the mass remains constant, or may do so. We can see the reduction of mass when we see a leap in complexity in an ecosystem of forms, the arrival of the first life forms on our planet for example.

In this case we have a very large mass before the birth of life on this planet (the whole globe) containing a very limited amount of information (matter that is inanimate does not need a great deal of specific information).

For anyone particularly interested in getting to grips with the whole concept of spiritual physics, I would recommend that you read Coyote Cardo's excellently comprehensive book, *Spiritual Physics: The Philosophy, Knowledge and Technology of the Future* (Litoprint Editioni, Emilia Romagna, 2014).

The supreme amount of effort and determination that went into building the Temples of Humankind and a spiritual community with such significance is a monumental achievement. It should have been an effort that was far beyond a community of this size and complexion.

To defeat the enemy – that is what Damanhurians call the anti-life principle and that I have described in the chapter on the great battle depicted in the Hall of the Earth – the primeval divinity cannot clash with it directly, but must simply fight to affirm existence and strive to divinize matter before the given amount of time expires.

Mention of the anti-life principle may need some more clarification. The concept is of crucial importance in the Damanhur philosophy. Falco was asked, in a public meeting, what he considered "the enemy" to be. He gave a fulsome, considered reply:

> It's the concept of the opposer. It has nothing to do with yin, yang, which is the eternal dance of the opposites inside of form, but it refers to the idea of an external force that opposes the development of complexity. This force is... how can I explain it? I can't explain it in only a few words. This is not just an abstract idea of a force present within the universe. It also manifests inside each one of us. It thrives on our limitations, on everything that creates separation from others: pride, arrogance, anger, laziness, selfishness, pessimism. For instance, it can become more active when we give ourselves in to depression. If that leads us to self-annihilation, reduction of our interactions with others, moral suicide, and even more, then we can see this is due to having let this anti-life principle take the lead.

The questioner asked a direct question: "But, then, is this force also inside of me?" Falco, at his most mischievous, replied:

> Certainly, best wishes... (much laughter) It's inside all of us, there is always a contact, a connection inside each one of us. We have as many creative forces as we have destructive ones. We need to constantly choose to apply our free will and go in the direction of growth. It is an esoteric concept, the idea that the Opposer exists in order for us to express free will otherwise everything would be predetermined. Just as we have a divine spark inside of us, we also have a particle of this anti-life force.

If the primeval divinity reaches its goal to divinize matter, the enemy will lose any chance of opposition, but during the time in which the "game" is played, it influences forms and entices them to move in its direction. Paradoxically, because of free will and because it is their choices that can tip the scales of evolution, it is the more evolved forms that are to pay more attention and be aware not to fall into this trap. Inside matter, the nonexistent cannot manifest unless the more evolved forms give it space. The laws previously analysed do not provide for the possibility of intervention by nonexistence, which means that the nothing has no means of its own with which to intervene in matter itself.

Each one of us, willing or not, is influenced by this force which we can easily identify within all the more egocentric aspects that block our evolution and inhibit the extension of our consciousness towards others. So, the pull towards the nonexistent is also within us, and we need shared values and meaning to direct our will. Our will, if manifested through continuity in our choices, gives us the opportunity to turn the opposer into a stimulus for constant growth and positive transformation.

I'd like to say a word here about the thorny issue of "time travel", which frequently crops up in relation to Damanhur. It's a subject that Damanhurians don't really want to talk about any more, mostly because, when it does get talked about, it tends to swamp all other things that the Damanhurians have done. It diminishes the other major achievements in artistic and spiritual endeavour and becomes a receptacle for fundamental scepticism.

When I was writing my first Damanhur book, I had many friendly, yet heated, arguments with my late friend Ken Campbell as to whether I should write about time travel. At that time, 1996, *Kindred Spirit* magazine had published stories and accounts about Damanhurian exploits travelling in time. It seemed like it was all anyone wanted to talk about in relation to Damanhur.

I had interviewed Damanhur people who told me about their time travel adventures. These were told in detailed, dispassionate and highly credible ways, with no aggrandizement or elaboration. In other words, I did believe what I was told. Ken used to challenge me. At meetings of our writers' group, he would ask each and every one: "What percentage do you believe that the Damanhurians actually time travel?" The responses were always low or miniscule percentages. When he asked me, I would provocatively say 100 per cent and he used to explode and shout: "You can't have 100 per cent." I thought I could. I could think of no reason why the people I spoke to would have lied to me.

When my book was published, Oberto and Esperide came over for the launch, which was held at the Institute of Contemporary Arts in London. During their visit, we took them to meet with famous cosmological scientist David Deutsch in Oxford. Oberto and Deutsch talked about many things, the cosmos, multiverses, the possibility of time travel. Very enjoyable it all was. When we took Esperide and Oberto back to London,

Ken stayed on. He later told me that he asked Deutsch what percentage he thought the Damanhurians actually time travelled, and the great cosmological professor had said 50 per cent. I felt somewhat vindicated.

In the end, I decided not to write anything about time travel in my first book, preferring to write about all the other amazing things that Damanhurians had done in creating what might well be the "eighth wonder of the world". I later found out that the time travel was no big deal at Damanhur. It had been necessary for a specific purpose at a specific time, and when that purpose had been achieved, the incredible efforts required to bring about the time travel were best employed elsewhere. That's all I intend to say on the matter; lancing the boil, so to speak.

CHAPTER 8

SPIRITUAL PHYSICS AND BIG QUESTIONS

In the myth of the shattered mirror, mentioned earlier, the fragments of mirror are known as "divine sparks", little bits of godliness (or the nearest thing we are going to get to godliness) that came through and lodged themselves in each of us, as well as in everything around us. In Damanhurian cosmology, the realm of the Absolute is "the Real" and the divine sparks, the flying shards of broken mirror, pass backwards and forwards, from form to real, as life begins and ends in its perpetual cycles. To be precise, there are three different states of being that are called "Form" (matter), the "Threshold" and the "Real". The Threshold is termed an intermediate dimension, which is found between Form and the Real, and represents a condition in which the laws are still primeval, though partially modified, with time and matter omitted, while the dominant element is information, or specifically, the memory of forms.

What drives the whole system is the Real, a spiritual dimension that unites the unknowable realm of what is described as the Immoveable Mover, all the way to the universes of form.

The Immoveable Mover is Oneness, and contemporaneously participates in and defines all the lesser forms. The Immoveable Mover expresses itself and passes through the world of ideas, of numbers, through the Demiurge, then the laws of the universe are created and everything cascades from there. The Real is the element connecting the sets of interpretations of the descents of possible worlds.

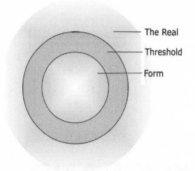

The Real
Threshold
Form

Each state – Real, Threshold and Form – has a different vibration quality, so that they actually all co-exist in timelessness. The first creation is contemporary with all the others, because it is out of time. But if we are to imagine this inside of time, we could say that the Absolute exerts its influence as the Real descending into Form in a continuous flow. This flow is carried out by structures called "attractors", which bring the potential of the Absolute within matter.

Before bringing their pure potential into the world of form – the multiverse in which Form exists – attractors transit through the Threshold which can be understood also like the complexity of the astral planes, containing the recording of everything that ever happened and everything that ever existed in each one of the universes, where they assimilate specific information, according to their purpose. Currents of attractors flow from the Real to the domain of matter, passing through the Threshold. Attractors whose purpose is to attract enough complexity to sustain human beings, will attract memories, past lives, and all aspects connected to the assemblage of a human soul. Attractors that will inform the correct functioning of just an organ, for instance, will assemble that kind of programming.

Damanhurians commonly refer to macro-attractors for evolutionary forms more complex than individual human ones, attractors for human forms and micro-attractors to define the level of complexity of information these energetic structures carry. This structure, composed of attractor and information, proceeds to matter, where it starts to animate Form.

Each attractor has the purpose of ensuring that the interaction between the information, transmitted through its failsafe intelligence, produces evolution as more complexity for the Form itself, so that it can add to the general complexity of the universe. This is another way to explain how consciousness can expand inside a universe of matter.

Looking at this flow in the opposite motion, information that resides within the Threshold has the function of preserving the complexity that is produced within matter until the moment in which this complexity obtains a high enough level to be able to directly access the Real.

In recent visits to Damanhur, I enjoyed my talks with Gnomo Orzo and Coyote Cardo – the champions of what is now known as spiritual physics – and their love for quantum mechanics and the work of the late Stephen Hawking. Similar to Falco's way of thinking, Hawking had a positive take on the idea of why we are here. In a book he left uncompleted when he passed from this world, *Brief Answers to Big Questions* (Random House, 2018), he set out his deliberations for writing that book and the importance of his final thoughts:

> People have always wanted answers to the big questions. Where did we come from? How did the universe begin? What is the meaning and design behind it all? Is there anyone out there? The creation accounts of the past now seem less relevant and credible. They have been replaced by a variety of what can only be called superstitions, ranging from New Age to *Star Trek*. But real science can be far stranger than science fiction, and much more satisfying.

The latter thought is just what might be expected from a scientist, albeit a great one. Even so, Hawking does see the relevance of creation theories from the past, though is less content with what he thinks have replaced them in contemporary thinking.

At Damanhur, there has been much research on inner selves. Over the years a theory has emerged that has come to be known as "personalities within". Based firmly on Damanhurian spiritual physics, the theory refers to the complex composition of the human soul, which gathers experiences of other lives, creating what we are now as a compendium of different personalities. It's a neat little theory on a big subject, in just the same way that Hawking had contemplated.

A soul that incarnates continues its constant evolutionary path; following the fragmentation of the mirror, Oneness recomposes itself by experiencing the forms. This makes it possible for it to evolve while allowing the expression of free will within a higher purpose. Indeed, human souls contain a divine spark, and with it the possibility of regaining memory and consciousness that we are divine ourselves and we can in turn divinize matter.

The attractor, that little "piece" of Real that passes through the Threshold, collects information, memories and experiences and then connects to a physical body at the moment of a new incarnation. The "Bridge" forms are those that have this potential to grow at an evolutionary level thanks to the divine spark; reincarnation is a quick way to continue on this path of exploration of matter.

Time to consider what the human soul consists of. A body, about to be born in the material domain, is the signal that attracts a soul. A corresponding attractor moves from the Real to the Threshold, where it finds some personalities. The attractor's intelligence summons a certain number of personalities, a minimum of eight, with no maximum.

The peculiarity of this theory lies in the fact that these personalities are recordings of the experiences of other humans, each with unique characteristics, who have lived in different periods of time, have different ages, tastes, morals and convictions. The attractor summons them, and they become parts of a newly formed structure, attractor plus personalities.

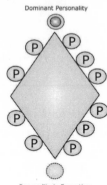

Personalities, as they are like memories of different individuals inside of us, are both young and old, male and female, but this has no specific relevance to the baby's gender. According to mythological tradition, human beings were once androgynous, which means their male and female aspects were not separated. The separation is a limiting condition, imposed on humans as a consequence of their defeat by the enemy. Every individual contains a group of personalities, interacting among themselves, and they are all essential for our life experience: integrating them with the new life we live with the identity that starts being created at the time of our birth is what defines our soul's evolution.

The personalities settle in precise body parts or organs of the person in question, and so there may very well be a personality that lives in the heart, another in the lungs, in the liver, in the kidneys and so on. All the organs are involved, this means that each of our physical organs have a memory represented by a personality, in addition to the cellular memory relating to their genetic code, their DNA and the memories of all the experiences of the current lives.

Amongst the organs, the brain, as the coordinator of the active presence of personalities that, at any given moment, surface to consciousness, has a very particular function. In the brain there are at all times two personalities: it is their conversation that is what gives us the possibility of making choices. As we grow wiser, the new "I" that is the personality that is being formed, becomes more and more one of the voices, integrating the impulses, desires and stimuli coming from the other personalities.

At a fascinating meeting with Gnomo Orzo, we explored how spiritual physics fits alongside cosmological physics. He pointed out that in 1912, the proof that special relativity was wrong had a strong resonance. As was shown by Einstein, the only form of accelerated motion that cannot be described is the one due to gravitation, since special relativity is not compatible with the equivalence principle.

Having just read Gnomo's book, *How Many Holes Does a Ring Have?* (Devodama, Vidracco, 2017), I expressed admiration for the way he had contrasted and compared the accepted methods of physics and the Damanhurian spiritual physics. I told him that I had found his book a beautiful read. He replied:

> Thank you. This is the base, the first, of a series of books around this aspect, because we are working hard to create a model that is official, and scientific, and so it's very nice. It's funny, because we'd like to do a review of the engineering of Falco's equipment, because he never completely explained everything to us. But in some ways, he spread a piece of his knowledge over to all Damanhurians. So, the only way to recreate this knowledge is to create a union within the people.

In coming to any understanding of the physics of the esoteric, it is important to remember the processes of evolution. Humankind, just like any other life form, is in a continual state of flux, persistently changing and evolving. That is why there are some differences between races, and even between species, who share virtually the same DNA. In spiritual physics, the most important facets are a broader understanding of time, appreciating the importance of synchronicity, and a full comprehension of the conception of complexity in all things natural.

The material universe obeys completely different laws to those encountered in the divinities' own dimension, so their attempt to enter this new realm involves a certain amount of risk. At this point something of a superior nature, even to that of the primeval divinities, intervenes and establishes conditions they will be obliged to follow in order to enter matter. We are now living in the era of the fourth primeval divinity, known by the Damanhurian school as the primeval divinity humankind, whose descent into matter took place around 30 million years ago.

Spiritual physics concerns the experience of the divinity humankind within form. I asked Coyote Cardo what the importance of spiritual physics was, in the overall philosophy of Damanhur:

> Today it is more difficult to answer this question than previously. From my point of view, it is important because Falco's vision was, and continues to be, a futuristic vision of physics. Maybe that the world of physics will keep in step with esoteric physics. Falco talked about a time in the future when this would become self-evident. This is not only relevant to physics, but to all the aspects of Damanhur. He brought this vision from the future and placed it here in the present. Esoteric physics was born out of that context.

Humankind is currently a player in a sort of huge game in which the jackpot is its very existence. This is an actual game, with all the usual components such as the adversary, the referee, and rules that must be obeyed. Beyond the playing field, which is this entire universe of form, superior forces watch the game without ever directly intervening. The concept of divinity, according to Coyote, means giving this word different meanings and functions, so it is necessary to focus on this topic at the outset and try to clarify it as much as possible.

> We are working in the field of magic, so let us take a look at how this topic is presented in the language of magic. As defined by magic, divinity is a concept that becomes an OBJECT by means of directed thought and which, then, thanks to its own perception of matter, allows what exists to exist.

To better understand what this means, divinity can be considered a concept, an idea, therefore an invention of mankind. Humankind is able to give this idea density through the power of focused thought. This means that if thoughts about an idea are focused in a certain way and for a sufficient amount of time that idea will become a real object. Herein lies one of the fundamental principles of magic: *thought creates*. This newly created divinity assumes a consciousness and an identity of its own and begins to perform a very important function: it perceives reality.

Once bonded to the project of the primeval divinity, humans were in a conundrum, having to deal with the reality of a short physical life on one hand, yet with the desire to attain goals that required decidedly longer timeframes on the other. Consequently, they began to search for continuity of existence after death as well as the possibility of being reborn in order to continue towards the realization of distant goals. To fulfil this need, something had to be found that would be able to contain human essence, the memory of the dead, and that would also be able to direct rebirth.

This is how the idea of reincarnation was first conceived, as well as the reason why divinities were invented, to contain the souls of the dead and to preserve their memories. Motivated by this need, humankind began a process that continued for thousands of years to develop the necessary technology, which today we define as magic, in order to create and control a divinity. Therefore, a divinity is basically a container, which necessitates direct focus in order to be created.

I asked Gnomo how he thought that spiritual physics fits into the overall philosophy of Damanhur.

> Esoteric physics, I think, from 1993 started to be one of the main translations of the magic in Damanhur. In some ways, from the moment Falco started to teach... not only teach, to discuss... it was listed there in a sheet from the first formation of Damanhur. So, it is a new sensation, a feeling, a resource of a completely new way and point of view, a magical perspective. Falco showed to the people, to the Damanhurians, that it was possible to look at the world as a creation using logic.

Maybe, I surmised, there had been something of a demystification of things magical within the community. Gnomo felt that this way of explaining things had helped a lot of people to understand Damanhur's emphasis on magic and the purpose of the mystic.

> For me, for example, I was not interested in religion, magic rituals, and the like. I prefer this logical way to express myself and for me it was the best channel to understand Damanhur. That's why I am constantly working around spiritual physics and I want to create a model, for example, for the Selfica, a mathematical and physical archetype.

Coyote explained that physics still lives with the dichotomy between Einsteinian physics and Newtonian physics, and now also quantum physics. These lines of physics are not compatible; the search is on for a "theory of everything". He felt it was important that a line of physics would be found to explain everything. The people who research esoteric physics in Damanhur really do believe that this is the area of research that will find common ground for the dichotomy of physics.

Coyote said that he wouldn't be surprised if, in the near future, someone who is more connected to such ideas, say a scientist working in that area, would understand that this aspect taught by Falco was not so crazy, after all. Such a person would be interested to know everything that happens at Damanhur, and so have greater insight as to how work should develop within the scope of his or her scientific discipline. "That would also be the moment", Coyote said, "when the topic would be of significantly general interest here. Currently, it is not the most important aspect from a Damanhurian point of view."

As far as projecting these ideas into the whole wide world, Coyote considered that, if ever there were the right sort of synchronistic signals contiguous to that direction, they would surely put their energy there. The researches of the gifts that Falco left behind are in that direction, to be able to grasp important aspects of spiritual physics. "Those aspects that keep us anchored," said Coyote.

> One of the categories of the gifts given is the aspect of keeping the two planes detached, where there is a need to understand in detail all the aspects of the separated planes. Then you have concepts, for example, of neutral events and saturated events, that in order to be able to use these gifts, you have to understand. Just like other gifts that require research, in spiritual physics you have to be able to comprehend the new vision to the maximum.

Spiritual physics features in the work of other Damanhurian centres round the world. For the intrepid Damanhurian researchers, their research is a two-way process. They are learning from cosmological physics all the time. There is an abundance of new discoveries being made in that branch of physics, and there is a distinct confluence between what Damanhurians are doing and what the quantum physicists are researching, and they are gradually coming closer together. The main stumbling block appears to be the way, at the moment, that regular science is in danger of becoming a religion and the concept of being a heretic in scientific terms is prevalent.

Many scientists have been branded as heretics, as if science is a religion. The scientific community is strictly controlled by an autocratic elite, with similar dogma to a religion. Coyote said this aspect was particularly prevalent in the 20th century:

At the beginning of the century, many individuals, like Einstein and others, but mainly individuals, would make discoveries that would change the world. Today, I'm convinced that the scientific approach is posited in groups of people, groups of researchers, while the discoveries of singular individuals does not count for much any more. If you are a scientist and you want to make significant researches, it is necessary to adapt yourself to that system. What happened, for example, with CERN and the work on the Large Hadron Collider, where millions of euros are spent annually – but how does what they do change our lives today, practically? The big discovery, celebrated in 2012, of the "God particle", the so-called Higgs boson, was loudly proclaimed, but what did it practically change?

The Higgs boson is an elementary particle in the standard model of particle physics, produced by the quantum excitation of the Higgs field, one of the fields in particle physics theory. My good friend, the late Ken Campbell, interviewed Peter Higgs for a Channel 4 series, *Reality on the Rocks*. This was before the great discovery of the Higgs boson, which was vaunted for a long time by the scientific establishment as the "holy grail of science". In fact, Higgs told him that it was gravity that was "buggering everything up", as Ken reported back. Ken attempted to explain the Higgs boson theory to me, but I couldn't make head nor tail of it. "Look," he said, "it's all about a field. Now, you're a field, aren't you? A Merri-field. Everywhere you go, you spread fields of merry. Well, it's something like that."

It appeared that gravity could not be fitted into quantum theory. A problem for many years had been that no experiment had ever observed the Higgs boson to confirm his theory. On 4 July 2012, the Atlas and CMS experiments at CERN's Large Hadron Collider announced they had each observed a new particle in the mass region around 125 GeV, which was later confirmed to be the elusive Higgs boson.

Higgs has lately revealed some remarkable things, including this: "I wouldn't be productive enough for today's academic system." And he feared he might have been sacked by Edinburgh University had it not been for the possibility of him being awarded the Nobel Prize. After the discovery at CERN, the award-winning Nobel scientist made clear the crowning achievement of his career had come at a heavy price. He said: "My life has been ruined by people recognizing me on the street and wanting to take a selfie with me."

The current scientific policy makes it almost impossible for an individual to break through, in the sense that Einstein did, and make discoveries that bring about real change. In the past, individuals made discoveries and we still feel their impact today. Now, Coyote thinks, we have this kind of religion-science, where a scientist has to go along with, and behind, this kind of elite in a surge that strengthens their grip on power.

> There is an evident niche of people who believe in making contact with esoteric schools. I have read about Rupert Sheldrake and his researches on "morphic resonance", and I must say this is very important work. He has a concept that is similar to some of our concepts in esoteric physics.

In recent times, there have been a considerable number of visits to Damanhur by a variety of indigenous peoples. Coyote feels that this is quite important, that it is a philosophical aspect when there could be talk about the beginning of the universe and the origin of the human soul. In recent times, he had engaged in research into peoples with esoteric traditions. These were perfectly compatible with Damanhurian research work. Some of these shamanic cultures, like the ones from South America, resonated considerably.

Here was an example of Damanhur going out to the world and the world coming to Damanhur. The project of the Parliament of Peoples appears to have already attracted particular indigenous peoples who are in danger of their cultures being driven to extinction. They come to Damanhur to protect their cultures and try to prevent their destruction.

Above all, Coyote wished to express the concept that Damanhur attempts to anticipate the future, with an aim to regain the power that humankind has, but has now apparently lost. "That is the most important thing," he said. Before modernity invented specializations, creating distance between things, philosophy, science, art and medicine were united, and there were no categories of scientists, doctors and artists. Further along we

will see that, if there is an obstacle to understanding the universe, it is precisely that excessive specialization.

While writing this chapter, some fundamentally important events came to light in the world of science. First, astronomers took the first ever image of a black hole, located in a distant galaxy. It measures 40 billion kilometres across, three million times the size of the Earth, and has been described by scientists as "a monster". The black hole is 500 trillion kilometres away, captured by the Event Horizon Telescope, a network of eight of the most powerful telescopes in the world linked together.

The initial research was set up by Professor Heino Falcke, of Radboud University in the Netherlands, who said the black hole was found in a galaxy called M87. "What we see is larger than the size of our entire solar system," he said. This event was crucial in bringing a positive level of proof to the theoretical theorems of black holes from Hawking and his cosmological fellow travellers.

The second event was the emergence of incredible pictures of the totality – and, therefore, the edge – of the universe, made possible with the Hubble telescope, and which have raised speculation about the expanding of the universe and the inevitability of such expansion.

Edwin Hubble initially made the observations in 1925 and was the first to prove that the universe is expanding. He proved there is a direct relationship between the speeds of distant galaxies and their distances from Earth.

This earliest possible snapshot of the entire universe – probably "the mother of all baby photos" – shows the cosmic microwave background (CMB). With new technology that has allowed scientists to measure it more accurately than ever before, the CMB gives us clues as to why the universe turned out as it did, and even how it all started in the first place.

Scientific thinking is increasingly coming to a conclusion that this expansion is not infinite and that there will come a time when the universe starts to shrink. At such an event, all the natural laws will go into reverse. Gravity will push rather than pull, time will move backwards rather than forwards, we will grow younger with each passing minute.

What are the chances that we will encounter some alien form of life as we explore the galaxy? If the argument about the timescale for the appearance of life on Earth is correct, there ought to be many other stars whose planets have life on them. Stephen Hawking had an open mind on such matters, as he wrote in *Brief Answers to Big Questions*:

> Some of these stellar systems could have formed five billion years before the Earth, so why is the galaxy not crawling with self-designing mechanical or biological life forms? Why hasn't the Earth been visited and even colonised? By the way, I discount suggestions that UFOs contain beings from outer space, as I think that any visits by aliens would be much more obvious and probably also much more unpleasant. So why haven't we been visited? Maybe the probability of life spontaneously appearing is so low that Earth is the only planet in the galaxy – or in the observable universe – on which it happened.

Other planets in the galaxy, on which life has developed, may not have had a long enough collision-free period to evolve intelligent beings. Hawking talks of a third possibility, a reasonable probability for life to form and evolve to intelligent beings, but the system becomes unstable and the intelligent life destroys itself:

> This would be a very pessimistic conclusion and I very much hope it isn't true. I prefer a fourth possibility: that there are other forms of intelligent life out there, but that we have been overlooked. In 2015, I was involved in the launch of the Breakthrough Listen Initiatives, which uses radio telescope observations to search for intelligent extraterrestrial life, and has state-of-the-art facilities, generous funding and thousands of hours of dedicated radio telescope time. It is the largest ever scientific research programme aimed at finding evidence of civilizations beyond Earth. Breakthrough Message is an international competition to create messages that could be read by an advanced civilization.

However, he urges caution, stating that perhaps we need to be wary of answering back until we have developed a bit further. Meeting a more advanced civilization, at our present stage, might be a bit like the original inhabitants of America meeting Columbus. In this, I share Hawking's caution.

The Drake equation is a probabilistic argument used to estimate the number of active, communicative extra-terrestrial civilizations in the Milky Way galaxy. The equation summarizes the main concepts that scientists must contemplate when considering the question of other radio-communicative life. While working as a radio astronomer at the National Radio Astronomy Observatory in Green Bank, West Virginia, Dr Frank Drake conceived an approach to bind the terms involved in estimating the number of technological civilizations that may exist in our galaxy.

The Drake equation:

$$N = R_* . f_p . n_e . f_l . f_i . f_c . L$$

N = Number of civilizations in the Milky Way galaxy whose electromagnetic emissions are detectable.

R_* = Rate of formation of stars suitable for the development of intelligent life.

f_p = The fraction of those stars with planetary systems.

n_e = Number of planets, per solar system, with environment suitable for life.

f_l = The fraction of suitable planets on which life actually appears.

f_i = The fraction of life-bearing planets on which intelligent life emerges.

f_c = The fraction of civilizations that develop a technology that releases detectable signs of their existence into space.

L = Length of time such civilizations release detectable signals into space.

The Drake equation was first presented in 1961 and identifies specific factors thought to play a role in the development of such civilizations. Although there is no unique solution to this equation, it is a generally accepted tool used by the scientific community to examine these factors. Stephen Hawking, again:

> I would like to speculate a little on the development of life in the universe, and in particular on the development of intelligent life. I shall take this to include the human race, even though much of its behaviour throughout history has been pretty stupid and not calculated to aid the survival of the species. Two questions I shall

discuss are "What is the probability of life existing elsewhere in the universe?" and "How may life develop in the future?"

Within the limits of our existing technology, any practical search for distant intelligent life must necessarily be a search for some manifestation of a distant technology. In each of its last four decadal reviews, the United States National Research Council has emphasized the relevance and importance of searching for evidence of the electromagnetic signature of distant civilizations. Besides illuminating the factors involved in such a search, the Drake equation is a simple, effective tool for stimulating intellectual curiosity about the universe around us, for helping us to understand that life as we know it is the end product of a natural, cosmic evolution, and for making us realize how much we are a part of that universe.

A key goal of the SETI Institute, which had a specific remit to search for extra-terrestrial intelligence, is to pursue further high-quality research that will yield any additional information related to the factors of Drake's fascinating equation. The SETI Institute's first project was to conduct a wide search for narrow-band radio transmissions that would betray the existence of technically competent beings elsewhere in the galaxy. Today, the SETI Institute uses a specially designed instrument for its SETI efforts – the Allen Telescope Array (ATA) located in the Cascade Mountains of California.

One of my life-long heroes is Carl Sagan, who first sparked my interest in extra-terrestrial intelligence. He was the American astronomer, cosmologist, astrophysicist, astrobiologist, author, best known for his work as a science popularizer and communicator. He died in 1996 and was way ahead of his time in his thinking, and popularised the word "cosmos" to describe the vast nature of the universe:

> There is a place with four suns in the sky – red, white, blue, and yellow; two of them are so close together that they touch, and starstuff flows between them. I know of a world with a million moons. I know of a sun the size of the Earth – and made of diamond. There are tiny grains between the stars, with the size and atomic composition of bacteria. There are stars leaving the Milky Way, and immense gas clouds falling into it. There are, perhaps, places which are outside our universe. The universe is vast and awesome, and for the first time we are becoming a part of it. (From: *Planetary Exploration*, University of Oregon Books, 1970)

Sagan had that genius sort of mind that was easy to admire. One of my very favourite films is *Contact*, an adaptation of a Sagan novel, starring Jodie Foster, who portrays the film's protagonist, a SETI scientist who finds strong evidence of extra-terrestrial life and is chosen to make first contact. The scene where she enters the pod in a complex machine, which is then dropped into four rapidly spinning rings, causing the pod to travel through a series of wormholes, is one of the most powerful in cinema. She eventually finds herself on a beach, like a childhood picture she drew – Pensacola, Florida – and a figure approaches that has the appearance of her deceased father. The scientist recognizes him as an alien taking her father's form and attempts to ask questions. The alien tells her that the familiar landscape and form were used to make their first contact easier for her, that this journey was just humanity's first step to joining other spacefaring species. It's a very compelling idea. And in line with Damanhurian thinking, methinks.

There may well never have been another intelligent technologically advanced species in the entire history of the universe. Unquestionably, that was the dogmatic view of the medieval church authorities. When you take into account that there may be 400 billion stars in the Milky Way, up to three potentially habitable worlds in many of these star systems, and some two trillion galaxies in the entire universe, it seems intelligent life is an inevitability. Our intuition can often lead us astray, but "supposing" exists alongside science. The magnitude of the unknowns that biogenesis, evolution and long-term habitability of a planet bring into the equation throws many of our assumptions about life into doubt. It's true, there are an astronomical number of possibilities for intelligent technologically advanced life forms, but the equally huge uncertainties make it a very real possibility that humans are the only spacefaring aliens our universe has ever known. Contemplating the vastness of the universe and our chances of meeting alien beings might be beyond the supposing of most human beings, but the Damanhur story does appear to make it more probable than we might previously have imagined.

And let's not forget that as well as being a legendary scientist, Albert Einstein was also a creative man, just like Falco. Einstein shared another aspect with the founder of Damanhur: his view of supposing, his view of imagination. He famously declared: "Imagination is more important than knowledge. For knowledge is limited, whereas imagination embraces the entire world, stimulating progress, giving birth to evolution."

CHAPTER 9

THE SACRED WOOD

On a snowy winter's day, I visited the Sacred Wood of Damanhur, located near the community nucleo of Tin and above the Temples of Humankind. It is a huge forest, a lush enchanted woodland, ripe with magnificent plant life. In the thick white snow, this was a magical place indeed. In the Tin nucleo, I met Lucertola Pepe with a group of others and we headed, in the deep snow, into this exceptional place. It looked marvellous, with the new snow and the clear fresh air. As far as I could see, there were endless trees, all looking wonderful in their bright white attire.

I was told that everyone at Damanhur had their own particular tree that they related to, and which were decorated with personal totems and objects that made the relationship with the tree more intense.

After some time walking deep into the forest, I was guided towards a huge tree, monumentally imposing, with a strangely powerful presence, situated at the centre of a spiral. It is regarded as a guardian of the forest. I was introduced to this tree, which is known as Diamentel, and asked to attempt a communication with it.

I approached this great tree with some trepidation and cautiously placed my forehead against it and my arms partially around its hefty circumference. As I meditated on this, I think I was "instructed" to try my best taking the message of Damanhur into the world. I also had a guilty feeling that I should be going back to Shetland in order to plant trees. We don't have many.

As I was writing up this chapter, "Thought for the day" came up on BBC Radio 4. It was a piece by Rob Marshall, a church rector from Digswell in Hertfordshire:

Some believe that trees have figured in ancient myths, folklore and religions, because of three things; firstly because of the huge variety

that exists, second because of their size, and thirdly because of their longevity. My goodness, we think that these trees have seen a great deal more than we have, but their longevity, it seems, is threatened more than ever following the news that deforestation is on the increase. The New York Declaration was signed in 1914, aimed at halving the rate of deforestation and the increased planting of new trees, when we have heard this week that 26 million hectares of trees, covering an area the size of Britain, is being lost every single year. Yes, every year.

The rector told us that such a statistic is honestly too much to digest, and he quoted Jo House, a reader in environmental science and policy at the University of Bristol, who described the continuing loss as "shocking" and "tragic", not least because of the incalculable value and irreplaceability of these trees. He added that all of these statistics don't yet account for the ongoing crisis of the Amazon rainforest fires, that are "only adding to a whirlpool of despondency". In many ways, the tree is a modern-day icon. It can easily represent an interdisciplinary fight to rescue our planet from the ravages of human destruction. We often talk of what might seem tokenistic gestures or protests. He went on:

> They are all well-meaning in their own right, but none of them in isolation really addresses the attacks on the creative order, of which we are clearly poor stewards. The story of the tree of knowledge, of good and evil, versus the tree of life in the Garden of Eden story, is a

reminder that possessing all the knowledge in the world doesn't mean we are making the right choices or doing the right thing. The tree is an icon for us to do more and more, doing not just saying. Philip Larkin's poem "The Trees" ends with the romantic supposition that trees die and then return again to what he describes as "fullgrown thickness" returning every year "afresh, afresh". But no longer is that always going to be the case, unless, of course, we begin again to cherish this icon, begin to behave responsibly, and all of us do a whole lot more.

With regard to the environment and the care of our planet we are all capable of doing a lot more. The news coming into our homes has been both alarming and optimistic. Alarming because of the raging fires in the Amazon rainforest and the escalating incidence of deforestation in the Congo and other parts of Africa – all this for commercial interests and monetary greed, while demonstrating a complete disregard for the effects on the planet. The "whirlpool of despondency" that the rector spoke of. While cutting through such despondency, like some environmentalist televisual Colossus alerting us to the dangers and calling for immediate action, is David Attenborough, surely a prophet sent to help us change our ways. The optimistic news is the admirable actions being taken by children and young people with their climate-change strikes and demonstrations, all the more admirable by the fact that they grew out of the passionate concerns of a Swedish young person, Greta Thunberg, and rapidly mushroomed into a world-wide campaign with millions of young people demanding action on climate change.

All of us could do more, and sometimes fundamental action is being taken to do exactly that. I spoke with Lucertola, who lives in the nucleo community of Tin, right in the heart of the Sacred Wood. She told me that the wood is now regarded as another temple and I asked her how this came about:

The story of the Sacred Wood is to accept that the origin and the heart of the wood is the underground temple. After ten years of people investing their time and effort building a sacred space for all the divine forces of our planet, the first stages of the Temples of

124

Humankind, at a certain time Falco indicated another action. He had a sensitivity for all sorts of subtle structures and subtle energies. He announced, around 1996, that the underground temple was sending more and more energy to the surface above. This meant that the trees were becoming antennae for the temple underground and the space above the temple.

Damanhurians started to call it the Sacred Wood, cleaning the space for the plants to grow again. They reinvigorated their efforts in reforestation, cutting back deadwood and carefully nurturing the growth of the best trees. Lucertola said that it was not easy to create an ecosystem:

> But we are still working hard to achieve it. For sure, it is not perfect yet, but we have made great progress and the wood is in a healthy state. Many animals have come back, many birds, 30 or 40 different species, we have wild pigs, foxes, bears, squirrels and hares. They find food now, berries, plants, vegetation, insects, and little by little life is once more returning to the woods. There are also human beings. Humans, in a way, have a very special presence in this wood. There are two nucleos, Tin and Sorgente, and we people living in these communities are challenging ourselves to integrate harmoniously into this sacred space, where we are entrusted with taking care of the wood, the ecosystem, while at the same time finding different ways of living ourselves, being more sustainable and able to adopt ever more ecological ideas and practices.

Both communities involved in this project call it a "cradle project", because the wood is like a cradle for the consciousness of plants and other forces connected to nature. Since this is a Sacred Wood, it is the place where special rituals take place, celebrating solstices, equinoxes and other commemorations. As a consequence, the woods have an increasing presence on a subtle plane. Lucertola told me another interesting thing:

> Falco came here to design all the spirals and labyrinths that you see all around us in this place as expressions of the mandalas, sacred language in a way. He came here, walked the area, often whistling, but he did not measure out the distances. He knew what they were and where they should be. He drew up the plans and over the next two years a group of us laid out the stones into the vast complex you

see now, modulating the energies from the temples below and from the synchronic lines above.

She then told me something that was quite remarkable, that the Sacred Wood was the place where human, plants and spirits of nature, will be reconnected in a spiritual unity:

> It is the reconnection project. In esoteric physics, there is an ancient knowledge where the three mother worlds of humans, plants and spirits of nature were formerly united in harmony, but then due largely to human neglect they got separated, and that is the condition they are in now. It is now up to us humans to take the first steps to reconnect them. In this place, we are making our first attempts at reunification. This is an activation point for initiatives happening all over the world, a world in a tragic situation.

She pointed out that in the Sacred Wood they had the synchronic lines, the trees as antennae to amplify the message, and the people who lived in this place and in the whole of Damanhur, all of them, for 20 or 30 years, contacting the trees, one by one, to create a new alliance for humanity. The trees and plants will have a higher state of consciousness and an ability to communicate this globally through the synchronic lines.

And we humans will be influenced by that, positively, because it will be a place similar to this wood where you will be honoured to get a spiritual orientation with the trees and the plants.

CHAPTER 10

MAKING MUSIC WITH PLANTS

As we have seen in the last chapter, Damanhurians have always been active in researching communication with the forces of nature, guided by the desire to re-establish a harmonious balance in the relationship with life on the planet. In the Damanhurian vision, humans are part of a spiritual ecosystem with extra-planetary forces and intelligences, and it is important to establish a conscious contact with them, as it is with life forms present in the environmental ecosystem that surrounds us.

Our human evolution is inextricably linked to the alliance and reunification with the physical and subtle forces that inhabit this and other worlds, as discussed in the previous chapters, which Damanhurians consider the "mother worlds". They can be conceived as dimensions vibrating at a slightly different vibration than ours. Humans live in one of the mother worlds; plants and nature spirits are the beings who inhabit the other two. A large part of research in Damanhur is dedicated to opening channels of deep contact with plants and all beings who inhabit natural environments, so that we can bring the three dimensions on to the same frequency, and live in a world where all beings and intelligences are connected in one living web.

It's no coincidence that one of the symbols of Damanhur is a flower, the dandelion, the Italian name for that distinctive flower (Tarassaco) was bestowed on Falco a short time after his demise.

Over many years a group of Damanhurians have researched communication with the plant world. As part of this research, they created an instrument able to perceive the electromagnetic variations from the surface of plant leaves to the root system and translated them into sound. Science increasingly supports the concept that plants operate with an innate intelligence and logic diverse from our own. The fascinating experimentation of the perceptive links between humans and the plant world is called "music of the plants". Emotional experiences come about through these experiments, where beings that are seemingly quite diverse are able to establish a harmony and communication between them. As Stevie Wonder once said: "For these are but a few discoveries we find inside the Secret Life of Plants."

From a technical point of view, communication takes places through the transmission of very-low-voltage electric currents between the roots and leaves and variations of resistivity in the plant, which is then translated into music through a sound generator. The actual device for linking to the plants has gone through many developmental stages. The latest device is now commercially available and is used by practitioners and musicians throughout the world.

Communication with plants mainly involves the emotional sphere of both humans and plants. The plants appear to relish the sound and learn to produce the sounds themselves through the technical instrumentation. Over the years, many recordings have been produced and made available, featuring music made by plants, whether potted or rooted in the ground. This music has been played live, as well at concerts in which plants and humans sing and play music together. The pleasure that the plants experience with these sounds becomes particularly evident during these sessions, when the sounds of the plant musicians harmoniously resonate with those of human musicians.

I was told about an incident that, to some extent, confirms that plants experience this musical connection. A Damanhurian singer was performing in a concert inside the temple. She was singing, with trees situated on top of the temple – in the Sacred Wood – connected by long cables to a sound system inside the temple. There were five such concerts scheduled, to accommodate the numbers wanting to attend in manageable groups. The first four concerts went remarkably well, with the singer and the trees interacting harmoniously. However, on the fifth night she found it almost impossible to communicate with the trees, whose music appeared angular, disjointed and somewhat angry. She had great difficulty singing with the trees and certainly not harmoniously. It was later revealed that a great storm had been raging outside. The trees were obviously reacting to the emotions that the storm raised within them. The music had to take second place.

I have experienced lots of concerts and workshops with the plants and the music they make. A funny, yet strange, incident happened when

I took a group of people from Essex to Damanhur as part of a youth exchange programme. We all attended a plant music demonstration workshop. There were a few other people already in the room, listening to the plants playing as we entered. The Essex young people sat themselves down, but the plant music subsided somewhat, before eventually petering out. Try as he may, the man conducting the demonstration could not get the plants to play. He apologized and we had the young people get up and leave. As we were going down the path, one of the group said that she had left her purse and could she go back to get it. I said that I would go back and find it. As I entered the room, I saw and heard that the plants were happily playing and the other folks there were enjoying the music. It made me smile.

Another time, we went to the Sound Symposium in St Johns, Newfoundland, and put on a demonstration of plant music, which was much appreciated and became one of the highlights of the festival. Musicians played with the plants and really enjoyed the experience.

I have a plant music device, one of the earlier models, and have used it in concerts of jazz and improvised music, primarily in concerts with the Shetland Improvisers Orchestra. I intend to experiment more in the future, linking into a piano keyboard and other instrumental devices. You can find out more about the music of the plants from the Damanhur website, their new portable Bamboo Music of the Plants devices and tracks of recorded plant music.

CHAPTER 11
RITUALS AND CEREMONIES

The universe is inhabited by many subtle beings, those kinds of energy that don't need a physical form to exist. There are realms, in addition to the animal, plant and mineral, in which intelligence and life are conveyed. This collection of subtle beings, ranging from the world of nature spirits to the realm of divinities related to the rich variety of peoples and cultures of the world, is known as the ecosystem and is fundamental for human evolution, and that of the universe itself. Ancient knowledge and new discoveries can be united through magic, which in Damanhur is defined as the "science of all sciences", and whose study and application helps develop the potential within each person, and theurgy, those techniques and languages in rituals that allow for communication with other dimensions.

The mystic philosopher George Ivanovich Gurdjieff talked of the way we all drift through life in a state of sleep, that most humans do not possess a unified consciousness and thus live their lives in a state of hypnotic "waking sleep", but that it is possible to awaken to a higher state of consciousness and achieve full human potential. In his youth, he studied Sufi dervish philosophy and Tibetan Buddhism, studied their language, ritual, dance, medicine and, above all, psychic techniques. In his later life, he developed a system he termed "the work", which emphasized ritual as a means of reawakening consciousness. I once attended a Gurdjieff school in southern England, where every month a different particular word was designated unusable, to keep us on our toes and to think about what we said before we said it. This was a simple ritual, yet effective. Gurdjieff built his methodology on a range of rituals. When I first came to Damanhur, I was delighted to discover that there was a comprehensive number of rituals, most of them related to the natural phenomena of the planet and the universe(s).

130

In Damanhur philosophy, the field of existence includes many universes. The one in which we live is characterized by diverse forms of life and matter, and by the interaction of these forms with time, whose flow does not move linearly from the past to the present to the future, but rather in a complex geography with the contemporaneous presence of times and parallel universes, as quantum physics has also hypothesized.

Over the millennia, humanity has felt the presence of many different forces all around us, and we have sensed the magnitude of these forces. This is how the pantheons, gods of all the mythologies considered collectively, have come about in history, including the major contemporary religions. Smaller fragments of this primeval origin are the nature spirits, which are present in the legends and traditions of many cultures, as inhabitants of the forests, springs and glades.

Even plants and animals are manifestations of the same divine nature. Some beings, including humans, are "bridge-forms" capable of bridging the material and spiritual planes, because they are aware of the divine spark within them. All beings have a divine spark. The divine spark is always awake.

The relationship between human beings and gods is thought of as an alliance rather than a submission, as they all emanate from the Absolute, and the divine nature permeates both, although at different levels of awareness, consciousness and power.

Solstice and equinox

The ritual of marking the transition between seasons of the year has been carried out on all continents since the beginning of human history. At Damanhur, they consider the equinoxes and solstices to be particularly sacred times of the year. The entire Damanhur community comes together to celebrate these important events inside circles of stone. During the solstices, a central fire represents the sun, and a second fire symbolizes the moon. At the equinoxes, as day and night have the same length, one central fire represents both the sun and the moon. The ritual is divided into three phases: the lighting, culmination and extinguishing of the fire(s).

Damanhurians enter the circle wearing robes of varying colours, according to their attainment level within the Initiation Path of Medit-Action. They offer herbs to the fires, meditate, sing, and recite hymns and prayers composed by Damanhurians. All phases of the rituals are accompanied by ritual music, music of the plants and sacred dance.

Due to the increased number of Damanhurians in recent years, the rituals take place two or three times on different days to allow everyone to participate. These are joyful occasions, and guests are encouraged to join in by registering in advance at the Damanhur Welcome Office.

The ritual of the Oracle

On every full moon night, the Open Temple of Damjl hosts the Oracle ritual. The ritual celebration of the Oracle takes place in the open air, with the attendance of many Damanhurians and guests, accompanied by the rhythmic sounds of the drummer and percussionists of Damanhur, and by the movements of the sacred dancers.

It is commonly known that the time of a full moon is a moment that exalts personal mediumship and makes it possible to receive intuitions, ideas and answers, gathering them from divine forces who are open to communicating with humankind during the full moon.

This is an occasion where each one of us may be particularly receptive to messages and indications that come from the spiritual ecosystem. Those attending the Oracle do so not only as spectators, but they may seize the opening of synchronicity that is brought about by the full moon. The Oracle of Damanhur is connected to the oracles and divination traditions of the past, those which were the subject of extensive research by the group that conducts and is involved with this matter, aiming to create a bridge between our material sphere and the diverse ramifications of possible futures.

The Oracle of Damanhur, therefore, is not a person. It is a group of divine forces that oversee the paths of time. The Oracle comprises also all the Oracle gods of ancient times, integrated with the new forces of the third millennium. The Oracle is a kind of antenna between our dimension and more expanded and apparently distant realities.

The Oracle can be consulted by all those who wish to take advantage of this possibility for human and spiritual growth. Individuals and groups from all over the world have requested a response as a precious source of inspiration and insight. The responses are prepared through many different ritual processes, along the different phases of the moon, to deliver it to the person who requested it after one or two lunar months, written on a leaf, at a successive celebration of the Oracle ritual.

I asked Sirena Ninfea, who usually leads these Oracle rituals, about their nature and purpose:

Each month many rituals are carried out to make contact with divine forces, in order to prepare the way for the Oracle, to receive the signs sent to us. The rituals are all linked to the phases of the moon. There are specific rituals related to the waning moon, the new moon, the crescent moon and the full moon. These are reserved for those Damanhurians belonging to the Way of the Oracle who are activated for this contact. The Oracle ritual of the full moon, held in the Open Temple, is the final phase of the monthly work, and it is open to anybody who wishes to assist, just as you did. You saw the Oracle in the full moon, which is the last ritual of contact with the Oracle, with divine forces linked to the Oracle.

Sirena was referring to an event that had taken place a couple of nights previous to our interview. I had been a privileged observer of the final part of the rite of the Oracle. This is a precise, detailed ritual incorporating sacred contact that spans, as Sirena had said, over all the four lunar phases. It requires specially prepared and consecrated places, so that questions can be sent to the Oracle and the answers "felt". It is the female members of the Way of the Oracle who are specially prepared for contact with divine forces and they are called Pythias or the "Oracle contactors".

The night I participated in the Oracle ritual, we assembled in the appropriate place, as directed, at around 8.30 pm. I remember that at the beginning of the ceremony there was no visible moon, but the general lighting around the temple and the fire that burned in front of the altar steps illuminated the proceedings in a highly evocative way. There was excellent drumming and the Damanhurians all wore their ritual robes, in the usual white, red, yellow and blue. Sirena Ninfea led the ritual, dressed in a blue robe with silver embroidery, the same robe worn by all the officiants, women and men.

There were lots of different stages to the ritual, involving moving sacred instruments around the fire, readings, meditations and the preparation of questioners. The night we were there, three people asked questions of the Oracle, or rather, received their answers, for they had asked their questions a month or so prior to the ritual. They were called, one at a time, into the heart of the temple, guided by one of the Oracle members carrying a candle. The answer to their question was then ritually read to them. All this was accompanied by drumming and flute music. It was a strangely moving experience.

There was a lovely moment when I saw people looking up into the sky. I looked up too. There it was, a beautiful, big, shining, full moon, radiating its light over all the proceedings.

All three questioners received their answers and the ritual ended as the drumming subsided. The Damanhurians removed their robes straight away and we headed down to the cars to be transported home. As we were loading up the car boot, I became aware that the only light was that from the street lamps. I looked up and there was no moon at all in the cloud-filled sky.

Later, I asked Sirena about the questions that were asked at an Oracle ritual. She explained:

A reply is passed to the questioners through the ritual, like the old Delphic oracle. It is always different and depends on what we have received by way of answers. People sometimes ask for interpretations, to deepen the meaning of the answer.

The questions vary. They might be about family, or work, or how to guide the entire community. Someone might ask for insight into something, how they might guide their spiritual evolution better, whether it would be better to do one thing rather than another. There might even be questions as to how to help the dead. The only questions that cannot be asked are those with any material or egotistical aspect, so you can't ask for the lottery numbers! The rite of the Oracle is a most important event for all Damanhurians and is highly respected.

Commemoration of the dead

Another important ritual at Damanhur is a celebration dedicated to the commemoration of the dead, which takes place every year between late October and early November.

According to Damanhur's understanding, the world of the living and the world of the dead are both expressions of spiritual life. At times, it is possible to open a channel of communication between these dimensions. Rituals are the most important moments of connection, for sending and receiving thoughts with Damanhur citizens who have passed, as well as other loved ones who are no longer in physical form. It is an act of celebration for life in all its manifestations.

As with the solstice and equinox rituals, the commemoration of the dead takes place in a stone circle around a fire, with meditation, prayer, song and offerings to the flames. In this case, though, the ritual is celebrated in the early evening, not during the phases of the sun.

Damanhurians stand inside the circle of stone, each wearing a ritual robe, and guests gather close around the outside of the circle. As the ceremony proceeds, these moments become an opening of energy and emotion for everyone, the citizens of Damanhur, guests and friends.

Alchemy

The concept of alchemy in Damanhur is based on the idea that the body is the most important alchemical laboratory. We can learn to use it to produce substances and guide emotions so that we can be in control of ourselves and transform reality around us. The human body is the main athanor, a furnace used to provide a uniform and constant heat for alchemical digestion, which the alchemist has at their disposal, a laboratory of extraordinary complexity and physical, emotional, subtle energies. This is what in Damanhur is referred to as "alchemy of living forces".

Alchemical gold, in this vision, corresponds to the full awakening of the individual, so that their divine spark can fully manifest its brilliance. Damanhurian alchemy acts through an individual's emotions, memories and thoughts by means of continuous exercise and experimentation. The objective is always to create the conditions for personal growth. At Damanhur, they use prepared instruments, stone circuits and collections of pure elements (air, water, earth, fire) to work in contact with natural essences and time.

Falco had always made his knowledge available to anyone who was willing to explore such subjects more deeply. The research that he conducted, including alchemy, has been organized and structured into a proper School of Alchemy, which can be attended in person and partially also online.

Academics have also looked at rituals in Damanhur. In a doctorate thesis at the Laurentian University of Ontario, Carol Ann Koziol points out that many rituals and celebrations are built into Damanhurian culture to "perpetuate place connectedness" and that these rituals communally honour the seasons and cycles of nature. She talks about a "first fruit" ritual, when a new type of fruit or vegetable ripens for harvest, and then a ritual is performed in gratitude for the crop. Dr Koziol backs this up with a quote from another academic study, by Dr Kara Salter of the University of Western Australia:

> When a new type of fruit ripens enough for harvest, there is a ritual performed that offers the first fruit or vegetable in gratitude for the crop (to what or whom this offer is made is unclear, although I assume that it is offered to the plant world or nature spirits). This ritual is done every year on all Damanhurian properties for each new ripe fruit or vegetable. When I asked why this was done the answer I received was that "it's part of the ethos of growing our own foods in connection and harmony, the plant world and nature"… but has essentially to do with practices that promote self-sufficiency within Damanhur.

Dr Koziol also noted that the "greeting tree" at each nucleo is an example of maintaining an individual's connection to place: "acknowledging the seen and unseen elements of the natural world educates people to treat the natural world as an equal." She reflects that the emphasis on both individual and collective rituals builds a "balance of relationships between the human and the more-than-human world". For her, this balance of rituals reinforces the many aspects of community relationships from an individual to a nucleo and finally, the federation. "The rituals are an example of the remembering flow of panarchy, a form of governance that encompasses all others, with the federation reminding communities and individuals about the importance of honouring the natural world." She regards this as an example of honouring the natural world that occurs within the temple complex.

CHAPTER 12
WAYS AND QUESTS

The School of Meditation has long been at the core of Damanhurian philosophy, a spiritual research pathway based on sharing and self-transformation, with the intention to awaken the divine within each human being through the creative power of positive thinking. In more than 40 years of history, the School of Mediation has stimulated and enriched the lives of many hundreds within many Damanhurian community groups around the world and has welcomed thousands of spiritual seekers. Now Medit-Action, its areas of experience and research, the course of meditation and the path to spiritual freedom, are open to everyone, without cost, because the knowledge that is accessed cannot be counted in monetary terms.

The course of meditation is a direct path to the heart of Falco's teachings and involves the triggering of a direct relationship with the forces of the spiritual ecosystem through an initiation. In the first meetings, the meaning of life is explored, as well as the laws and forces that govern the universe. The research then takes on a chosen direction through "spiritual ways", nine specific pathways to express spirituality in practice, according to one's personal characteristics and preferences.

The spirituals ways are groups within Medit-Action, where every initiate develops specific points of interest according to their aspirations and talents. They complement the general path of Medit-Action and lay the foundation for individual growth by exercising the qualities of each person, expressed not only individually, but also within a group.

Each Damanhurian chooses a main spiritual way to follow, and, if they like, a second one as well. Many of these are interconnected. In this choice they deepen their research, individually and in groups. Citizens are free to leave one way for another but are encouraged to persevere with their chosen one, as it is important to be on a path that you feel is truly serving your growth. There is a deeply held principle at Damanhur that if you start something you should see it through.

But the overcoming of personal hurdles and inhibitions is a fundamental part of personal development. The nine ways are intended to help people develop inner strength, to realize their spiritual identity within the context of the day-to-day world in which they live. Currently, the nine ways from which Damanhurians may choose are:

The Way of the Word, which involves the transmission of messages and refinement of the arts and of communication.

The Way of the Arts, which unites all Damanhurian artists.

The Way of the Monks may be chosen by singles who wish to focus on how they contain and direct their vital energies. It is a pathway based on ritual and devotional aspects.

The Way of the Couples, chosen by couples who wish to contain and direct their vital energies towards the creation of a condition of spiritual androgyny. They give advice to other couples, and support them in the planning and education of children.

The Way of the Knights, which involves security and protection on all of the lands of Damanhur, as well as engagement and participation in the construction of the temples.

The Way of the Oracle, which is dedicated to deepening exploration of the ritual language, and keeping the contact with the divine forces of the Oracle. They carry out past-life research, carry out complex devotional and ritual works in the temples and take care of a special Oracle Temple, immersed in nature, called Baita.

The Way of Well-Being, which creates a pathway of growth through care and wellness, and the relationship with the pure force of the Grail as an instrument of healing. Olio Caldo (Warm Oil) is a sub-group dedicated to pursuing health through nutrition and sustainable living.

The Way of Work, which supports and promotes development of activities and services, with the objective of turning all work into a tool for spiritual advancement.

And, last but not least, **the Way Damanhur**, established in recent years to elaborate meanings and directions for the whole community.

Within the major ways are sub-groups known as "directions", related to specific topics within the theme of the way itself; for instance: ritual music, sacred dance, education in the context of family and school. At present there are nine ways, but they are undergoing changes.

Here I shall explore just three of the ways in some depth to illustrate how they are incorporated into the everyday lives of Damanhurians.

The Way of the Word is the way of communication. Visual, musical and written. Citizens on this path might be extensively involved in the myriad of artistic endeavours within Damanhur, teaching in schools, running the newspapers and the internal broadcasting network at Damanhur, or dealing in external relations and politics. In short, they try to make Damanhur understood, both by its inhabitants and the world outside. They spread the message of Damanhur. There is also the path of music, which uses the word in another sense – because it is a vibration, a sound, just like the voice is a sound. Orango Riso explained something of this way to me:

> The common link among all the expressions of the Way of the Word is communication. It is, therefore, important to have many people who can bear witness to and communicate accurately what Damanhur is all about. People have grown in such a way that they can now hold conferences, without being afraid of speaking in public.

For people of the Way of the Word, this taking of the word outside of Damanhur is an essential and primary path. However, it is also necessary to create a common culture within the community. Therefore, this way has the task of developing new ideas, opinions and debates. For example, the daily newspaper QDq, in Italian and English, printed and online, is a central feature of communication among all the Vajne citizens in the world; it is managed, administratively and spiritually, mostly by members of the Way of the Word.

This path is very important to those involved in creativity, in all manner of ways, whether creating artwork for the temple, creating a website interface with the world outside or producing artefacts that have a commercial potential, and those who deal with the technology at Damanhur, setting up links on the internet, implementing alternative technologies or maintaining computers, as well as working with video and the internal television channel.

Theatre is also included within the Way of the Word. There has always been a strong tradition of theatre in Damanhur, with regular performances by established groups of actors. The plays often draw on Damanhurian myths or the re-telling of historical events from the lives of these industrious and colourful people. There seemed to be a preponderance of comedy dramas, but there have also been more serious interpretations of classical topics. Falco wrote a number of plays, some of which were translated into English and collected into an edition entitled *Tales from Damanhur*, published by Edizioni Horus with introductions by Ken Campbell and this author. Many other plays have been written and directed by Stambecco Pesco and Cormorano Sicomoro, as well as other Damanhurian playwrights. Stambecco told me:

> Theatre is one of the ways in which we Damanhurians prefer to express our philosophy. Ours is a magic theatre: the texts are based upon the principal concepts of our spiritual and esoteric path. It allows us to understand better, to elaborate our ideas, to present them to a wider public and naturally have fun while we are doing it.

Stambecco thought it important that each performance contained as many different artistic expressions as possible: Recitation, song, music, scenography and so on, and that the characters represented human beings of different ages, their different states and characters. For him, life appears in many forms and it is best represented through its diversity.

Above all, theatre is a privileged way of working on oneself: not only as a means of overcoming shyness or learning to work in a group but to express parts of ourselves that would otherwise never be discovered. Reciting is a good method of working on one's personality encouraging it to manifest in a harmonious way. Theatre is a formative element, be it for the individual or the People as a whole. The audience is also an integral part of the magic scene because, thanks to its energy, the will of the protagonists is transformed into art.

These varied strands illustrate how every aspect of life is intertwined at Damanhur. The people believe that they grow spiritually when they do something materially, productively. "For us," Orango said, "action is the first movement." The spiritual path that someone is on is often closely related to their occupation.

A very important manifestation of this way is the active commitment to the development of the valley and region through politics. In 1995, Damanhur founded a new independent political movement called Con te per il Paese (With you for the Country). This political movement is very active in the local politics of Valchiusella; the first Damanhurian mayor of Vidracco was elected in 1999 and since then the mayor and members of the council of the municipality of Vidracco are Damanhurians. Other members of the community are regularly elected onto valley councils.

The activity of the movement regards cultural initiatives, from conferences to the elaboration of projects in the area of civil protection, to the presentation of proposals for a law on the legal recognition of intentional communities, eco-villages and co-housing in the Italian Parliament and the European Union.

Plate 1
The Hall of the Victory
in the Temples of Humankind

Plate 2 – The Hall of the Earth

Plate 3 – The Hall of Spheres

Plate 4 – The Labyrinth

Plate 5 – Apollo is one of the gods
represented in the Labyrinth

Plate 6 – The battle against the enemy
as depicted in the Hall if the Earth

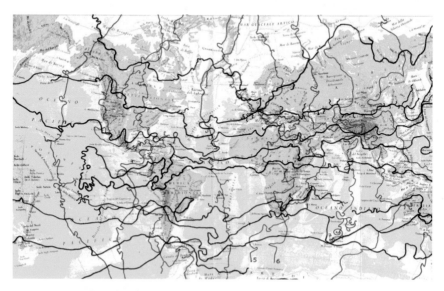

Plate 7 – Synchronic Lines – a communication system
that traverses the Earth and connects to heavenly bodies

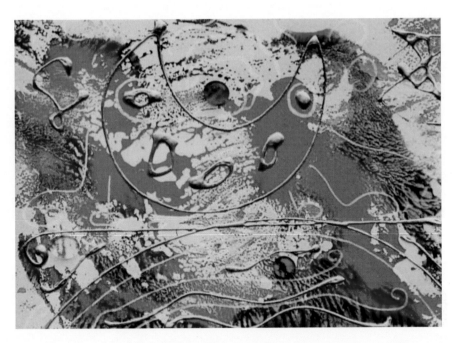

Plate 8 – Selfic painting by Oberto Airaudi,
presented to the author in 1997

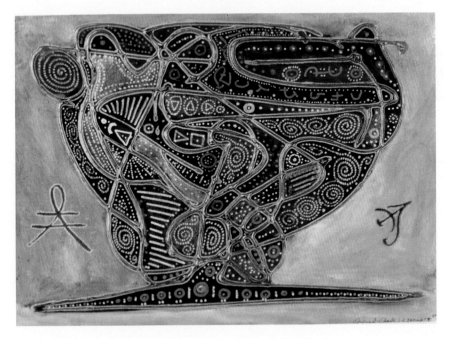

Plate 9 – Selfic painting by Oberto of the Grail
connected now to the process of healing

Plate 10 – Landscapes filled with spiral circuits

Plate 11 – Visualisation of the new development

Plate 12 – A human spiral

Plate 13 – The magnificent artwork in the
Time of Peoples dedicated chamber

Plate 14 – Eric Maddern reciting in Jung's garden

Plate 15 – Pilgrims on the way to CERN

Plate 16 – The Pilgrims – now known as the 69ers – a Superindividual

The movement involves representatives in six towns of the area, who periodically share information about various situations: elaborations that include the possible orientation of votes in the political, administrative, European and referendum elections, participation in initiatives for the safeguarding of water as a public resource, and supporting organic cultivation, as well as statements on international issues such as war and the question of immigration, from financial systems to the living conditions of some peoples of the earth. I asked to read the political manifesto of their movement. Here is how it starts:

> The distance between the hands and the soul is more subtle than we think. Spiritual growth means assuming responsibility for the environment around us, for the well-being of others and for the growth of society. It is not enough to sit and meditate for an hour a day to consider how we ourselves evolved. It is necessary to work and manifest spiritual conquests through concrete actions that change things.

Macaco Tamerice is a singer and musician, as well as a prime mover in the Global Eco-villages Network organization. Prior to settling in Damanhur, she regularly performed around the major jazz venues of Europe. Now she teaches, consults and works as a coach for people interested in creating community, continuing musical exploration as a part of her spiritual endeavour. She explained the role that music plays in the Way of the Word:

> Musical research started many years ago and it developed in two directions: the vocal direction, the choral work – the choir is one of the oldest groups in Damanhur – then the direction of the musicians. There has been a lot of experimentation with music. For us, music is a means of inner growth.
> In our concerts, music is developed by both the musicians and the dancers, because they need music to dance to. We try to develop new music, new compositions. A lot of this research has been done within the temples. When you are inside the temples, you are in connection with higher forces and you have to have a clear mind and be focused in order to express this emotion through your music.

This is a perfect example of a spiritual way being employed as a practical aspect of life. As Orango said: "For us, the material and the spiritual are intertwined."

The Way of the Arts, is the path that has art and aesthetic research at its heart. They are tools capable of giving substance to a creative expression that is most obviously displayed in the Temples of Humankind but pervades many other aspects of life in the community. The sacred in Damanhur is a concrete reality, created by sharing the offering of creative efforts and strength in the realization of a common ideal. For those on this path the development of heightened creative faculties is part of a sublime process, a way of getting in tune with themselves at the same time as getting in tune with the divine.

The development of the art in the temples is a direct reflection of the quality of the meditation, the results of following a particular spiritual path. There is a quality about the artwork that raises it above the mere application of paint or the sculpting of terracotta. The emotion most people experience when seeing the temples for the first time is undoubtedly connected to the high level of spiritual energy that has gone into their creation.

Piovra Caffè is always ebullient, always ready to talk about the temple artwork. When I asked her what she thought I should write about it, she was profound:

What is most important is to put across a feeling of the complexity of it, not in a numerical or a practical sense, though the quantity of the artwork is in itself significant, but more in terms of the inner complexity of the experience, as it has been developed and as it will continue to evolve. What I would like to happen is that when someone looks at the temples, they become aware that every millimetre of it has significance and represents that inner complexity. I would like them to realize that every millimetre has some meaning, both for those who created it and for those who encounter it.

She had a special request for me:

If you can, in the book, please put forward the idea of just how much meaning there is in the temples. It is important, not only in terms of complexity itself, but also to remind people that humankind has no limits. This is the significance of the complexity that humankind has limitless potential. Possibilities are infinite. I hope that the temples will stimulate people to evolve in themselves, their own souls. That, I think, is most important.

Since 1985, the members of the Way of the Oracle work in deep and dedicated ritual to bring forth messages from the divine forces. When I was preparing, some many moons back, for an important first meeting with Sirena Ninfea to discuss the Way of the Oracle, I was quite nervous. She seemed to be a very important person at Damanhur. I girded my loins and tentatively began. "So, Sirena. Sigh-rain-ah?" I ventured as a way of breaking the ice. "See-rain-ah," she replied. "Sirena. In English, Mermaid." I was getting a little bolder. I thought some light-heartedness might be appropriate. "Siren. That's the one that calls the men in from the ships and they crash on the rocks, is that right?" She smiled serenely. "I chose my name. The second name, the vegetable name is Ninfea." "Which means?" I ask. "It is a big flower, on the water. Waterlily." I'm impressed, "It's Mermaid Waterlily, then?" I told her that I really want to talk about the Way of the Oracle, which I understood was a big subject and most dear to her. She spoke in a precise and deliberate way:

A big subject, yes. But it is very important for us, here in Damanhur. This way deals with the rituals. It is the ritual body of Damanhur. There are other ways, but our ways in Damanhur are spiritual ways, and the characteristic of our way is the ritual body. For a lot of years, we have been working with these sacred aspects, temple rituals, the life in Damanhur, Damanhur people. In Damanhur we don't separate the spiritual and the social aspects.

The Way of the Oracle is an important aspect of Damanhur. If each of the ways is the spiritual expression of a facet of Damanhurian life, the Way of the Oracle is that part devoted to the contact with divine forces. It is a demanding way, requiring devotion, inner refinement and self-discipline. The principle embedded in such an essential transformation is that of bettering oneself in order to become a channel to the divine. It requires a particular calling, a certain predisposition, a vocation. Though in recent times, many things have changed, the rules are now much softer.

The operations carried out by the Way of the Oracle are a constant magic interaction in the daily life of Damanhurians. As far as I can gather, "magic interaction" means a series of precise and well-thought-out actions, based on the knowledge of laws that govern things and events in this material world. Actions at Damanhur are subjected to constant contemplation, as are all the cycles of life. As the Way of the Oracle is specifically directed towards the spiritual, magical and sacred, it utilizes processes and research at a variety of magical levels and, according to exacting ethical rules, all directed towards a positive evolution of humankind.

The Way of the Oracle also operates in particular fields of high magic research. Theurgic magic is practised to maintain a constant dialogue with divine forces, addressing and awakening their specific energies, to help create and maintain a harmonious relationship between the divine and the human plane.

As discussed in the previous chapter, the way is named after the Oracle of Damanhur, a group of divine forces involved in "time prospecting", which is described as "an investigation in time able to move and modify events". Damanhurians claim to have "re-conquered" and revived these investigative processes in 1985, some 2,500 years on from the Oracle of Delphi. Sirena told me something about the nature of this path:

> This way is the ritual body of Damanhur. For many years we have been working on sacred rituals and how they relate to the lives of Damanhurians. Here we do not separate the spiritual and the social aspects of life. They are interwoven.

At Damanhur there are several temples in which the Way of the Oracle operates, in particular the Temples of Humankind and the Baita, a very special place. The Baita has been prepared over time for hosting high-level magical operations. It is a place of clean energy, where elevated thoughts and positive energies come more naturally.

It is kept constantly and meticulously clean so that the physical and the spiritual can embrace. Here barriers between dimensions are more easily overcome and divine contact made.

In such places of spiritual retreat, everybody directs their attention closely to every subtle aspect of the ritual. Each nuance of each action must be followed, wanted, sought after – dances, movements, words in the sacred language, ancient gestures, everything must be supported by the right energy, brought in by means of special magical instruments. The first magical instruments were made by Falco and since then have evolved, little by little, over time, according to what was needed, as Damanhur progressed through many different magical and ritual phases. Rites are also only effective if those performing them are pure, so that they can be free conductors for the evoked energies.

Members of the Way of the Oracle work with modesty and constancy, with the pleasure of serving their ideal, working in friendship. Meditations and studies are carried out, including prayer practices, the learning of formulas, the investigation of silence, of spirals and the potentialities of the mind. They use dream as a tool to inspire ideas and creativity, to reveal hidden depths, leading to experiences with dimensions that cannot be otherwise contacted. Time itself is researched as part of this path, with researches being conducted relating to previous existences in other points of time, for Damanhurians and people from all over the world. Past-life research is one of the most popular seminars offered by Damanhur University. Many rituals are necessary for accessing the time roads and the matrixes of the different spiritual forces. Synchronic forces are channelled through specific rituals, so that small and important actions are nurtured and protected.

Fire is the element of particular importance to the Way of the Oracle. It is guarded with special care, because it is considered sacred, a symbol of light and a particular vehicle for contacting higher forces. It is used as a part of all major rituals and often the ashes from fires are preserved to guide create a basis of connection and memory for future rituals.

Another function of the Way of the Oracle – in support to the functions of a special group of people devoted to this highly sacred and special work, and called the "Charons" – is to help the passage of the dead through the different phases and levels they encounter on what Damanhurians call the "Threshold", maintaining, through the structure of the People, a connecting thread to this life. This aspect of the Way of the Oracle changed after Falco's death, after the creation of the Charons.

Sacred dance is a sub-section of the Way of the Oracle. The importance of dance in Damanhur must not be underestimated. It is part of the Way of the Oracle because dance, as performed in Damanhur, is always a direct interpretation of texts from the sacred language. Each of the movements is related to specific words and concepts and can be read as if reading a book. Consequently, dance is used in many Damanhurian rituals, both in the temples and the solstice and equinox ceremonies. Damanhurian sacred dance has a natural beauty and gracefulness about it. It is probably one of the most refined of the Damanhurian creative arts and one of the most easily identifiable as Damanhurian. In Damanhur, where this language is studied, it is widely used for composing songs. It is also included as decorative elements in the halls of the Temples of Humankind and other prayer halls on Damanhur lands.

Sacred dance is often part of ritual celebrations and is also present in community dances. Many symbols in the sacred language, or other similar sacred languages, can be traced back to various ancient alphabets, which supports Falco's message about the ancient origins of this language.

145

According to Falco's teachings, this archetypal language dates back to an era when humankind had mastery over the deep meanings and values of life. One mythical interpretation asserts that this sacred language is a ritual language for poems, formulas, prayers… Every concept in the sacred language is expressed in three forms that all carry the same meaning: as an ideogram, a spoken word and a sacred dance movement. The language can be written, drawn, spoken, sang and danced. Here is a sentence written for me by Sirena Ninfea in the sacred language of Damanhur, in three different ways: as ideograms, numbers and script:

**BE OLAMI CAO LAOR BAV DAMANHUR
EEJ ATALJI JAE CAO**

I hope that your days in Damanhur
bring you very much help

The Way of Couples: one aspect that has been worked on has been to unite the nucleo family with educational aspects within professional departments, such as that of the schoolteachers. The Way of Couples has created a path for professionals and parents, who have chosen to make the education of children their spiritual path. For instance, arranging trips to places of interest outside of Damanhur, sometimes to places abroad and doing whatever is necessary to help children grow in an open and holistic way.

There is a Damanhurian tradition where children of six or eight years old, when they feel ready and their parents and those around them think the time is right, perform a particular rite of passage, called Prova di Coraggio, a demonstration of personal strength and fortitude. Boys and girls that choose to do it, walk alone (there are adults watching, hidden, but the kids do not know that) across the hill behind Damjl, and need to reach the Open Temple where Damanhurians wait to celebrate them. They are helped by the sound of drums that guide them to the destination.

Another aspect of education is creating a common ground, culturally and philosophically within the population on all that concerns the education of the children. They acknowledge that what they are trying to arrive at is a definition of the Damanhurian way of education, pulling together the best of everyone's experiences, a way of education of the People, instead of your way, my way and his way.

I'm recalling something that Plato said, in a favourite quote of Sir Herbert Read, pioneer arts educationalist and active anarchist:

An aesthetic education is the only education that brings grace to the body and nobility to the mind.

Damanhur is a place where people grow, refine their creative nature and find the highest order of aesthetic education, where education is considered to be an opportunity for intellectual, social, ethical and spiritual growth – not just for children but for educators, teachers, parents... and the entire Damanhur family. The diversity of cultures and nationalities at Damanhur contributes to the richness of the educational environment. For both children and adults in the community, it expands their capacity to think creatively and welcome new ideas.

In this fertile environment, children are educated from an early age to be responsible individuals and citizens of the world who are capable of determining their own future. At 18 years of age, or even a few years before if they have the prerequisites, Damanhur young people can choose whether to continue living in a nucleo community with their parents or have other experiences. For example, one option is participation in a project called Casa Ragazzi, a community run by Damanhurian youth from 15 to 23 years of age.

The Quests (Quesiti)

Since the beginning of its growth process, Damanhur felt the need to trace a path to guide every single individual and the community as a whole towards a harmonic and synergic spiritual evolution. This is a sort of spiritual vade mecum, a handbook or guide that is kept constantly at hand for consultation, with behaviour rules which represent basic formulas of individual and collective growth. I once came across a saying in a Damanhurian book of prayers: "It is not difficult to realize the human being; it only takes a second. It is the preparation for that realization that is long and difficult..."

Damanhurians live by a set of principles called the Quesiti. This interesting word has no direct equivalent in English. It is somewhere between a "question" and a "quest". There are currently eight Quesiti fully formulated and applied. They are active and dynamic concepts that, if followed, provide a path to enlightenment. For this reason, the Quesiti are central to an understanding of Damanhur. The Quesiti are living formulas, to be meditated on and translated into action, according to individual talents. Every Damanhurian reads and meditates on the Quesiti each day, using them and finding ways in which to apply them practically in daily life.

The Quesiti can be compared to the different floors of a building: the ground floor supports the first, the second and all the others, and it is impossible to get directly to the top floor without going through the preceding stories. Damanhur's spiritual building is composed of eight Quesiti, but as it is a growing reality, organic by nature, the capacity to intensely inhabit all the floors might open up new levels of spiritual growth.

The Quesiti are based both on the inner development of individuals and on that of the People of Damanhur as a whole. The first Quesito was developed in 1983, when Damanhur first began to see itself as a newly directed spiritual path. It placed the focus on action, on never being static, on living life to the full. It is better to act and make a mistake than not to act for fear of making a mistake. It requires the continuity of the action you have undertaken, not to leave a job half finished, to always follow through on any decisions you have made. It focuses on constancy and fulfilment, acting every day, choosing to act every day, keeping on practising, keeping up the rhythm.

These principles were brought into being after considerable experience. Every nuance of every term was considered in relation to how it might be applied to people's lives. Each was concerned with a return to the sacred and each related to each person making their own inner transformation, even as the community itself was transformed around them. Indeed, this was the time when the concept of a People evolved. The first three Quesiti all worked towards defining the People as an idea.

While the first three Quesiti set the Damanhurians off in a positive direction, the fourth caused them to shift their way of thinking quite substantially. This Quesito encourages everyone, men and women, to discover the feminine aspects within themselves, to cultivate them in all areas of their lives. There was a long period over which this one developed and it was accompanied by a huge amount of artistic activity. Much of the artwork for the temples was created using the energy transformed by the work on this Quesito.

The full outline of the Quesiti, in the order they were developed through discussion and meditation, is included in Appendix 1. Here I will explore two of them and illustrate some practical applications. For example, the fifth Quesito was concerned with change, transformation, movement. Thanks to the steps taken in previous Quesiti, people should have reached an inner point of balance. As stated in the description of this quest:

> How much do we act out of habit, out of fear of ridicule or judgement, out of respect for conventions we do not subscribe to? Let's look for our real identity, our own personal values and let's slough off our skin, but still remain the same person. Perhaps, paradoxically, by keeping the same tendencies, the same attitudes as before but now they will be the result of the application of our will, in a process of evaluation and choice which is a more evolved level of action.

Habits are false friends, a result perhaps of the conditioning of our education and our environment. By use of the intelligence a person possesses, it should be learned not to take things for granted. Only by so doing can habits be discovered and chosen, so that they become an aware power, a new strength capable of giving a vital rhythm to actions. Feminine characteristics, from a social and spiritual point of view, make it possible to consolidate and to build any situation. If we compare men to bricks, women are the mortar. Thanks to the specifically feminine capability of cohesion, of keeping a wider knowledge and of facilitating deeper relationships between individuals, we obtain stability with a different strength than that of a pre-eminently masculine one.

The masculine capacity to invent, to drive, to move, must bear fruit through a conscious expression of free will in order for tradition not to become a habit, but a springboard to create new ideas and effect change and growth. Change is a positive dynamic. This is the Quesito of resolution, in which the elements of stability and firmness of a person ought to become stronger through continuous inner evolutionary movement.

I remembered a legendary story about Falco. When he was with a large group of citizens who had gathered together one day, at the very beginning of Damanhur, he asked everyone to take off their wristwatches and to place them in a basket that he took round. Everyone did it happily, thinking that Falco was going to perform an experiment in time travel or some such wonder. When he had collected all the watches, he took the basket round again and asked everyone to take one out without looking. Of course, those who had put in a cheap plastic watch might take out a top-quality gold one or vice versa, until those at the end were left with whatever was left. Then the whole exercise was repeated once more. Falco did this to show that people should not be too attached to possessions and also to unite everyone's individual sense of time, to bring about a communal time. People got to keep the watches they had finally chosen and so, even years later, someone would see another wearing "their" watch and be reminded of the importance of the People, the importance of change.

The eighth Quesito opens to others. It is the integration of all the other Quesiti: after enlightenment, metamorphosis. This is the Quesito related to an irreversible choice of the ideal, of reproduction and love, as a path to one's inner god. All that has been learnt through the path of the previous Quesiti can now be brought outside to nourish others and the world. Transformation must not just function as a support for the self, but it must become a factor of evolution which finds its maximum expression in reproduction. Reproduction defined as knowledge, as the capacity to create something superior to oneself in the direction of evolution.

This is the Quesito of maturity, of knowing one's unique gifts and choosing to give them to others, with humility and a sense of service. It is the awareness that once the ideal is chosen, it is irreversible, and all behaviour will follow from it. This is the path towards the full expression of divine nature, as the result of the unfolding of life's mission. In this, discipline is very important, as a tool to create an inner order and as self-determination towards the ideal:

> The path of the eighth Quesito, if fully lived, has made us strong enough that we have learnt to trust, and we have no fear of losing our role: we are now authentic and really able to listen to others without preconceived ideas, to welcome them and exchange with them. All that we have learnt in our life is not something we can possess and use just for ourselves.

This is the Quesito of direct personal commitment to improving society, in making all actions follow the chosen ideal, in bringing a concrete contribution, without pride or prevarication, but service and trust, teaching what has been learnt through empathy and respect to transmit a living message. It should be transmitted through example, not with any presumption, not with a sense of superiority, but being aware that teaching works best when learning comes from it. Teaching and learning do not exist one without the other. They are two aspects of the same phenomenon, which allow us to fertilize without losing anything. The master who is teaching a poem, is not deprived of what he knows by giving it to his pupils. On the contrary, he himself is enriched by sharing with others new interpretations and by the pleasure of the meeting of minds all enjoying the same beauty. Those who teach well generate, those who teach badly kill: culture should become like a trampoline to reach increasingly higher levels of comprehension, not a cage to imprison the mind and the imagination.

Study therefore becomes a spiritual necessity to learn – and then transmit – keeping alive a magical sense of life, with pleasure, with humour, with love. In nature it is through the change of the previous season that everything can be renewed and born again. This is the Quesito of the meeting of generations, of experience with vitality, it is the formula to turn the conflict between old and new into an exchange. Different generations cannot understand each other completely and this is exactly what facilitates growth and change. If there were complete communication there would be stillness, a society able only to simply perpetuate itself. What the older generations have conquered must be given to the young in order that they can grow beyond their parents, then the point of arrival of the former is the starting point of the latter.

> The eighth Quesito is a door to welcome others and the world inside one's own transformation, so that the fruit of our growth will not be only inside of ourselves but will be donated to others. This Quesito has a special link with aspects of the first Quesito: complete and responsible action. Purity of intentions; of the second Quesito: continuous choice instant by instant. Respect of the given word, at all costs; of the fourth Quesito: unselfish availability of oneself. Being an element of union; and of the fifth Quesito: harmonious inner revolution as the ability of changing one's mind.

The Quesiti of Damanhur are central to an understanding of almost everything about the Damanhurians and their socio-spiritual philosophy. They are strictly interwoven with all other aspects: the primeval laws of esoteric physics, the spiritual ways, the chakras of the body, positive and negative characteristics. This is further evidence as to why, when you ask a question at Damanhur, you rarely get a simple answer. It is not that they are being evasive, but that the complexity of their view of life is not so easily described in cut-and-dried, black-and-white terms. Subtle shades and depth are important in their big picture.

CHAPTER 13
THE TRIAD, A SWEET REALIZATION

The Triad is one of the major achievements of Damanhur during their four decades of its development. When I first visited the community, back in the late 1990s, the concept of the Triad was beyond its embryonic stages and was emerging into a fully fledged philosophical pursuit. The Triad refers to a new alliance of all the divine forces. The bringing together of the vast number of divinities and spiritual entities of humankind was a profound endeavour, demanding a powerful focus of the whole community.

The names which define this new divine Triad, containing all the spiritual forces of the planet allied to humanity, are "Horus", "Bastet" and "Pan". These name-frequencies, not specific deities but their essence, and do not refer only to the traditional Egyptian and Greek divinities. Horus is the main force of the third millennium, the spiritual sun, stellar divinity, motor to the awakening of the god within every human being. Bastet contains in herself the forces linked to the feminine principle, to water, to Mother Earth, to love, healing and the arts. Pan has in himself the generative masculine force of the planet and is cooperating with humanity to save the Earth from an ecological and environmental point of view.

Damanhur philosophy states that the evolution of humanity is connected to the evolution of its gods, and vice versa, just as it is connected to the life of the plant and animal species, as well as the entire planet. There is no separation in the concept of spiritual evolution in Damanhur, but rather deep union with the diverse aspects of existence, while respecting the differences that characterize each. In Damanhur, the highest vision of the relationship between human and divine is represented by the Triad. In the Triad, the divinities of all peoples of the planet, often separated and in conflict, are connected in complete harmony. The ones with similar myths and characteristics are united with each other, in order to strengthen a new global alliance between humanity and the divine, able to reawaken consciousness and a sense of unity, rather than separation, in all of humanity.

Damanhurians believe that every divine force is composed of three primary sources: energy, will and knowledge, echoing the concept of the "the Triad". These divinities are entities that can interact with and influence universal laws. Throughout human history, people have attempted, and often succeeded, to connect with these forces by developing religions, rituals and pantheons of divinities, many of which still exist today. Within the Triad divine forces that are benevolent to humanity are brought together in a single interconnected spiritual ecosystem that contains, receives and gives back inspiration and thought. The goal is to achieve a state of harmony among all of the planet's divine forces.

Every Sunday afternoon a ritual connected to the Triad takes place at the Temples of Humankind; it is open to those who wish to be immersed in a mystical atmosphere and experience. The officiants make offerings to the divine forces that represent a mirror to the divine contained within each person. The offerings have many forms: music, sacred dance, poetry, scents, sounds, coloured lights and silence, always accompanied by soulful presence. Participating in this ritual is regarded as a serene opportunity to connect your own human and divine essence with the higher pure energies.

In striving to create a spiritual ecosystem, the Damanhurian researchers have acknowledged a divine energy divided into a thousand forms. In Damanhur philosophy, the field of existence includes many universes, similar to the way quantum physics has also conjectured, as was discussed with Coyote Cardo and Gnomo Orzo in the earlier chapter on spiritual physics.

The underlying hypothesis is that life in this universe, in all its manifestations, originates from a single divine matrix. This force is greater than the universe itself, so in order to enter into the world of forms, it had to fraction into many smaller forces. Some of them have a physical form, others do not. In Damanhur, this force is called the human primeval divinity, and all the manifestations of its essence on the subtle or nonmaterial planes form what is commonly called the spiritual ecosystem.

Over the millennia, humanity has felt the presence of many different forces all around us, and we have sensed the magnitude of these forces. This is how the pantheons, gods of all the mythologies considered collectively, have come about in history, including the major contemporary religions. Smaller fragments of this primeval origin are the nature spirits, which are present in the legends and traditions of many cultures, as inhabitants of the forests, springs and glades.

Even plants and animals are manifestations of the same divine nature. Some beings, including humans, are "bridge-forms", capable of bridging the material and spiritual planes. Bridge-forms carry fragments of a divine spark, and, when reawakened, the divine spark has the power to reunite different planes of existence.

The relationship between human beings and gods is thought of as an alliance rather than a submission, as the same divine nature that permeates both. Damanhur philosophy supposes that evolution of humanity is connected to evolution of its gods, and vice versa, just as it is connected to the life of the plant and animal species, as well as the entire planet. There is no separation in the concept of spiritual evolution in Damanhur, but rather deep union with the diverse aspects of existence, while respecting the differences that characterize each.

In Damanhur, the highest vision of the relationship between the human and the divine is represented by the Triad, where the divinities of all peoples of the planet, which have often been separated and in conflict, are to be connected in a complete harmony. Those with similar myths and characteristics are united with each other, to strengthen a global alliance between humanity and the divine, able to reawaken consciousness, a sense of unity, rather than separation, in all of humanity.

The guardian of this important spiritual philosophy in Damanhur is Sirena Ninfea, a quietly spoken woman of deep intellect and serene disposition. I have spoken to her on many occasions about this concept of the Triad and am deeply grateful to her for giving me even a smidgeon of understanding of this complex subject. I asked her recently about her own introduction to Damanhur:

I have lived and experienced things that I couldn't imagine were possible. I can look back to a time when I didn't know about the existence of Damanhur and I was talking to someone about it, more or less 35/36 years ago, I don't recall the exact time. But I started to live experiences and moments which connected me, though I didn't know it at the time, connected me to Damanhur. I met some people who had relations with Damanhur, although I didn't know this link. At home, I found some magazines with articles about Damanhur, and it was only later that I realized this as another link. So even though I was not aware of it at the time, I was already linked to Damanhur.

She looked serious for a moment and told me about the moment which was transformational for her. It was the time when she had a car accident, and it changed her life, for it was at that time, because of the accident, she came into contact with people who then linked her directly to Damanhur. Today, people come into contact via conferences, courses, the internet or from media articles. There are many possibilities for coming into contact with Damanhur, but she had nothing like that, it just appeared to happen.

It seemed that I was destined to come here. I moved close to Damanhur, I came to visit, I did courses, I enrolled in the School of Meditation, and also in the Game of Life. And all that led to me becoming a citizen of Damanhur, which was the path that many other people took at the same time.

Meeting Falco accelerated considerably my interest in Damanhur. He brought me into contact with the subtle world, that I wasn't aware of, and the magical world. He helped me in discovering this aspect and talent, which I realized I could use in the service of Damanhur.

I have learned in all these years that I have left a trace and impact. If I were to die today, or to do something else, this trace would still be behind me, because I have left it. I dedicated myself completely with heart, soul and body to be with the magical aims of Damanhur. I was a creator, I created a lot in this project and brought into fruition my feminine part and my lunar part.

I asked Sirena about the changes and growth of Damanhur over the years, over the time she had been there. From where it was in 1983, she told me, when she first came to Damanhur, up until today, she had seen many changes. Damanhur she considered very intense, but very much in the past it had to focus on realizing, defining and creating itself. From the very beginning, she had seen and experienced how rapid these changes were. "But you just had to go with the flow during such changes," she said, "and after a while you would be completely transformed."

The subject of the Triad had been a very important one for Damanhur and for all Damanhurians, who are important people in this project.

It is an undertaking everybody had been associated with. For sure, in a highly personal way, people for many, many years had carried out ritual work, with the help of Falco, so that all the divinities of the planet, of all peoples and from all times, could have their places at the Triad project, if they so wished.

I told Sirena that as long as I had been coming to Damanhur, she had always appeared to be at the centre of the ritual and magic parts of the community's activities. When I first came, she was the only one to wear a blue robe during rituals. I had therefore assumed her to be regarded as someone of importance. I was intrigued to know what it was like to be at the centre of magic and rituals like that, and to be such a profound influence on people's lives. The spiritual, the art and the magic.

> For years, for many accumulated hours, I have been engrossed in the ritual and magical aspect. I was always right in the heart of this project in the temple. When the heart beats, it gives impulse to the whole flow of blood to circulate and transfer throughout the body. Mine wasn't an executive aspect, but a very creative role in the spiritual and magic. Not only that, but also in all the aspects surrounding them, ensuring that the ritual is done properly.
>
> It was also my role in bringing and taking the artistic aspects of the ritual and to develop myself as a model and pass this on to everyone else to develop the inner sense of the divine sacred.

When I was writing the first Damanhur book, two decades back, I always felt that I was walking on eggshells when I spoke about the Triad. It seemed to be a thing that was most important, secret in many ways, and that it was part of the initiate school. I found it hard to talk about it outside of that, in case it appeared as if I were intruding on a fragile and intimate community aspect.

I've changed my response over the years and I now think that the Triad has become part of the vocabulary, being often mentioned in books, in talks, on the internet, in videos.

I asked if I was right in thinking that at the time of this development and thinking of the Triad, that all these aspects were integrated into the ways and quests of Damanhur, the balance of masculine/feminine in a practical sense. Sirena replied:

> All the aspects of Damanhur are always linked to the community life, for the research and for the development of Damanhur,

territory-wise. Falco was always stimulating us, for example, he would ask you what the first Quest was, then he would ask philosophical questions which were designed to inspire your thinking and it would be connected to discovering what the Goddess was, because at that time we did not know her name. We knew it was a divinity connected to the sea, a feminine divinity, what could be her name? And then many people were researching myths to discover which could be that divinity. Our research brought us to the point where we said there is a divinity with three names Gaia, Demeter and Aphrodite.

From that moment when we gave him this answer, we used these three names for all the rituals, and we carried on using them. It's not as if Falco said they were right or wrong, it's something else; it's just from that moment on we were using the name Gaia. It was one year later, when a very important ritual took place, that he expressed this name of Bastet. Because, what was most important was this research of the divine, of the feminine divine, not of the name itself. The name came later.

A similar thing happened when we were researching for the third divinity, given the name of Pan later. We knew there was one divinity that was related to this planet, which we needed to reawaken. And he said, find the name. Again, a lot of research, what could it be, and only later it came to be that this name was Pan.

The project completing the Triad had been a complex and stimulating work, an advanced form of ritual alchemical operation, ritual operation to reawaken from their sleep ancient allied divine forces. This work had taken on board other massive interventions of an alchemical and ritual nature, leading to the tangible rejoining of thousands of divinities into a single central body, appropriate for the type of universe we now live in. These magical operations, of a theurgic nature, had a goal of the union of divine forces, with different dimensions and intensity, their decomposition, new births of divine nature, and recomposition in a new useful form for the evolution of humankind and liberation of the planet.

By completing this project, we will have validated and participated in the union of the parts of the fundamental mirror of this space-time. This implies unifying the systems, extrapolating the fundamental divine rules – laws for an extraordinary humans–gods relationship, as it has not existed for at least 20,000 years.

I asked Sirena what she thought of Damanhur today. Is it in a comfortable place, after the passing of Falco? Is it a settled place, a good place? She was pensive, deep in thought:

> Falco's passing was a huge step for us. He was our spiritual guide and he would be providing inspiration from many directions, and he was very influential in that sense. His passing was sudden. From the time of the discovery of his terminal illness to him actually passing away was such a short time. Now, it is several years since his passing, which for us was a huge step of discovering and making a switch from the practical, because everything was very practical for him. Now, we are going more into theory, in the sense of understanding all that happened. From a theoretical point of view. Now, we are refining and making projects out of that.

I pointed out the possibility that Falco's passing could have been traumatic, could have been a big problem, but now it appears that a positive has come from it. A great amount of positive. What does Sirena think of the future, what are her hopes for this new vision, this broader vision, what does she hope will come from it? The answer was as positive as the huge smile that accompanied it, and she answered in some detail and at some length:

> All Damanhurians have this huge dedication and devotion to the overall project and the magical aim of Damanhur, the reasons why it exists. Falco's passing did not disperse that, didn't disconnect us, but made us even more connected because of our faith and belief in that project. We are saying that we are all on the same boat, and we are trying to help each other in guiding this boat, even though he is not here anymore.
>
> I don't look very far into the future. I am looking at today and now, how we are living in Damanhur now. What I consider important is to continue to work in a direction of helping the world, this planet, humankind. I have the same aspirations that the ritual and magical aspects of Damanhur realize and complete themselves in a way where Damanhur people become not only a people, but an enlightened people. Not only on this planet. I have aspirations as well that we reach out to touch other worlds.

This had been a very important day for me at Damanhur. I had learned how better to understand the spiritual work of the community, especially in relation to the connection of the divinities and divine energies in the Triad project. This had been fundamentally important work with significant repercussions for the whole of humanity. It had been meticulously accomplished through serious effort and constant striving over many years. We should embrace its significance.

CHAPTER 14
SELFICA AND SELFIC PAINTINGS

Selfica is a field of research that has been explored since the early years of Damanhur, introduced by Falco Tarassaco and subsequently developed by Damanhurians, foremost by Cicogna Giunco. Selfica makes it possible to tap into specific frequencies of our universe, by creating objects made of metals, minerals, special inks and alchemical liquids. It is based on the basic form of our galaxy, the spiral, and on a specific mathematics of forms and proportions.

According to the Damanhurian researchers, Selfica connects us to the life force of nature to increase our vitality and well-being, and to cosmic forces in order to amplify synchronicity and our ability to interact with the energies of the universe, which is considered as a conscious entity. Selfica, departing from a two- or three-dimensional physical object – copper bracelets, larger installations, paintings of different sizes – makes it possible for that object to host a purely energetic intelligence that exchanges information with the person who owns it. In this sense, selfic items can be considered living objects that exchange energy with their owners – energy directed towards the well-being, equilibrium and rejuvenation of the person.

Esperide Ananas Ametista has lived in Damanhur for nigh on 30 years. She conducts extensive practical research in the field of Selfica and the energy structure of human beings. Esperide explained to me the importance of this area of research:

> The energies that transit through selfic objects adjust to the energy field of the people who wear or use them, or to those of the environment in which they are placed. Selfic bracelets that are used frequently often

change their shape, and all more or less in the same way on the same person. This is because they adjust to the wearer's aura, to the shape of their energy field. During a series of experiments conducted at Damanhur in the 1970s, at the beginning of the research on Selfica, a Kirlian camera was used. In this way it was possible to capture this image of the vital aura of a few selfic bracelets.

In Italian, selfic devices are called "selfs", and in English this term is very interesting. The dictionary tells us that a "self" denotes a person or thing referred to with respect to complete individuality: one's own self, nature or character.

I might not have even happened upon the world of Damanhur were it not for the selfs. When we were thinking of visiting Alpine regions to research several sorts of controversial phenomena – such as spontaneous combustions in the French Alps, solar temple burnings in the Swiss Alps, and the unfathomable science at CERN – Ken Campbell was uncertain whether to embark on the journey as he was in the midst of researching the great philosophers of the world for a Channel 4 series called *Brainspotting* and had uncovered the notion that philosophy was about the "search for the self". He was due to interview Derek Parfit, a British philosopher who specialized in personal identity, rationality and ethics, widely considered one of the most important and influential moral philosophers of the late 20th century. Ken was to interview him about his new book, *Reasons and Persons* (Oxford University Press, 1986) and should have been reading it at the time of our suggested journey.

I convinced Ken to come on the trip by pointing out that at Damanhur, they made "selfs" and he could maybe talk to a person who made them. That swung it, and he came, learning a speed-reading course on the outward journey and speed-reading Parfit's book on the way back. After the interview, the eminent philosopher told Ken that he thought that he had a well-founded understanding of his work. Oh, the joys of such splendid synchronistic lives. And we joyfully "discovered" Damanhur, to boot.

Selfic objects can be very simple or very complex, and they can take on various forms such as bracelets, rings, necklaces and other objects which can be placed in the environment. They have different functions such as supporting memory, protecting the aura and personal energy fields, and many other purposes. There are also special paintings called "Selfic paintings" that use colors, shapes and symbols as energy conduits and can be used as mandalas for personal or group meditation.

In his most recent book, *I Make Things Happen: Selfica, Spiritual Technology for the Third Millennium* (Devodama, Vidracco, 2020), Gnomo Orzo gives a passionate tribute to the history of Selfic technology and its current development. It is a testament to how that which is most complex is also extremely simple in its essence.

Metal is made of time. Its encounter with light ignites the power of making things happen. The archaeological findings and myths of our planet show that in the connection between human beings and metals, a great power is concealed. It is the power of making things happen, and it has determined human events since the dawn of time. Today, as we embark on the third millennium, after a long period of research, a technology arises that can bring us close to this extraordinary potential – that technology is Selfica.

In his first experiments, Falco developed a series of very large Selfic healing structures, which looked like hospital scanning machines equipped with many selfic metallic selfic devices, but were built to focus the energy, the life force of nature through Selfica directly onto a particular organ or system in a patient's body. I remember, we were filming once, just after one of the large healing machines was unveiled. I was filming with a guy called Roger, who used to work for the BBC as a production AV technician. We were left alone with the device for a short while and Roger had a closer look behind and around the Selfica. He said, "Well, I don't really know, but there does seem to be some sort of logic going on inside there." As I said, it was a struggle for me to understand some of the more reified aspects of spiritual physics, when I was here more than 20 years ago. Esperide, rather pointedly and with some perspicacity, asked: "And do you understand them now? I am not sure there is anyone here who fully understands Selfica, yet…"

The person with an overall responsibility for Selfica at Damanhur is Cicogna Giunco. It was she to whom Ken spoke in order to find out about the making of selfs. She told him about selfs that were used in healing and

meditation, those that helped in the realms of dreaming, "…and supposing," he added. He told her about John Joyce buying one for his memory, at the Damanhur Sunday market, so he could learn his lines better when acting. "But he forgot where he put it," added Ken.

I talked to Giunco (unusually known by her plant name) recently, in the main Selfica workshop at Damanhur Crea, a place of great wonderment, with all the glitzy sparkle of jewellery made in Selfica form and an air of mystery as to what it was all for. I asked her about her role, the idea of Selfica and its importance in the development of Damanhur.

I reminded Giunco that selfs were the reason we first came to Damanhur and that she was the first person we interviewed. I remarked that she was very much identified in our minds with the development of the Selfica and was the guardian of its importance.

> In the last year before Falco passed from this life, I was given the role of being the person responsible for Selfica. And now it is my inheritance. It was quite difficult to inherit the knowledge about Selfica and I can now appreciate how difficult it will be to pass this knowledge on to others.

It appears that the development of Selfica is an important part of the overall Damanhurian philosophy. The esoteric tradition explains that Selfica were found back in the time of mythical Atlantis, as well as in civilizations of historical eras, such as Egyptian, Etruscan, Celtic and ancient Minoan. However, it was always reserved for specific social classes, that is, the priests and rulers. Selfica is a science that is widespread throughout the universe, and its history on our planet begins with a fundamental cultural change, shifting from a vision of the universe as a place where everything happens because of divine intervention, to the understanding that there are other forces on a par with human beings, which can be used to obtain the desired effects.

Selfica came about with this realization that there can be non-divine forces involved in changing events. It was a rationalization of magic. Falco defined this quite succinctly:

Selfica is a border science that goes beyond the pure and simple concept of magic, where the only way for anything to happen is by passively repeating rituals, and it introduces a creative phase in which human beings are active agents. As such, we can conceive of theories, create circuits, improve the system, establish the forces that flow within a circuit to a greater or lesser extent, in order to receive and direct these forces that exist in the universe.

In everyday lives, Selfica are used for channelling vital energies through the use of instruments, though practitioners don't refer to them as "instruments", but regard them as vital intelligences that have been imbued with functions. For example, the function of recharging oneself during sleep, easing a sore knee, or taking care of an open wound that needs to heal, and many other functions.

Giunco again:

Two aspects I have learned from working with the selfs, first that there is no "no", only a "not yet". There is no absolute "no". In the answer to any question you might have there is no "no", only "not yet". Another aspect is the modality and emotions you have when working with Selfica. When you might be angry or unwell, it can be very difficult to work on the selfs, often you just cannot do it.

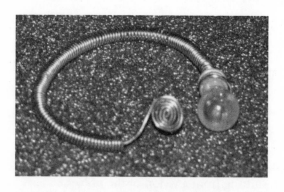

I remember, during one of my earlier visits to Damanhur, seeing Giunco rushing out of the studio where she had been working, clutching a handful of Selfic bracelets and announcing to everyone that here was a new function for Selfica that she had just succeeded in developing. The bracelets were copper wiring wound tightly round a flexible core, with a spiral at one end and a small globe of alchemical liquid at the other. They were intended to sort out the personalities within a person, bring them into equilibrium and resolve the potential conflicts.

I had recently done a "Personalities Within" workshop with Falco and Esperide. From previous researches and writings, I had come to a firm belief that I may be a reincarnated Cathar, or that one of my inner personalities was a Cathar. To my utter surprise – nay to my profound shock – I had discovered that one of my inner personalities was probably not a Cathar, but a mercenary soldier who had burned Cathars. This had come so far from left field and had been a "wow" moment for me. As one of Shakespeare's characters says: "The heretic is not the one who burns in the flame, but the one who lights the burn." (Plain English re-write from *The Winter's Tale*, Act 2, Scene 3.) When I saw the new bracelets in Giunco's hands, I felt I should have one. And there it is, a couple of decades on, in the photograph here. I'm not sure how many times it has succeeded in resolving the conflict among my complex inner selves, but I still wear it much of the time.

The ancient history of Selfica has always been stressed. One of the Damanhur founders, Fenice Felce, once took me to the Egyptian Museum in Turin and showed me the Selfic bracelets on the statues in there. Selfica is, indeed, knowledge that comes from ancient Egypt. Several different cultures have used Selfica in past times, including Celts and the people of mythical Atlantis. Falco discovered the knowledge and techniques from his researches and began himself to experiment and develop new devices based on the ancient information. As Giunco acknowledges:

Falco was the one who brought this ancient knowledge back here, but now we can continue working without him being present. Sometimes people come to me and ask me for specific functions. In this last period, I have concentrated on work with circuits.

The whole concept of Selfica appeared complex to me and I asked Giunco if this work required a lot of personal energy.

No. There is a lot of energy present when working with Selfica. When I work with them, I feel fulfilled. It has a return which is greater than what is lost or used. It is a happy experience, not a draining experience. There was never an experience that brought me down, it was always an enriching experience.

Selfic items might be small or enormous, from the most delicate piece of activated jewellery to several tonnes of Selfica constructed into the very fabric of the temples. Giunco pointed out that in the temples there are many kilometres of Selfica, behind the walls, under mosaic floors, along the corridors, all encased in the construction. She said that the temple has been built in order to help, to intensify, the growth of people, or to bring out into the universe a signal, as well as energizing new instruments.

In the making of Selfica, the use of materials is crucially important. If copper were not used, for example, but gold, it would necessitate less complexity of instrument, because the material from which you build Selfica has a different conductive ability, not only on the physical plan, also in how selfic intelligences can flow to them. There are a few cases of selfic tools made in gold or in copper with the same function: they look completely different, with the one in copper being larger and needing more coils. Being somewhat provocative, I asked if the future was, therefore, golden. The Giunco icy stare and broad smile came in response:

We are working in that direction. We have to be able to detach from our past and believe in our vision. When I say past, I do not mean historical philosophy behind our building of reality, but those memories that I am happy to bring forth. We happen to have a solid belief in our principles, with fresh important building blocks to be discovered, and it will bring us the "gold" of a spiritual life.

Esperide Ananas has written a most interesting and useful book about Selfica, *Spirals of Energy: The Ancient Art of Selfica* (using her original name, Silvia Buffagni, Devodrama, 2013) that I heartily recommend. She talks about her own earliest experiences with Selfica:

The first time I saw a "self", I was profoundly captured. A small spiralling copper structure placed on a shelf among books, medallions, and a plethora of other objects, and it stood out to me, as though a spotlight was shining on it. The identification card said that it was an "environmental balancer", built to keep the atmosphere of a space energetically "clean"; its function was to direct to the outdoors any traces of disharmony so that they could dissolve back into nature. Even though it was simple, it had harmonious proportions, and the coils, which tightened horizontally until they came to a point with a single copper wire, seemed like it was actually creating a direction – the direction where, I imagined, the self was to invite stale thoughts to go out the door...

Selfica is a field of empirical research, initially introduced into Damanhur through Falco's studies and experiments, conducted with other people in the community. The Selfica discipline makes it possible to focus and direct vital and intelligent energies to perform

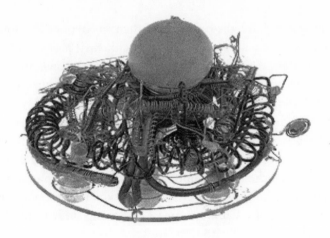

different functions connected to wellness, as well as amplifying perceptions and personal development. Allied to this work was the considerable contribution Falco made in the development and execution of a particular form of artwork that was termed "Selfic paintings".

He painted prodigious numbers of such works, which he declared, have always been present in the human unconscious. These symbols can therefore open channels of insight and intuition in those looking at them, as the paintings are meant to be mandalas, signs that mirror our inner landscapes. On the back of the canvas, Falco wrote the title of the painting, in the form of a poem. Falco has exhibited his paintings in Moscow, Tokyo, New York, San Francisco and Turin.

His images might be thought of as being pregnant with a sense of expectation that the viewers are able to define by themselves. It constitutes a mysterious vibrating of colour, an unpredictability of rhythms, and sometimes resembles or alludes to further development, perhaps to an apparition of the shape of the drawing. These are the simplest images, set with a warm and affectionate care in the space of a very soft and trepid light. This is the "data" of a nature to be wondered at and contemplated with surprised eyes for the inner beauty that gathers and breathes in them. There are hints and traces of that occult truth that is denied to us but is nonetheless a part of our fate.

He painted a picture for me, at the time when I wrote my first book about Damanhur (see Plate 8). As in many of Falco's paintings, each colour corresponds to a different vital frequency, a two-dimensional expression of the selfs, typically acting through three-dimensional objects that are a complex intermingling of different metals, minerals, liquids and inks. My picture was resplendent in splashes of vibrant colour, covered in scrolls and patterns of gold, with jewel-like stones to enhance the work. Each painting is connected to the owner's preferences and sensitivities. On the reverse side of my painting, Falco wrote (original in Italian):

> Spatial bridge, supporting the tired moon, so that part of us may rest and gather even more strength than before... The waters are soft and enveloping, the light, coming from the very close moon, intense and reflecting... So, the mind itself learns, to reflect thoughts and concepts, knowledge, with the aim of possessing them fully... 4–7 November 1996 (259) with three stones.

Falco used a visual language, suitable for a style of painting that is narrative and evocative. Every Selfic painting is a page from a book of knowledge, written with alchemically prepared colours and components, combined with forms and signs passed down from ancient mystical and esoteric traditions (See Plate 9).

Selfic paintings keep their functions active through light. Their colours, forms and symbols are alive, animated, so they need light like plants needs water. To understand the relationship that is established with a Selfic painting, Damanhurians like to think that they are not so much purchased as "adopted" by their owners because they are living beings, not just inanimate objects. Just like every self, the Selfic paintings establish a special connection with the person who uses them, creating an energetic symbiosis that allows for a kind of "dialogue" with each work of art.

There is an affinity that expressionist artists tend to share with each other. The illustrious Russian painter Wassily Kandinsky, generally credited as a pioneer of abstract art, has said:

> There is in my paintings a calm acquiescence of life – and not only life. It gives me great satisfaction to reach that point, what had originally been a dream of mine (unconscious in the beginning). Earlier, I wanted more "noise", but in 1914 – that is, before the beginning of the war and the revolution – I started dreaming of an immense calm. I began working with a most rigorous limitation of expressive means, which has been very salutary for me. Today this quiet "yes" remains even in the most complicated paintings.

The abstract expressionist painter Jackson Pollock made powerful discoveries in establishing a free-form style of artistic expression, defining an art of applying paint to canvases that was both radical and inspirational. That said, his work was often subjected to popular ridicule, of the "I could do better than that" or the "What is it supposed to mean?" ilk. Pollock, much more thoughtful than that, said:

> When I am in my painting, I am not aware of what I'm doing. It is only after a sort of "get acquainted" period that I see what I have been about. I have no fears about making changes, destroying the image, and so on, because the painting has a life of its own. I try to let it come through. It is only when I lose contact with the painting that the result is a mess. Otherwise, there is pure harmony, an easy give and take, and the painting comes out well.

People generally misunderstand. This defined form of painting is not in any way supposed to represent. It is what it is, paint on canvas, to be judged by its visual intrigue and by its emotional response in the observer. I have stood in front of many Pollock artworks, filled with feelings of amazement and awe – in particular, the magnificent 1950 large canvas, *Number 31*, in the Museum of Modern Art, New York. It is indeed an awesome experience. A painting that takes you over, that you can get lost inside. It is one of Pollock's largest paintings, in which he dropped, dribbled, or threw paint onto a canvas laid on the floor. His looping cords of colour register force and speed yet at the same time are graceful and lyrical, animating every inch of the composition in an electrifying and profound emotional experience.

The large Selfic paintings of Falco have similar characteristics, plus a spiritual aspect of particular significance. The curator of Falco's Selfic paintings was Eraldo Tempia Valenta, commonly known around Damanhur as Parsifal. He arranged viewings and sales through a number of different gallery spaces throughout Damanhur, sometimes bathing the pictures in ultraviolet light for a truly alternative view of the works. In 2004, Parsifal published a book of some of Falco's paintings and the text that goes with them. In his introduction to the book, echoing the thoughts of Pollock above, he wrote:

> In many of Falco's paintings the object is lacking or is not recognizable. An abstract painting does not represent but is. It is, *per se*, a universe without relationship to any aspect of the viable

world. It creates, through purely pictorial means, an atmosphere, a climate, a state of being that offers the observer every possible interpretation and evocative association produced by shapes and colours. It renounces the representation of the material world to make a spiritual world visible. Shapes and colours complete themselves, disassociate, harmonize.

The tensions and the reactions among the different parts of a painting matter more than the parts themselves. It is they that create the expression and the true content of the painting. They provoke an echo, a resonance in the observer and evoke a memory, a gesture, a melody and a poem, which, albeit different in aspect, has the same emotional content.

Those "abstractions", which do not hide but reveal, are the keys that Falco adopts to give shape to the multiple voices of the silence of objects and colours. (Eraldo Valenta, *Oberto Airaudi: Quadri Selfici*, ValRa Damanhur, 2004)

Falco's paintings are strong, joyful and expansive. Emotion is the catalyst for a connection with the viewer, a mutual celebration, a constant expansion of awareness, a love affair with life and its origins. The joy engendered by Falco in the commission of these works helps to explain their extraordinary quality. When asked about his artistic endeavour, Falco said:

When I create Selfic paintings, I use specific systems to spread out the colour. These systems are part of the language, and in particular, they give the direction of the reading. There may be layers of colour overlapping each other in weaves, diagonally or in other ways. This technique makes it possible to project the meaning of a solid figure, as it determines three directions indicating which dimension is considered in that moment.

Thanks to the colour that is applied with these particular systems, the flat shape of the painting has a different relief in some points. So, the keys of interpretation are based on techniques that use the way of tracing the sign as a reality in and of itself, regardless of the aesthetic result.

Sign and mark constitute expressive nuclei; every sign, every mark has a meaning: They are not lost in confused arbitrariness. The vital charge that supports them expands in space, dominates it with an excited rhythm that is stimulating and always clearly determined by an emotional impulse.

Some say that Falco's Selfic paintings call upon the observer to be directly involved in their reading and interpretation through sensorial and rational experience. They can provoke dreams, facilitate new insights and interact with one another. Falco produced a vast number of Selfic paintings.

As Falco felt that is was important for the art of Selfic painting to continue – and that book of knowledge he was writing was not complete – before dying, he instructed a group of four Damanhurians on how to channel these energies through painting. They can do it only when they are all together and paint in Falco's original studio. In more recent times another group of four Damanhurians has started to create Selfic paintings, following the same modalities. All paintings of the two groups are signed "Oberto Airaudi" through mediums, to acknowledge Falco's function as a gatekeeper to the realm of Selfic intelligences.

Falco's paintings serve a communal purpose for Damanhurians. Certainly, the paintings are works of art and are purchased as such by many non-Damanhurian collectors. Further than that, Selfic paintings, health cabins and Selfica machines are much more than mere artistic creations. Their ultimate purpose is to generate energies that benefit Damanhurians, whoever comes into contact with them, in the community or in the wider planet.

In Damanhur Crea, at the Niatel Gallery, there is a permanent exhibition of Selfic paintings, which can be viewed in normal light and comparatively viewed under ultraviolet light, where the character of each work is significantly changed. Standing in front of Falco's paintings is indeed an awesome experience.

One time, when I interviewed Sirena at Aval, the nucleo that was Falco's home, she showed me into Falco's studio, the place where he did most of his artworks. It was still as he left it. His brushes and paints lying there, as if waiting to be used on the next piece of creative expression. A wait that will no longer be fulfilled. I was overcome by an immense feeling of wonderment, where the word "awesome" was rendered completely inadequate. Tears welled in my eyes and I felt a shaking feeling throughout my body. This was indeed the place of a creative and spiritual master and it was imbued with a profound spiritual energy that was hard to understand, yet easy to contemplate. For sure, I was moved.

CHAPTER 15

HEALTHY LIVING, HEALTHY LIFE

Damanhurian medicine is characterized by a humanistic view of care, where the individual is the main character. The body is regarded as a temple, as a precious instrument for the soul. For this reason, physical and spiritual wellness are equally important. Each of us has the responsibility to engage in lifestyles and behaviour that protect overall health. However, optimal health doesn't just depend on the individual, it is influenced by other factors, such as genetics, relationships and interaction with the environment.

Health is not the absence of illness, but the fullness of living. It means getting up in the morning with a dream and having the necessary strength to realize it. Good health is about having a balanced lifestyle that nourishes the body through nutrition and hygiene, as well as the mind and spirit through social relations, creative pursuits and the capacity to get out of routines, to be adaptable to any situation. Prevention plays a key role.

Antilope Verbena is one of the lead practitioners in the Damanhurian health programme. She confirms the idea of personal well-being over the cure of illness. "It is important to take care of ourselves," she told me, "not just when we feel ill but also when we are well – by engaging in wellness disciplines, as well as scientific ones in emergency situations."

A prime aspect of Damanhurian thinking is that healing is always based on choice.

It is a process, a potential pathway that can accelerate self-awareness and personal growth. Health is a collective concept, just as human beings are gregarious beings and social animals. Being healthy is the result of lifestyle choices, harmonious thoughts, prevention and identifying treatment that is appropriate for each condition, using the principle of maximum benefit with minimum risk, and applying synergy between different therapies.

I shared with Antilope my view that, if there is anything at Damanhur that has been indubitably constant throughout its history, it is the healing practices that have taken place. She told me the basis of this successful approach:

> The main focus of our healing is pranatherapy. Prana is a Sanskrit term that refers to the pure life force of the universe, which also contains complex information for evolution. Currently, the two leading healing practices are pranatherapy, where the healer opens an energy channel through which the client can access vital prana in the atmosphere, and a new discipline that is called PranaSelf, a combined use of pranatherapy with specially designed Selfic structures and instruments. Vital prana brings the overall physical, emotional, mental and spiritual dimensions of the person back into equilibrium. The Selfic intelligences help direct the healing energy and expand their effect throughout time.

Antilope told me that Damanhur has had a School of Spiritual Healing for over 40 years, with students from all over the world. Healing courses are a very important part of the Damanhurian system. There were healing courses before there was a Damanhur, in the days of the Horus Centre in Turin. The Damanhurian University is the organ through which the healing courses are taught, internally and externally. For a long time Antilope was head of the University, so important was the healing process. She explained that a healer has to raise their frequency to a level that embraces the illness and the person:

> We have to be aware and conscious that our body is like a suit in which we move ourselves in this point of reality. The part of ourselves that wears this suit is complex and has a divine nature. The suit is most precious, but at the same time it has a very dense vibration.

Spiritual healers trained through Damanhur's School go through a deep process of self-knowledge and spiritual awareness to activate this energy channel. "It is the energy itself that helps the transformation, the changes of our mind, body, and soul," Antilope said. "It is this coherent field of pure energy, held collectively, that initiates and supports the changes."

In Damanhurian philosophy, disease is considered also as the possibility of major change that, for different reasons, we manifest in each of our lives. It is regarded as an opportunity to have a significant experience. Indeed, it can be like a Grail that pours profound life lessons into us. It is a signal that, in addition to getting the most appropriate care, we are being challenged to transform something inside of us. The journey from illness to healing is a journey of self-discovery towards finding greater new balance.

Another fundamental illness–wellness concept is personal responsibility. Each person is the creator of their own health and pathway to healing. The therapist, healer, doctor, the surgeon, when necessary, can offer crucial help, but real healing takes place when we become accountable for ourselves.

Orango Riso, one of the six sages, is the Director of Damanhur's School of Healing. He has a particular responsibility for health and is one of the most respected healers in Damanhur. He explained more about the ideas behind PranaSelfica:

> This new Selfic healing technology gives us the possibility to work with the field of possibilities contained in time, selecting the timeline that can lead to transformation and healing. We can, for instance, make a severe illness less impactful by "diluting" it in time; or we could make time "denser" for the illness to heal. Or even attract a plane of existence in which the illness does not exist for that person. We believe this will be at the basis of many healing techniques of the future. Whereas time itself is a dimension we can grasp, when we talk about illness, we do not normally talk about time as its main container and landscape.

Orango speaks with a calm determination that has to be admired. "We are interested in working on things that still need to happen, and this is the reason why we use Selfica," he said, adding that schools of human growth work mostly in clearing the trauma of the person's past, whilst Damanhur works also on the future.

He went on to say that as they are not yet sufficiently advanced to accomplish this fully consciously, and they are using Selfica, with which they have developed an experimental relationship. He considered that, with PranaSelfica, they thought this was an area that could be sufficiently developed in the future. He added that he thought modern physics was also beginning to develop similar ideas.

In their healthcare, Damanhurians have chosen to adopt methodologies that are natural and respectful to both humans and the environment. When appropriate, they incorporate the best of contemporary science and technology. In a model with different steps, they advocate moving from prevention – with pranatherapy, nutrition, breathing techniques, preparation for pregnancy and natural birth – to health maintenance, which includes all wellness disciplines, and finally restorative medicine, herbal medicine, homeopathy, flower essence therapy, conventional medicine and surgery.

At Damanhur, there are doctors, spiritual healers and holistic researchers who are available by appointment for anyone who wishes to consult with them. The Damanhurian doctors work in the Centre for Integrative Medicine Crea Salute and FisioCrea at Damanhur Crea.

Orango said that it was important to understand that the Damanhurian definition of illness is very broad. Illness is not only thought of as a structural problem, but of everything that prevents a relationship amongst people:

When you are well, you express yourself to the world and you love it. When you are not so well, you tend to close yourself up. All this stops us from entering a relationship with the world: this in itself is an illness, a condition of the spirit. This separation from others and the flow of life is a widespread disease in today's world. We regard that a spiritual part of humankind today is illness.

Healing is a collective concept, not an individual one. "There is no such thing," said Orango, "as my healing. There is our healing." The calm determination coming through again:

If you are not feeling well, then I am not feeling well. If I am to feel good, I need to be in a good place. I need to be in a family that loves me, in a work environment where I feel supported, with friends I can feel good with, who give me the opportunity to express myself and feel happy. Humankind needs to reawaken to a wholehearted consciousness. Who am I? Who are we, today? In this respect, it might help to understand where we came from.

Orango is adamant that the Damanhurians are so confident of these matters that, according to the teachings of their School of Medit-Action, the Grail in our epoch changed form and can now be found inside human beings, not outside them. I must have looked surprised, so Orango felt obliged to explain:

The actual form of the Grail is not a chalice anymore, it is the meeting of an illness with an aware human being. The person who enters the path to healing becomes the container of the Grail. This is the reason we believe why, in the future, a spiritual awakening is the path of healing, being mediated by the Grail.

In this way, healing and the inner transformation it requires and promotes become the search for the Grail. Orango and Antilope consider this a huge epochal change. A symbolical aspect of this, but not only the spiritual meaning behind the thinking, is that the Grail is no longer reserved for the elected ones, the knights or priests, but is in reach of everyone. "We are now ready," said Orango, "to tell this to the whole world." He continued:

A person who doesn't feel well should be aware of the possibility for change and awakening that is within them. It could be depression, it could be existential crisis, but a person needs instruments to realise that things are moving in a very different way to what the person imagines.

There is a catharsis that is happening that involves all humankind. Today, more than ever, there is an opportunity of a collective reawakening. "Let us say that the healers are priests of the Grail," he pronounced, "and the ones who are ill are all on a quest for the Grail." Or, as Antilope pointed out, we are no longer searching for the Grail, but it is the Grail that is searching for us, and this is another switch in perception. "Sooner or later," she said, "we all be in a position of encounter illness, and if we are aware if its potential to transform us, we will all be touched by the pure force of the Grail."

The commonly held perception of the Grail is the search for perfection, of something to be attained. The Damanhur view of the Grail is not about perfection, but about the inner alchemy of healing. This is a seismic shift in human consciousness. Consider the ills of humankind. Well-being is difficult if there is disease and a sense of not achieving in the background.

Indeed, this is a monumental change in concept, aligning our thinking about the Grail to our thinking about illness. If a person feels ill then that person should not feel bad about that. It is an important part of a person's spiritual development and the person becomes an instrument through which the process happens. "This is why we say that illness is not an individual concept, it is a collective concept," Orango explained. "There is no such thing as my health, but a concept of our health. It requires a future in which we have to raise our trust."

The self-healing powers we all have inside of us can be examined, revealed and expressed during the process of healing. This is one of Damanhur's great success stories and is work that is ongoing and vitally important.

And then, in early 2020, the COVID-19 pandemic came to Europe. Italy was one of the first places to feel its significance. At the height of the outbreak, northern Italy's high-density cities were struggling to contain both the virus and its more insidious counterpart: social isolation. As restrictive quarantine measures swept the region, news reports were of deserted streets, funeral homes swelled to capacity and individual families huddled together in apartment blocks above the cities of Bologna and Milan. In the alps of Piedmont, however, the Damanhur community, less than an hour north of the city of Turin, was having a different experience. Elfo Frassino, who is also the elected mayor of Vidracco as well as being a long-term resident of Damanhur, told me about its impact:

> COVID changed our lifestyle, though I think, in a small village near a large wood, it was less of a problem than in the city. There was a particular threat to the elderly. March and April were beautiful months and the old people used the time for a short walk in the woods to help keep healthy, or to work in the garden growing the first vegetables. One of the advantages of living far away from big towns and cities.

On the Vidracco website he put the text of the ordinance of the Minister of Health of 20 March 2020, which introduced measures to counter the spread of the virus. These stated that:

- public access to parks, villas, play areas and public gardens is prohibited;
- it is not allowed to carry out play or recreational activities outdoors; it is still allowed to carry out physical activity individually in the vicinity of one's home, provided that in any case respecting the distance of at least one meter from any other person;
- food and beverage outlets are closed, located inside railway and lake stations, as well as in service and refuelling areas, with the exception of those located along motorways, which can only sell take-away products to be consumed outside the premises;
- those located in hospitals and airports remain open, with the obligation to ensure in any case compliance with the interpersonal distance of at least one meter;
- on holidays and days before holidays, as well as on those others that immediately precede or follow these days, any movement to homes other than the main one, including second homes used for holidays, is prohibited.

The unique societal structure of Damanhur meant few changes to physical closeness were necessary, even as coronavirus began to ravage nearby cities. When lockdown became law, nucleos were able to quarantine together with their extended family, sharing meals, working their gardens and meeting regularly to discuss family matters as usual.

A renewed appreciation for closeness was a common theme among Damanhurians, with families emerging more united than ever. This positive outcome might have been helped by the community's methodology regarding conflict resolution. If disputes arise, community members are constitutionally bound to offer each other "one more chance" while also having access to three members of the College of Justice – elected representatives who mediate upon request if things get out of hand. There were also new commitments to slowing the pace of life.

Capra Carruba told me about her own experiences during the difficult time of lockdown:

To deal with uncertainty has been a challenge in spite of my nature that loves change. In Damanhur we believe that uncertainty is actually an essential part of the nature of reality and to embrace it takes maturity. My work stopped since my clients were blocked. I saw many people getting busy on the net, becoming super-efficient in smart working and this put me in performance anxiety. How should I navigate this period strategically to turn it into an advantage? I did create some videos but I also dealt with my ambivalence. I simply loved slowing down and resisted working at the usual pace.

Life in Damanhur is usually cram-full to the limit, eclectic, never boring and lacking idle time. I loved working physically supporting our self-sufficiency which boosted thanks to COVID. So did my five-year old son, driving on the tractor with us or collecting eggs. We live in a family of 12 adults with eight hectares of land around and having everyone in lockdown was an enormous boost to finally direct resources to clean brambles, prepare the land, plant vegetables, prepare shelter for 50 chickens and two pigs. I am aware that we live in a very privileged situation, the lockdown was a relaxing quality time while people in Milan had breakdowns! We ate a lot (too much) and spent much time together growing as a group.

We followed our internal medical protocols which meant that members of the family with flu symptoms isolated themselves staying in their room and were taken care of by the family. The other members of the family took precautions in regard to hygiene to avoid a potential spreading to other parts of the community. This happened to two of us during the entire period. Most of us were actually particularly healthy – maybe thanks to all the prevention with pranatherapy, vitamins… The most touching event for me was assisting one of our family members suffering a heart attack during one of our joint activities around the house. We were all there immediately, ready to intervene with the shock defibrillator at hand and our friend survived against all odds. It was a miracle.

In the nucleo residence of Magilla, Formica Coriandolo had her own mixed feelings about the pandemic. She told me:

Life in COVID time has been very intense and, even if it seems a paradox, beautiful and meaningful. I have been spending much time in nature, with my family, staying at our home, working all together in the land, appreciating the community life even more than ever. On the other side, I have been affected by the shadow of COVID, which has deeply affected my father, in a bad way. His depression increased and he fell down a very dark tunnel. I think this is the result of different life choices.

Life before the coronavirus was already set in this very efficient way. You have to be a harmonious part of the chain. We believe in the fact that in every human being, there is a divine spark that can be reawakened. We believe in human beings, in the potential that we have, the goodness that we carry.

Betsy Poole, a long-time citizen of Damanhur with strong links to the US and the UK, found herself locked into a travel nightmare:

Travelling to England for a video production assignment, I left Damanhur on this voyage just after all of Italy locked down in quarantine. There was not a car on the road as we drove to Caselle airport and I saw about six people in there and transferring through Rome, the airport was equally bleak and devoid of humanity. I arrived at Heathrow and things appeared relatively normal. I rented a car and drove to Worcester; however, the hotel would not allow me to set foot in the venue, as I had just arrived from Northern Italy. My friend Victor and his wife graciously hosted us in their home. A few days after we arrived, England locked down as well. We became trapped there for two weeks as this happened, with our flights cancelled.

When I eventually got back to Damanhur, I was on strict quarantine for the next 14 days, not allowed to step out of our home for anything. Other Damanhurians brought food, leaving it for us on the doorstep. Even after we came through our 14 days of strict quarantine, we were still not allowed to leave our homes except to go to a doctor's appointment, pharmacy or grocery store. Then, any travel required a signed document stating the reason for travel – one document for going and a second for returning home. I basically did not leave the house for three months.

There are no doubt as many COVID stories as there are citizens of Damanhur. But there is a spiritual side to the pandemic as well. Esperide reflected on the situation in a Damanhurian blog:

I don't believe we can ever be fully aware of the effects of our actions. This is a blessing because the weight of our responsibility would probably fill us with horror and discouragement. At the same time, it is a curse: no one, on an interconnected planet, can be free of suffering until every other being is. The web of life binds us to each other through space, and also through time. And in the time in which everything is present, our essence plays many games, in many different situations and circumstances. We are at the same time those who suffer and those who create the pain.

I was reminded of a favourite Kevin Ayers song "Why Are We Sleeping?", which opens with these words, "It began with a blessing and it ends with a curse, making life easy by making it worse." Esperide continued:

> The COVID-19 pandemic has distracted the world's gaze from the ongoing conflicts – and the number of victims that wars produce – yet the consequences of the virus in conflict zones are even more tragic than in better organized, peaceful nations. And the same is true for those areas devastated by the effects of climate change.

For Esperide, there is no separation between material and spiritual reality: this is a principle we find in many sacred texts and philosophies, from Spinoza, to the Advaita-Vedanta, as well as in Damanhurian philosophy. The Absolute is in everything. But the perfect balance, the full divinization of everything, is in the totality. In our little piece of the universe, on the plane of material reality, which defines much of our experience, however illusory, the game is still open, the result still uncertain. It is not possible for us to fully understand the mysteries of the Absolute, as long as we are in a finite reality; its presence in us, however, can guide us like a scent showing the way to a blindfolded wanderer in the night. Every human being is an electromagnetic antenna: something in us is predisposed to receive the impulses reaching us from the spiritual and divine energies that participate more consciously in the design of the Absolute.

Other community blogs amplified the story and the experience of COVID-19, declaring that the community is living through unusual times:

> The pandemic diminishes... then it seems to reappear; possibility to travel and meet each other returns... but not for everyone just yet. In Italy and in Damanhur we see the guests coming back, domestically and from the EU, though many governments have already announced that things are likely to become unpleasant yet again in the coming autumn.
>
> For this reason, we feel for the remainder of this summer it is important to focus, maintain optimism, and show that we take care of ourselves and others by behaving with presence and responsibility.

In this way, our joint action will pave the way towards a new, more fulfilled quality of human civilization to re-emerge after the period of quarantine – a useful pause, which gives many of us a fresh perspective on our priorities and an unexpected possibility to redefine our intentions for the future.

CHAPTER 16

MAKING YOUR WAY
TO DAMANHUR

Damanhur has been described as "a remarkable living laboratory", and
the people of Damanhur take great pleasure in sharing their more than 40
years of research and experience in spiritual, artistic and social fields, with
guests from around the world.

I'm often asked how to organize a visit to Damanhur. Well, it appears
to be easier now than it has ever been. However, you shouldn't just
turn up unannounced. It's necessary to make a reservation before you
arrive. But that's easy to do through their website, which is remarkably
comprehensive. Over the years, they have got their organizational act
together. Whether you just want time to relax or to delve deeper into the
many different layers of Damanhur, visits offer a memorable experience
planned to be both educational and enjoyable. You also choose your own
length of stay and the activities you want to take part in.

A basic visit programme has been designed to suitably introduce
yourself to Damanhur, experience its wonders, and may then lead to
other more in-depth experiences. The one-day programme, for example,
includes an opportunity to explore life through science, research,
community and a spiritual philosophy in harmony with nature. You will
visit the main centres of Damjl and Damanhur Crea, have an opportunity
to walk the stone labyrinths, or spend time in the Niatel Selfic Art Gallery,
where you can meditate upon the mystical Selfic paintings.

Then you will have a guided visit to the Temples of Humankind, which,
as we have seen, is more than a work of artistic achievement, it is a direct
pathway for profound spiritual experience. During the visit of the temples
you will be guided through each of the eight halls and learn why the

structure is a living conduit that connects the energies of the planet that travel via the synchronic lines. You will experience listening to the specific sounds of each hall as a way to more deeply connect with the energy there.

To this basic programme, there are now add-on additional activities. You might wish to organize such things as a meditation in the temples (if you have been there before), a visit to the Sacred Wood, an introduction to spiritual physics, a meditative session where you make a clay model of yourself, or sacred dance in the Sacred Wood Temple. Or you may wish to participate in rituals and other ceremonies. All this is possible.

Over the years, I have introduced many of my friends to Damanhur. I was interested to know what they thought about the experience many years afterwards. Lisa Temple-Cox is an excellent painter of grand murals and has worked on many projects with me over the years. Ken Campbell loved her work, and after he had seen the wall paintings in the Damanhur temples, he duly commissioned her to paint all the rooms in his house with Campbellian imagery. I thought it only fair to show her what had inspired Ken, so we had a journey together to Damanhur in order that she could witness for herself the artworks that had so influenced Ken and me. Here's what she thought about Damanhur:

> The bushes outside sparkled with fireflies. Water trickled and splashed down the rocks and around the small stone temple to that element. Everyone was friendly and smiling. Alas, most of these friendly and agreeable people spoke less English than I do Italian, and consequently I spent much of my first few days completely ignorant of what I was meant to be doing, or where I was meant to be. But I felt honoured by being adopted by the various families I spent time with in Damjl. I loved the look of the place: murals, mosaics, embossed copper plates, everything decorated and lovely, art everywhere.
>
> But I really loved Etulté – the Sacred Wood, the mountains, a monolith among the trees, paths bordered by white rocks, and in the sloping meadows spirals and symbols marked out in rocks painted blue, red and yellow. I found it strange and beautiful. There was a stark difference between these woods – spacious, airy, full of ferns and blueberry bushes, stone seats and menhirs – and the woods opposite Damjl. That offsite place was dank, dark, with unpleasant undergrowth: littered with rubbish, and slightly scary. The Sacred Wood had an air of tranquillity and calm. I would often take breaks

from painting to have a wander and enjoy the quiet. Just being there was like meditating, and as I write this now I wish I were there.

I was initially quite stressed: lack of sleep, cigarettes, coffee and the unsettling sensation of being a stranger in a strange land. I was, at one point, overcome by misery and tears. This upset the couple who were showing me round very much, but they took me to the nearest Etulté household and I was fed coffee and comforting words.

The householder had apparently been filled with rage against the world before she came to live in Damanhur, which I found hard to imagine, she was so giggly and bouncy.

The citizens, apart from being almost unnervingly friendly and cheerful (to an English person!) were all very down-to-earth, everyday people. The oddest (perhaps hippiest) people I saw were the visitors who came on open day.

Esperide told me that no-one judges you here, as long as you're happy. I slowly became more relaxed about the lack of formality. Despite the carefree nature, it seemed that everyone was studying: all the rooms were littered with books on a huge variety of subjects: natural history, mythology, Atlantean knowledge, the languages and aesthetics of every possible culture on earth alongside astronomy, physics, alchemy… it was fascinating.

I spent a lot of time walking the circuits. I walked the circuits designed to improve memory, increase optimism, improve the dream state, reduce insomnia and relieve fatigue… I came out feeling lightheaded, and my teeth slightly numb.

The visit to the underground Temples of Humankind was astonishing. I've never seen anything like it, before or since. The secret passages opened into the most incredible, indescribable underground site – it was too much to take in, or even think too hard about.

In retrospect, I see that I was going through a challenging and uncertain period of my life. The solstice rites that I participated in while I was there precipitated some of my worst nightmares – I wrote them down somewhere, can't remember the details but awoke unnerved and discombobulated. This is not a criticism: I suspect it was a purging. My time there made me realize how much I need periods of isolation and retreat. I also realized that Damanhur was not for me, and perhaps part of the reason is they have a wonderful sense of group belonging. I felt – and still do – like the cat who walks by itself. Looking back on my time there, and reading my diary, I realize that this experience was vital and necessary to my process of becoming more comfortable with my solitary self.

I began drawing a set of tarot cards during my time here, and although I never finished them, I still use the major arcana regularly. Oberto was, of course, the High Priest. (Though Esperide commented that he would probably preferred to have been The Magician.)

From my earliest visits, I had always been fascinated with the rituals of Damanhur and I recalled being swept away by the incessant rhythmical drumming from their excellent band of percussionists at one such ritual. I had a naughty little thought, during the ritual, of how great it would be the have some tasty Santana guitar soaring over the drumbeats. Well, by Jove, I actually made it happen. Within months, I had arranged for good friend Mo Nazam, a brilliant guitarist, together with another mate, John Maynard, a self-taught innovative keyboard player, to come along to Damanhur, the latter bringing his son Paul who we persuaded to play on a borrowed bass. We spontaneously arranged some workshops with a group of Damanhurian drummers and put on a gig for a thousand happy people in the newly built amphitheatre behind the Open Temple. The gig was an absolute sensation. Here are the views about Damanhur by the musicians:
Mohammed Nazam had this to say:

My first impressions of Damanhur were of a beautiful place and very nice people. Hot. Welcoming.

What I liked most about Damanhur, the Temples of Humankind and dinner with the time travellers. I liked the way communities were organized and self-sufficient. The level of expertise within the members and of course the food was excellent!

I'm not sure that there was anything that I didn't like. I would have liked to meet Oberto, but I wasn't too disappointed as my experience was so good.

Further thoughts about Damanhur... The story of how the temples were built is fascinating and to be shown the time chamber was also an experience to remember. Being a guest who was there to facilitate music was very enjoyable and of course the company was interesting!

John Maynard was equally impressed:

A highly creative community, with people who were clearly happy with their involvement and proud of their achievements. Friendly and enthusiastic to share information about the process by which the community was formed. The building programme is impressive and their attention to conservation ahead of their time.

The most impressive aspect was the recognition of all religions and the non-judgemental way in which they were portrayed. The arts and crafts were spectacular, as well as their aspiration for a three-part time allotment, where one third was dedicated to the community, one third to research and learning, and the final third for themselves.

Not much to dislike, except it seemed to me that some were so consumed by their own tasks and achievements that only a polite interest in the visitors was shown. I understand that things are much better in this respect, now. My personal thought is, I'm glad I had the privilege to visit and I would like to see how they have developed over the next few years.

Jill Slee Blackadder is a writer, artist, singer, composer and teacher, best known for her wonderful writings about the fauna and flora of the Shetland Islands. She visited Damanhur some years ago and sent me this piece that she described as "an attempt at conveying something, however inadequate, of the incredible reality of Damanhur". Here it is:

Damanhur, city of light, thousands of years ago and today, a serene, dazzling, place of light right now. I had read and heard about this extraordinary place, and as our friend Sergio drove us closer and closer, my excitement and anticipation was hard to contain.

We travelled through quiet lanes, thick, engulfing hedges of grass, trees, steep banks of wild shrubs and flowers, was this the right place at all? Early impressions were hard to focus on, but as we entered the parking area, glimpses of buildings, hinted at multiple activities, concentrations of calm work, a hub of books, art, courtesy and welcome.

Our visit was planned, the timetable fixed and practical needs, food, facilities met; choices of options to see in more detail were easy to make. But a growing restlessness demanded more time. Strange sculptures, natural systems celebrated, curious objects built within the landscape, each hinting at unifying significances. Evidence of traditions from every corner of the globe studied, and technologies learned, tested, developed, I needed to know more.

The temples were mind-blowing, the research and insights possible into human thought and history, astonishing and tantalizing. The workshops were staggering in variety and intensity. There was a strong sense of endless dedicated individuality, and that all who had come here had given as well as received. But overwhelmingly, the sense of continuous change and discovery flowed through the whole place, but not a trace of ego. Even the supermarket, which stocked all the food, materials and paraphernalia you could wish for, bore the stamp of creativity, serious selection, assessment of craft, quality, and manufacturing ethos. I wanted so much to stay for longer, and perhaps "wanted" isn't the right word. I felt I *needed* to stay for longer.

Lisa Louise Lovebucket has been in and out of my life for longer than I can really remember. She oozes exuberance and *joie de vivre* and always lifts your spirits by every encounter. She fell in love with Damanhur from her first encounter:

I was at the launch of Jeff's first book on Damanhur in 1998. I read the book in a day and, swept up by exhilaration and resonance, I signed up for the "Personalities Within" course led by Esperide and Oberto. That weekend transformed my existence. Damanhur has played a formative role in my life ever since.

My first visit to Damanhur was with Jeff Merrifield, and my husband Julian, around 2002. We went out there to teach the kids how to put on their own rave. We taught video recording/editing skills and electronic music production through the week and threw a dance party for Damanhur on the Friday night. This was a great opportunity for me to experience the community as something more than a tourist. We stayed as guests in one of the Damanhurian houses and became part of the social living environment, helping to prepare meals, and joining in with the day-to-day running of the house. This kept me grounded as my head ran wild.

Walking into Damanhur for the first time was like a homecoming. The first thing that struck me was the art. Everywhere. Everything. The Open Temple was under construction and it was an honour to get involved with some of the work. I had not expected the community to be so large and diverse. As well as spending much time in the school, we visited workshops producing textiles, stained glass, Selfica. We helped harvest food – some of the most delicious I have ever tasted – before enjoying one the most spectacular meals I have ever eaten. We joined in the solstice celebrations and attended a concert where we were played haunting music by the plants and the trees. But, as with most visitors to Damanhur, it was the Temples of Humankind that had the greatest impact. I will never forget the grin on Oberto's face as he pressed his magic button and the floor slid away to form steps down into another dimension. That magical place is a physical force that sweeps over you and transforms you from the inside out.

Claudia Boulton has been a long-time and much-valued stalwart of the greater Ken Campbell family. Known also as Claudia Egypt, she has been involved in acting, directing, providing an extraordinary array of costumes and props, an invaluable person in the production of epic plays. A totally irreplaceable right-hand woman, so to speak. She once organized a trip for me and her to meet up with Ken Kesey's Magic Bus, *Further*, for a drug-fuelled trip across Scotland, an experience I will never ever forget.

Claudia recalls her first trip to Damanhur:

I first went to Damanhur with Ken, Jeff, Irving and a motley crew, 30 years ago, a visit that meant a lot to me. It was where I managed to stop smoking: Damanhur has a policy of no smoking all over their territory. Despite several previous attempts to give up tobacco, it has stuck since that visit. We visited the temple through the original entrance, a sort of vestibule temple with a stone in the wall that moved, revealing steps into the interior of the mountain. It was exciting and awe inspiring, magick in the air.

Alan Watts says: "Underneath opposition there is love. Underneath duality there is unity." Damanhur expresses that entirely and moved us all towards that truth. Thank you, friends.

I'll be forever grateful to Claudia for the work she did in helping to make the later productions of *The Warp* happen, and for arranging the time we got to spend in Scotland with Ken Kesey and the Merry Pranksters on *Further*. Riding on that remarkable vehicle was just like Tom Wolfe had so eloquently described in *The Electric Kool-Aid Acid Test* (Bantam Books, 1971). And to have Neal Cassady's son, John, drive my car behind, so that I could be on the bus was just the icing on a very magical cake.

CHAPTER 17
OFF INTO THE FUTURE

What the future holds for Damanhur is now being discussed, deliberated and proposed. The word that has had most significance for most Damanhurians over the decades has been "change". The immediate prospects suggest that the coming period will be some of the most significant changes in the community's history.

Gazza Solidago was one of the first people I met at Damanhur as she was in charge of the visitors centre at Damjl during my earliest stays and we have maintained a friendship ever since. I met up with her in the Somachandra Café and asked her views on the future changes. "When I came here in 1985," she said, "Damanhur was already showing signs of being open, reaching out." Gazza has a firm grasp on what Damanhur is about and has always been open to sharing her views in the most lucid of ways:

Damanhur has always been open to the world since the very beginning. Even before the establishment of the first settlement, the first founders were invited in several towns all over Italy to share the dream of Damanhur and their experiences, in public conferences. Every Sunday afternoon Damanhur was open to visitors for a cup of tea and a chat, answering their questions. It was always a pleasure to welcome everyone and show them around. And Falco was with us for 40 years, from the very beginning in Turin to his death in 2013.

Now, we have completed a cycle of more than 45 years, after a period of building spiritual awareness, of solidarity and generational self-awareness.

When you turn 40 you begin to wonder who you are, who you have become, how much you have accomplished and where you are headed from there. So with the community. We wondered. Those 40 years built an identity, a spiritual awareness, a solidarity, a basis for reflection, as a means of evaluating.

In fact, we needed 40 years also to build a spiritual Popolo and a generational transformation – similar to what happened with the Jewish people who spent 40 years in the desert guided by Moses, even if our desert was a different one.

At Damanhur, looking where we are now, I feel that our direction now is to commit in being a community with full consciousness. Become fully aware of what we have created. In a relatively short time we built a complex social and spiritual vehicle, now it's time to have the courage to drive it. Maybe we will need to study, in order to reinforce our awareness, and go from practice to theory. Most importantly, go from the "I" to the "We". This is our great adventure, a birth of something that is not only changing, but growing out of the previous 40 years with Falco. Awakening our collective consciousness. It is a process that needs everyone's participation, everyone's contributions, dreams, ideas, opinions. We are bit like, wow! Where are we going? Comfortable in a way, exciting in a way, open to a new thing in another way. But at the same time, it is a process we have to go through. To then be in this new, little by little, to what we are creating, defining what it is to be a community.

Gazza pointed out that Damanhur is often visited by sociologists, including by famous sociologists, Luigi Berzano and Stefania Palmisano from the University of Turin, Massimo Introvigne from the Centre for Studies on New Religions (CESNUR), Eileen Barker from the London School of Economics, and Immacolata Maciotti of the University La Sapienza of Rome. Immacolata Maciotti had pointed out that, of course, there is no dogma at Damanhur because there is no religion. However, she further pointed out that, if there were a dogma, it would be "change". Change would be the dogma, but now, Gazza thought, it is not only a matter of changing, but making a big resolution, they were questioning it all. What does it mean to be a community today, both in this moment in Damanhur and in this moment in the world?

For Gazza, Damanhur is like a seed. A seed that needed a long time to grow, a long period of gestation and cultivation. That is a complex process with many stages to go through. The seeds are now blossoming and spreading in the world: they will grow with the flowers and the grass of the lands where they will fly to, called by the dreams of many people all over the world.

> A Damanhur group formed in Norway have now determined their community, and it is happening also in Germany and Spain. The future will be populated by communities. Falco was writing about this in his books in the 1970s, he was speaking of a future made of communities, which seemed improbable at the time. However, it is happening. So many people in so many different countries are getting together and creating communities and projects, around their dreams. People are awakening. There is a universal awakening of consciousness. A community model that was very innovative at the time was the kibbutz. It is curious that many people from Israel come and visit Damanhur today.

It is Gazza's impression that they find something here that resonates with them more than it does with other cultures.

> We were invited for a cup of tea and a chat on a Sunday afternoon to see whatever was going on here. You were invited to come, ask questions, to see what the dream was, to see how Damanhur was spreading in the world. The dream was there even before the building was underway, before the establishment of the community. It was there during the time of the Horus Centre in Turin.
>
> Now, it has had a cycle of around 40 years, after a period of building spiritual awareness of solidarity and generational self-awareness. When you are 40 you begin to wonder who you are, and where you came from, and where you are headed. So with the community, we wondered. We also needed that spiritual awareness and solidarity. Those 40 years are needed, as a basis for reflection, as a means of evaluating.

She has been working on projects in Israel for a number of years and feels that it is similar with the Jewish people and the kibbutz system, who also needed 40 years to build a spiritual awareness, with solidity and a generational transformation.

> At Damanhur, looking where we are now, I think it is a fascinating, delicate, crucial moment. And very important, because with Falco it was a story, it was a way, and he was catalyzing everyone's energy, attention and focus. That was all very clear, but he knew that he had time to do it, to put it into practice.
>
> So, we can look at how people came from all over the world, from the very beginning. And when I tell the story, I cannot believe it myself, what we have done. Not only the temples, but the building of the community, the schools, the artistic workshops. It is amazing what we have done in so little time. But now, it is like a new book. It's a birth of something that is not only changing, but growing out of the previous 40 years.

Gazza pointed out that Damanhur has been visited by famous sociologists, Luigi Berzano from the University of Turin, Massimo Introvigne from the Centre for Studies on New Religions (CESNUR),

Eileen Barker from the London School of Economics, and Immaculata Marchetti of the University of Rome. Marchetti had pointed out that, of course, there is no dogma at Damanhur because there is no religion. However, she further pointed out that, if there were a dogma, it would be "change". Change would be the dogma, but now, Gazza thought, it is not only a matter of changing, but making a big resolution, they were questioning it all. What is it to be a community? The big questions need to be asked, like the question the philosophers ask: who are we, where do we come from, where are we going? Big questions that require big answers. What is the community? Where do we want to go? What does it mean to be a community today, both in this moment in Damanhur and in this moment in the world?

The process of gestation and cultivation is complex. It has to be worked through many stages. The seed is blossoming, and Gazza sees it happening by synchronicity. It is happening because they thought of it, it is happening because it is meant to be, they witness it unfolding before their eyes. Not only in Italy:

> A Damanhur group formed in Norway have now determined their community. In Germany and Spain, we have groups. In these cases, the synchronicity is leaving us and now resides in them. If you read

Falco's books, those he wrote in the 1970s, he was speaking of a future made of communities, which seemed improbable at the time. However, it is happening. Because the good news is their own, we cannot be totally sure, but so many people in so many different countries are making groups, communities, projects. People are awakening. There is a universal awakening of consciousness.

In asking what is needed, Gazza concludes that the community is not just like a mission. The community is an instrument for transformation. Living together is the formula that is chosen to accelerate awakening. There can be many ways to awaken the divine inside, this method was chosen for many reasons. People are gregarious animals, even if taught to be separate from everything and everyone, and the ecosystem functions, but people are happier when they are with others than when they are by ourselves and all alone. Moreover, we are imperfect in the vision of ourselves, and thanks to the mirror that we can find in the others around us, we can see ourselves in a more complete way. "Also, it's fun to live together!" she exclaimed.

You know what Falco once said in a course he was teaching? About how other civilizations lived in other galaxies. Of course, we live like this here, but there can be other, and we believe there are, other civilizations following a different formula, with different laws, senses and circumstances.

One person once asked Falco: "How would you describe to other people living on another planet, how would you describe us humans living on this planet?" He remarked that this was an interesting question. "Let me see," he said, pausing a moment in thought, before continuing: "Well, I would describe them as people in whom part of the body the only part of the body that shows their inner life, their soul, and their deepest emotions – that is their eyes – is not visible to themselves but only to others."

"Isn't that interesting?" asked Gazza of me. "I don't see myself, the others can see me, only the others. Isn't that a key in our hands to use for our growth?"

Gazza has recently paid a working visit to Liverpool, where she and a group of people from the Liverpool Arts Lab constructed a spiral circuit, as well as discussions and seminars about Damanhur. Josh Ray wrote to me about this project:

One of the three magnolias taken on the Cerne To CERN Pilgrimage found its home in Damanhur's Sacred Woods. A Jungian symbol that, to the Liverpool Arts Lab and others who have the eyes to see, represents the creative life force that underlies everything in the city by the Mersey – it was a gift that cut right to the core of what Liverpool is about.

Bringing things full circle just under a year later, Damanhur sent a "magpie" with a gift that cut right to the core of what they're about. Gazza arrived in Liverpool on the cusp of the world locking down and gifted a group of individuals known as Astronavi Liverpool the wisdom to create a Damanhurian Spiral around a tree in Princes Park.

This Astronavi spiral has since become a beacon for community, self-care and creativity during these discordant times. The sign that sits aside the spiral explains further...

> The Spiral is a recurring symbol of life in the universe
> Expand your sensory perceptions as you slowly walk
> the path between the stones.
> When the spiral welcomes you to its centre,
> take some time to connect with the present moment.
> As you retrace your steps back,
> make sure not to step over the stones.
> We ask that you do not smoke or consume alcohol within the spiral.
> Please walk the spiral one at a time,
> Holding positive intention.
> A three-dimensional energy path,
> this spiral was created for the people of Liverpool
> with wisdom gifted to us from the "Popolo Spirituale" of Damanhur.
> Walking this Spiral helps clear the mind and elevate thoughts
> The Spiral was first developed in the Italian Alps
> with glacier-carved pebbles,
> however, the stones used here have a more urban origin.
> These "stones" began life as clay before they were shaped into bricks
> and hardened with fire, creating shelter for families,
> organizations and businesses throughout Liverpool.
> Then, over seven nights in May 1941 during the Blitz,
> many of these bricks suffered from the citywide onslaught,
> where far too many died and many more made homeless.
> Fragmented once again, these bricks found
> new life on a mile-long stretch of Mersey coast in Crosby.
> Smoothed by the elements over the best part of 80 years,
> they have since returned to a more natural form.
>
> ASTRONAVI LIVERPOOL 2020

Damanhur has devoted much of its time and energy to awaken and embrace the principles of the Divine Feminine, the Goddess. As 2020 melted into 2021, a new initiative was afoot in Damanhur. Announced on the Damanhur website was "a world-wide spiritual operation: The Earth is Calling! Respond with Us", it went on to say:

Our planet is changing frequency, freeing its power to help us ascend. Let's unite in a coordinated magical action, tuning in to the new divine frequencies and the new times.

Awakening the Divine Masculine

The presence of the Goddess, in many of her manifestations, is felt by all the sensitive souls on the planet. It is now time for the masculine to be activated and harmonized.

It is time to awaken the Divine Masculine, present in the earth as the propulsive force of the magma in the core of the planet, in volcanoes, and within the life force that animates nature. Some Native Americans call this force Kokkopelli, the ancient Romans Faunus, in China it is known as Tudi Gong. In Damanhur they use the name-frequency of the ancient Greek god of nature, Pan, a powerful, passionate and kind god, who loved music and poetry, and protected nature and the earth, as depicted here in this powerful drawing by Bruco Tartufo. Pan means everything: this divine force supports a renewed, harmonious, generous and creative Divine Masculine, ready to protect life in the loving embrace of the Goddess.

A series of events, celebrations and join-in rituals was announced for the months ahead. Lighting a bonfire for the Earth, Striking the Gong, Listening to the Voice of the Earth, and a whole range of dance, song and spiritual rituals in the hall of the Temples of Humankind. Life at Damanhur never stands still. Action, change and moving on are the watchwords of the community.

Summary and conclusion

What a long, strange journey it has been for me, the finding and exploring of this incredible phenomenon called Damanhur. Since the first synchronistic connection in 1997, I've enjoyed a sublime roller-coaster ride of amazement, astonishment and admiration. Damanhur began with a dream and that dream lives on. Starting from humble beginnings, the community has become a tower of strength.

I have had it said to me that I may be too uncritical about Damanhur and I have to admit about having an optimistic disposition. I also have to acknowledge that from the moment I first experienced Damanhur I have found more to like, to be positive about, than to dislike. I was aware from the very first that they had a great deal of negative energies railed against them and they had found a somewhat unique ability to turn all that negativity positive. Of course, there has been some criticism from without and within, but this has largely been by nature of personal grievance. Knowing what regularly happens in families, it is hardly surprising that with a community grouping of many hundreds, there was bound to be some disgruntlement and disenchantment. For me, the positivity I have experienced at Damanhur and the monumental nature of their attainments has been an inspiration.

The first 16 years were developed in secret, constructing the Temples of Humankind in a clandestine way, so that by the time the world found out about them, it was too late. They were there, to be admired, to be marvelled at. The next 20 years were a time of consolidation, making the community stronger and more stable, spreading a positive message about the temples, the community they had developed, and getting better known in the world.

Then came what could have been a catastrophe. The death of Oberto Airaudi, who had taken the Damanhurian name Falco Tarassaco, and who was founder of the community and the inspiration behind all its achievements. However, far from being a devastating calamity, through the grief and loss grew a renewed spirit of optimism. Falco had prepared for his own death by preparing the community for a positive future and a renewal of all they stood for.

This now is that time of renewal. The spiritual growth of Damanhur is embodied in the Initiation Path of Medit-Action, formerly the School of Meditation, stronger than ever in the lives of Damanhurians, and joined by thousands of people from all over the world. The ongoing work of further developing the Temples of Humankind and the Sacred Woods, in size and in artistic accomplishment, has attracted even more visitors to Damanhur than ever before, not as tourists, but as seekers of spiritual experience.

Damanhur has spread throughout Europe and the world, with thriving centres in the Italian cities of Bergamo, Bologna, Firenze, Milano, Modena and Verona. There are centres further afield in Australia, Germany, Spain, Croatia, Hungary, Israel, Kobe and Tokyo in Japan, Holland, Norway, Switzerland, Slovenia, California and Colorado in the United States, and Vienna in Austria.

Tobias Jones, a journalist with a theological bent, lived for several years in Italy and visited Damanhur, which he wrote about in his book, *Utopian*

Dreams (Faber & Faber, 2007). He writes with large dollops of scepticism, yet concludes that he was determined at the outset of his journey to be as positive as he could about communes, and that he remained impressed with Damanhur:

> It was, I'm sure, well-intentioned: the idea that anything dangerous could ever come out of Damanhur is hilarious, which is in itself a serious compliment. And I was fond of the people I met. But if I had started out imagining that religion was dogmatic and restrictive, I was beginning to realise that Damanhur was, for all its exoticism, rather predictable… It's a reduction, rather than an extension of the horizon.

Jones was writing at the time of greatest pressure on Damanhur, just after the digging out of the mountain and the building of the Temples of Humankind had been discovered by the world. I wonder, if he visited now, after nearly 30 more years of development and horizons certainly widening, his scepticism might be more blunted and his reservations less acute.

This growth in Damanhurian influence is a prelude to a new commitment to openness and extensive sharing of its experience and achievements. In real response to the dying wishes of Falco Tarassaco, Damanhur is reaching out to like-minded individuals and community groups throughout the world to share what they have learned over the past four decades. Indigenous people, shamans and spiritual guides have been increasingly making visits to Damanhur in a glorious example of mutual sharing. Ways of living in Damanhur are being made more open and accessible. Visits are being enriched and expanded, with most arranged around the learning experience of a specially prepared course, and a plan to have special days when people on limited incomes might visit Damanhur for free.

The community is in the midst of a big revolution, whereby every initiate in Damanhur or beyond is considered a Vajne citizen, with every different role and choice recognized at the same level of importance for its growth and development.

Vajne citizens are scattered throughout the world, actively striving in a common purpose to bring about spiritual awareness and social and environmental change.

Betsy Poole and Eddie Effron came to Damanhur nine years ago from California. In recent years, they have been collecting archival material about Damanhur and creating a story room that will serve as an information resource outlining the history and development of Damanhur. It has been an arduous project, but is now reaching fruition and by the time you read this, a video presentation of this archive will be online.*

In 2020, as a new decade started, Damanhurians were asking, what will be the colour and rhythm of this new time? It started with the pause imposed by the pandemics, as if to draw our attention to how they will be years of transformation, with new unprecedented crises, memorable moments that will transform the world. They say that it is a time when they need to be present and centred, in order to hear the truest voice within. One of the gods that the Damanhur calendar celebrated on the December 2019 page is Horus, stellar and galactic divinity, symbol of the spiritual Sun and life. Symbolically, Horus is also direction and energy for the god who lives within each person, a fragment of divine energy that gives light to the human being. A true protagonist of our new time, the spiritual compass that allows people to transform themselves and remain lucid, strong and able to be at service to others. Life is always "now" in every moment, as hands are moved, and hearts are touched.

The god Horus is one of the most significant ones in the mythology of ancient Egypt. From the fourth millennium BC, spreading from Edfu on the western bank of the Nile, to then touch every point of time and space in the civilization of Upper and Lower Egypt. He has the appearance of a falcon, and he is often represented as a human figure with the head of a raptor.

Horus – who is also called "Sun on two horizons" – is the personification of the pharaoh and his power: absolute, administered with wisdom, tinged with a deep love for the peoples he reigns over and for whom he is responsible. The divinity Horus became ever more central in the Egyptian pantheon until he was the most elaborate and complete divinity, a bridge between the celestial world and the human world. He was pharaoh, thaumaturge, one who ordered chaos, one who vanquished and pacified evil. He was a protector of his peoples and dynastic traditions. He was the inspiration for Falco Tarassaco, and consequently for Damanhur. One last thing, as written by Damanhur scribe, Stambecco Pesco:

Horus always acts in the first person, not delegating his responsibilities to others. Perhaps this is his secret, having gods as friends and allies but acting personally, and the secret of Horus can now become ours.

*The video of The Story of Everything, can be seen here: https://vimeo.com/ondemand/storyofeverything.

Horus, like all of the gods, is visualised in the magnificent paintings in the Labyrinth of the Temples of Humankind, with many featured on the 2019 and 2020 Damanhur calendars, always beautifully produced. This artwork has been developed to a quite magnificent standard, fully befitting the gods. Esperide came up with a perceptive phrase to describe this Labyrinthine space; "Gods walking among gods," she said. I liked that.

Approaching the end of this book, and what an incredible journey it has been. I'd like to briefly return to the Gauguin painting, *Where Do We Come From? Who Are We? Where Are We Going?* It is a little like Hitchcock's MacGuffin, a device that sets and guides the purpose of an event or situation. Unimportant in itself, it permeates the reasons and persons of the story. Another synchronic coincidence. I have just recalled that there came into my consciousness several years ago an interesting little book called *Sapiens: A Brief History of Humankind* by Yuval Noah Harari (Penguin Books, 2015). *Sapiens* showed us that where we came from – the main thing that separates us from our closest animal relatives, chimps and apes – is the ability to gossip.

> The apes can communicate effectively about dangers lurking around a corner and can co-operate in groups of about a dozen. We *Homo sapiens* can easily cope with a group of some thousands and express opinions about many of them. We thrive on stories, especially stories about gods and goddesses, which are ingrained in our history.

I loved this book and its quirky ideas about from whence we have come. Since then, Harari has added two more books that complete a philosophical trilogy. *21 Lessons for the 21st Century* (Penguin Books, 2019) is a book of essays on different subjects like "Disillusionment", "Work", "Liberty", and "Equality". The book has five parts: "The Technological Challenge" "The Political Challenge", "Despair and Hope", "Truth" and "Resilience". Harari's thoughts spring from the basic, but important question: what can we say about the meaning of life today? It is the book of where we are now. Free will has been substantially undermined by the algorithmic hacking of human beings, algorithms that in many respects know you better than you know yourselves and are thus able to manipulate you. Unless you are aware and prepared. Know thyself better than the machine.

Homo Deus (Penguin Books, 2017) shows us where we're going. War is obsolete. You are more likely to commit suicide than be killed in conflict. Famine is disappearing. You are at more risk of obesity than starvation. Death is just a technical problem. Equality is out – but immortality is in. What does our future hold? *Homo Deus* explores the projects, dreams and nightmares that will shape the 21st century – from overcoming death to creating artificial life. It asks the fundamental questions: where do we go from here? And how will we protect this fragile world from our own destructive powers?

Harari attempts to make a clear distinction for us, between intelligence and consciousness. Intelligence is the ability to solve problems, a task that modern computers are probably more adept at than we are.

Consciousness is about feelings: pain, hurt, love, hate, loss, bereavement. Machines don't have such abilities. Humans combine intelligence and consciousness. This makes us unique.

The opening out of their lives is no small matter for the people of Damanhur, in fact it has come as a considerable cultural shockwave. However, the realization is beginning to take hold that this is a significant moment in the history of the human race and that the opportunity to grasp the situation is of paramount importance. Over 40 years of preparation have been leading up to this moment and now is the time to go, go, go.

The future of Damanhur is assured. Like all communities, they will struggle to keep a financial viability and equilibrium, as they stride out into a superbly exciting and adventurous future that we can all participate in, that we can all encourage, marvel at, and be a part of.

A DISCORDIAN PILGRIMAGE

If we knew why, we wouldn't be doing it.

(Bill Drummond, KLF)

Some background may be needed here in order to get a clear handle on this particular adventure. It will be recalled that Ken Campbell, John Joyce and I had found ourselves, by chance, at Damanhur in the late 1990s. Many years prior to that, Ken had somewhat heroically dramatized *The Illuminatus! Trilogy* by Robert Shea and Robert Anton Wilson (Dell Publishing, 1975), staging it first at the Liverpool School of Language, Music, Dream and Pun, and then at the Royal National Theatre, with sets designed by Bill Drummond, who would later go on to found the KLF and the K Foundation.

The reason why the first *Illuminatus!* show was in Liverpool was due in no small part to Peter O'Halligan, who was obsessed by a dream that the Swiss psychoanalyst Carl Gustav Jung had had, in which he saw Liverpool as the "pool of life". Jung had written about his dream on page 223 of *Memories, Dreams and Reflections* (Pantheon Books, 1963). O'Halligan became obsessed and studied every possible link, connection and consequence of Jung's dream, identifying the precise location of it as an underground meeting of waterways, now covered with a manhole cover, on Mathew Street, home of the Cavern Club made famous by the Beatles.

Peter O'Halligan acquired an old warehouse building. It was a huge old property, at the point where a number of roads meet, at the end of Mathew Street. The building is still there. It is now an Irish pub and eating house, called Flannagan's. In those days, it was quite broken down. He built a market on the ground floor, where people would sell their hand-made crafts, the sort of clothes you could not buy in the regular shops, and aromatic perfumery. On the upper floor, he built a café,

where the Liverpool philosophical debaters would meet. It was a place where he could do dream merchanting, along with a lot of friends. Some ran the café and others ran stalls in the market. They called the market *Aunt Twackies*, which apparently means "something old-fashioned", in the scouse. Antiques. Anti-kwies. Aunt Twackies. The café became The Liverpool School of Language, Music, Dream and Pun. And it was here that *Illuminatus!* was staged as a twelve-hour epic play.

Subsequent to this, Ken hosted a TV series called *Reality on the Rocks* (Windfall Films, 1995), where he was to interview the great cosmological thinkers, including an episode on CERN and the Large Hadron Collider that straddles the border between France and Switzerland. Many mythological links were forged between *Illuminatus!*, Shea and Wilson, Jung, the number 23, Liverpool as the pool of life, Bill Drummond, the Justified Ancients of Mu Mu and CERN.

Fast forward to 2019, and Ken's daughter, Daisy Eris Campbell, conceived during the run of *Illuminatus!*, was becoming increasingly absorbed by her late father's interests and musings, using them as a foundation for her own transformational work. Having staged a number of shows and events, including a play based on another book by Robert

Anton Wilson, *Cosmic Trigger* (Hilaritas Press, 1977), where Wilson wrote about appearing in the Royal National Theatre production of *Illuminatus!* – the story to be found on page 223 (just like Jung's dream). From these adventures Daisy had dreamed up the idea of a "pilgrimage", gathered together a group of artists, musicians, poets, mystics, photographers, writers and dancers, all of whom had become immersed in a Discordian dystopia. Daisy proposed the trip and informed me about it when she came up to Shetland to perform her play *Pigspurt's Daughter*, based on spending her engaging and chaotic life with her dad. I considered the idea for ten minutes and I put myself down for it. A detailed itinerary arrived a couple of weeks later, reproduced in the section below.

* * *

CERNE TO CERN
Including:
The Liverpool-Lapis Express Jung Pilgrimage
A Heretical Caper
The Proposed Itinerary

FRI 19 APRIL
BICYCLE DAY – THE MANHOLE COVER,
JUNG'S DREAM, LIVERPOOL

Those who can physically be at the manhole cover, in Liverpool's Mathew Street, go there, others mark this start psychically, from the comfort of your own portals, via portable manhole covers.

It begins with a dream that Carl Gustav Jung (1875–1961), one of the founding fathers of psychology, once had and recorded in his book *Memories, Dreams, Reflections*. Though he never visited Liverpool, Jung dreamt that he was in the city along with several of his fellow "Swiss" and gives a detailed description of his precise dream location, comparing it to the more familiar (to him) Basel – a place where, among other things, "streets converged".

Here, he sees a vision of a mysterious "round pool, and in the middle of it, a small island… On it stood a single tree… It was as though the tree… was the source of light." Jung's Swiss companions in the dream could not see any of this.

"They spoke of another Swiss who was living in Liverpool, and expressed surprise that he should have settled here. I was carried away by the beauty of the tree and the sunlit island and thought 'I know very well why he has settled here.' Then I awoke." Jung considered this dream to be the turning point in his life which led him to study synchronicity and the subconscious.

In the early 1970s, self-styled scouse beat-poet Peter O'Halligan read about Jung's dream and it struck a chord with him. He began to investigate possible sites for the location of the dream based on Jung's descriptions and concluded that the best fit was the small square where several streets converged at the bottom of Mathew Street. Waterways met underground in a similar way and access is through a manhole cover. Then the adventure really begins…

SAT 20 APRIL
CERNE GIANT DAY

The journey begins in the large hard-on. The res-erection, the protuberential, the heretical. The male principle. Cerne Abbas is a charming and quaint village that is world renowned for the Cerne Giant, a 180-foot-high ancient chalk figure carved out into the steep sloping hillside above the village. The origins of the giant, now owned by the National Trust, are a mix of fact and speculation. Some believe that he represents the Roman god Hercules and is over 1,500 years old or that he is a pagan fertility symbol. However, there is no known historical record before 1694 and it has been argued that the giant is a more recent caricature of a historical figure, the most probable being Oliver Cromwell. Journey via minibus to Calais, or maybe a bit beyond. Set up camp in France, in readiness for the long bus journey to Damanhur in the Italian Alps.

SUN 21 APRIL (EASTER)
JOURNEY TO DAMANHUR

We embark on the nine-hour drive to the Temples of Mankind and the Federation of Damanhur. We rehearse and plan for our performance tomorrow. Set up camp in Damanhur.

MON 22 APRIL
DAMANHUR DAY

Workshops in sacred language and sacred dance – a visit to the underground Temples of Mankind and the Sacred Wood. Put on a show for the Damanhurian people.

The Damanhurians have rediscovered an ancient sacred language. Oberto Airaudi (Falco) developed the language and used it extensively throughout the Temples of Humankind. The sacred language can be interpreted through dance and we will be taught how to say a special message in sacred dance which will be delivered to CERN.

TUES APRIL 23RD
CERN DAY

After breakfast we set out for CERN, the ultimate orifice, the glorious gnothing. The female principle. We're now fully prepared for the ritual to reset the world. We take a tour of the large Hadron, and then immanentize the eschaton. Daisy Campbell:

> CERN is only a four-hour drive from the Italian community and the temples at Damanhur. This was the place I first visited with my dad when I was 16. Truly one of the great wonders of the world.

When I got in touch and told them about our proposed pilgrimage, they completely understood our quest and have invited us to prepare ourselves for resetting the world at CERN by preparing a special message in sacred dance form, with a day of temple-visiting, sacred woods, various extraordinary initiations and then to gift them a performance that evening.

WED 24 APRIL
JUNG DAY

Set up camp near Jung Institute. Visit Jung Institute and Jung's garden – Liverpool and Jung connection – The presentation of gifts – A deeper understanding of WHY. Jung's dream becomes LUCID. Pilgrims' last supper.

Carl Jung had a well-known standpoint. He believed in paranormal occasions and sometimes saw the harrowing creatures from the hell. According to some legend, he had an argument with Freud who was famous for a realistic approach to life and down-to-earth attitude to the things. Freud shouted that there were no ghosts or spirits on the planet. He tried to convince Jung that all the paranormal creatures were neither more nor less than the figment of imagination.

He made inscriptions on a slab of stone at Bollingen. When the stone arrived, the first thing that occurred to him was a Latin verse by the alchemist Arnaldus de Villanova. He chiselled this into the stone; in translation it goes:

Here stands the mean, uncomely
tone, 'Tis very cheap in price!
The more it is despised by fools,
The more loved by the wise.

This verse refers to the alchemist's stone, the lapis, which is despised and rejected. The Telesphoros of Asklepios came to him. Ancient statues show him wearing a hooded cloak and carrying a lantern. At the same time, he is a pointer of the way. Jung dedicated a few words to him which came into his mind while he was working. The inscription is in Greek; the translation goes:

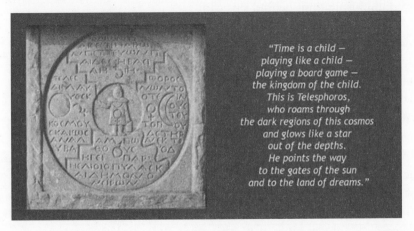

"Time is a child –
playing like a child –
playing a board game –
the kingdom of the child.
This is Telesphoros,
who roams through
the dark regions of this cosmos
and glows like a star
out of the depths.
He points the way
to the gates of the sun
and to the land of dreams."

In conclusion, under the saying of Arnaldus de Villanova, Jung set down in Latin the words: "In remembrance of his 75th birthday C G Jung made and placed this here as a thanks offering, in the year 1950." When the stone was finished, he looked at it again and again, wondering about it and asking himself what lay behind his impulse to carve it.

The stone stands outside the Bollingen Tower, like an explanation of it. It is a manifestation of the occupant, but one which remains incomprehensible to others. "Do you know what I wanted to chisel into the back face of the stone?" he asked. "Le cri de Merlin!" For what the stone expressed reminded him of Merlin's life in the forest, after he had vanished from the world. Men still hear his cries, so the legend runs, but they cannot understand or interpret them.

THUR 25 APRIL
HOMEWARD BOUND

*　　　*　　　*

Wow! Now that sounded like some cosmic adventure. And indeed, it turned out to be. A truly amazing, phenomenal and enjoyable journey. Inspiring, enlightening, emotional, spiritual, dream-catching, infectious, socially uplifting, gratifying, enjoyable and one of the most memorable experiences of my life.

As Alan Moore says in *Jerusalem* (W W Norton, 2018): "Snowy heard the self-infatuated kings and queens… the avenues and monument… It made him laugh, although not literally. Where did they think that everything, including them, was going to go?" Moore was another of the profound inspirations behind this trip.

We were all asked to give ourselves a newly designated name and to design a personal tarot card based on that name. So, I became The Sage (with Onion), along with The Bridge, The Sceptical Believer, The Toilet, The Authenticator, The Clamjamfie, The Creatrix, and, of course, Daisy Eris Campbell herself as The Bricklayer. The tarot card that we individually designed reflected our new pilgrim names. The designs were made into an authentic one-off tarot set, a "Pilgrim's Tarot" pack.

On the journey was a large contingent from the Liverpool Arts Lab, and they were our genial happiness inducers. Every time a journey stopped, for whatever reason, heartening songs would break out. "All You Need is Love", "You'll Never Walk Alone", "The Power of Love", "Ferry 'Cross the Mersey", and any number of Beatles songs. This was group bonding on

a ginormous scale. The double-decker bus we travelled on was the living incarnation of that in the *Magical Mystery Tour*; your mind transformed it into the multi-coloured vehicle of an enchanted dream factory of growing friendships and the natural birth of a superindividual!

I make this last point due to the organizational aspects of the trip, highly creative, highly participatory, highly inclusive. For starters, Josh Ray (The Rework), from the Liverpool Arts Lab group, produced a wondrous *Pilgrim's Guidebook*, including contributions from an array of members of the pilgrimage. Among ruminations on a *Destination Un-Gnown*, an investigation of *Dreams in the Oneirosphere*, an interpretation of quantum theory, a best wishes send-off by John Higgs, and some gorgeous illustrations, I contributed an essay on the Damanhurian concept of the superindividual that appeared to strike a chord and become a theme for the journey.

A weird performance piece, the *Pilgrim's Opera*, was devised, written and performed, with minimal rehearsal time, for a large audience at Damanhur. Three highly organized rituals were performed at Cerne, at CERN, and in Jung's garden at Bollingen. A plethora of entertainments and sound mixes were provided for the journey. Strangers got to know

each other, supported each other, friendships developed. And in these many creative ways the 69 became as one, a superindividual.

The adventure began when we all met up for the first time, in front of the great erect man of chalk, at Cerne Abbas. The ensuing ritualized celebrations included the recitation of traditional verse and specially written contributions from members of the entourage. The outstanding costumes, outrageous makeup and the high energy music, all made this a most memorable launch for the rest of the pilgrimage. Jonathan Harris (The Money Burner) summed up many of our feelings about this auspicious start to our journey:

> On Good Friday, from all around the United Kingdom, the pilgrims piled into 17 different vehicles to convene on a campsite near the Cerne Abbas Giant. Then early morning on Easter Saturday we gathered below the giant's giant testicles. After sermons, song and ritual, and with each of us dressed as an individual sperm, an ejaculation was enacted.

Suitably climaxed, it was off in our various cars and vans to the Portsmouth port, a ferry across the channel to Caen, and a meeting with a double-decker bus that would be our transport and home for most of the remaining journey. It had a small kitchen area from which tea, coffee and snacks regularly emerged thanks to The Cook (Simon Scanlan) and The Drummer (Mandie Buchanan). It had endless entertainment presented by the Liverpool Arts Lab mob and Kermit. Overall organizing and administration were attended to by The Money Burner.

Overnight was spent at a French campsite, rough ground and trees that threatened to drop branches on you. It was my first attempt at putting up a new tent, which didn't go too well. Morning came, with me stiff as a board, not able to stand, and I'd already decided that a 76-year-old man should not be living like this. It wasn't that my blue wigwam tent was hard to put up and take down, it was more that it was impossible for me to live in. I've done Glastonbury and many other festivals. I should have known this would have been beyond my ageing frail frame and rickety knees. It would be my last night in that tent. I'd try once more, then give in to the offer of a nice warm bed for other sleepovers.

Packed up and on the bus for the long journey over the Alps to the Canavese town of Vidracco, wherein lies Damanhur. Horton Jupiter (The Phonomancer) described the impact of our arrival:

Here at Damanhur, sobbing. Here's Horus, there's our kid Pan… earth, air, fire, water… holding on to Pigspurt's Daughter, for dear, dear life. I've wanted to be here for longer than I've known about it, possibly more than this lifetime, possibly much more than that.

Josh Ray (The Rework), superscribe of the Liverpool Arts Lab and editor of our much-cherished *Pilgrim's Guidebook*, further elaborated on how the feelings were being felt:

Waking up in a slight state of delirium following a heady first night on a magic bus with 69 pilgrims, we were greeted at the gates of Damanhur by Esperide. Basked in the same glow we would soon notice in everyone who chose to find a home in this esoteric corner of the Italian Alps, the initial impression was of a community from another world, less troubled than ours.

Larry Sidorczuk (Ch'angel of Synchronicity) is a celebrated Liverpudlian, who for decades has been a champion of the Jung dream of Liverpool as the pool of life. He concurred with Josh about the arrival:

First, was the warm welcome and reception we were given by Esperide, which was reciprocated by a strong feeling of fellowship, assembling in an amphitheatre where we all sang an impromptu "All You Need Is Love", accompanied by combs and paper kazoos.

Lisa Louise Lovebucket (Cilla Black) and several other pilgrims had been to Damanhur previously and I was able to negotiate with Esperide for a small group to visit to the brand-new artwork in parts of the Labyrinth. Lisa spoke with some pride:

Having visited the temples before, I was honoured to be invited to see the newly completed section of the Labyrinth, along with a small group of pilgrims who had also visited before. I spent the whole time in silent reverie, with tears flowing down my cheeks.

Eric Maddern (The Omphalos) is an author, musician, a masterful storyteller and denizen of the forestry retreat Cae Mabon, home of hobbits and wood lore in the wintry mountains of Snowdonia. He thought that Damanhur was a high functioning spiritual community, the most astonishing achievement of which was to have hewn out of the mountain caverns by hand the exquisite Temples of Humankind:

> Extraordinary painting, stained glass and sculpture illustrate human history and diversity; Earth landscapes from snowy mountains to steaming jungles; creatures of the natural world, many threatened with extinction; gods and goddesses from all religions; symbolic languages, crystal spheres, a hall of mirrors… I was in tears in the first temple. Never had I been so moved by such beauty.

Show us so we can understand (You – reveal – to us – how to do – with ability – and power – the knowledge). This was the message to be learned in the sacred dance of Damanhur and taken to the heart of CERN in order to be performed in the ritual to reset the world and immanentize the eschaton. From such reified aspirations to the practicalities of surviving on a pilgrimage. Camp was set up on the football field next to Damanhur Crea. It was a cold night and I'm afraid I was compelled to give up on another night in that tent and was delighted when someone found me a bed for the next two nights. Sheer bliss.

The next morning the larger group was split into smaller ones to take turns on a journey through the Temples of Humankind. Josh Ray felt that he had a particularly moving experience:

> My group was full of explosive extroverts that you'd normally expect to cause disruptions, but we all fell into deep silence as soon as we saw the enchanting beauty of the first temple. Each time we moved into another section we were greeted with a new profound experience; from despairing at the state of the natural world, to feeling elevated by higher beings, losing ourselves in spheres and finally having our minds blown together by an intense reverberating gong. None of us would be the same from this point forward!

Larry Sidorczuk spoke for many in the group when he espoused the awe-inspiring feelings of visiting the temples:

The next day, the pilgrims were split into smaller groups and transported to the site of the Temples of Humankind – often described as the "eighth wonder of the world". It's an awe-inspiring achievement with its foundations built (or rather excavated) on a vision of humanity which celebrates co-existence, spiritual enlightenment and above all, a respect for the natural and mystical world and our place within it. The place embodies a kind of worship normally given to deities but in this case, it's us – the human race – which is given credence. These temples within the mountain bear testimony to our unique place in creation.

Emma Watkinson (The Creatrix) is a painter, an artistic interpreter of the phantasmagorical, who has spent a lot of time exploring the sacred sites of the world: Ankor Wat, the Egyptian pyramids, Mayan temples, Buddhism in Thailand, the Ganga in Varanasi India, Stonehenge and crop circles. She found each place was like an initiation key that she still feels the resonance of today. "It's all in there if you look." For her, Damanhur is a place of shared artistic vision:

> I'm a visionary artist, and I have visited Damanhur previously from that artistic perspective, and, for me, the temples are a great example of what sacred art can achieve. I felt honoured and blessed to see the new wing, and as we gazed at the gods and goddesses, I felt light energy streaming through the archetypal forms. You could say this painting is my response to the experience in the temples.

I was struck by the Damanhurian vision of the history of humanity I saw painted along the walls, an understanding of our struggles with conflict, and collective aspirations for peace. I loved the invocation in the new temples of the old gods of war laying down their arms, transmuting into a more evolved and harmonious aspect. I really feel and cherish the vision they hold there, of the possibility of a harmonious and positive future for this beloved planet.

The feelings of most pilgrims were expressed to me in many thousands of words sent to me after the adventure was over, the consensus being that of an awe-inspiring experience for the remarkable achievements evident in these constructions and artworks. "The Temples of Humankind were awesome, and I use that word very carefully and precisely." "An amazing intersection of art, engineering, spirit, mythology, humour, love, plants and animals." "Utterly mind-blowing. All that history of Huamnkind, all that spiritual research. All that beautiful art." These were typical of the feedback freely given.

However, Kermit Leveridge (The Moment Maker), legendary genial rapper with Black Grape, the Manchester band that concocted a fusion funk and electronic rock and grew out of Happy Mondays, was certainly passionate and succinct in his response: "I came out and burst into tears…"

'Nuff said, eh?

The evening had another important event in store, when the esteemed tour manager of our pilgrimage, Jonathan Harris (The Money Burner), led our group back to the campsite for a mass money burning ritual. Just before coming on the journey, I had acquired a copy of *Burning Issue*, a new print magazine about burning money. This first edition highlighted the most recent ritual mass burn, which took place in 2018. About 100 people came and half burned their money, more than £675 in total. Inspired by the legendary burning of a million quid by Bill Drummond and Jimmy Cauty of *KLF* – money that they said they never craved or particularly wanted from their music – a movement has grown, proudly

espoused by Jonathan Harris, who had also been fully involved in the organization of our pilgrimage.

Jonathan insists he doesn't know why people burn money. He makes a point not to ask. "One of the rules I set myself was to never ask or tell anyone to burn their money," he says. For him, it's less about why he does it, more a question of "Why not?" Burning money seems almost like a religion, one leaning far towards the pagan end of the spectrum. It's a symbolic way to get back to the roots of civilization, for which he believes "sacrifice is the founding act, and burning money becomes the primary form of sacrificial ritual". So, we had our own ritual burning ceremony in the cold April evening at Damanhur.

Then to the performance of the *Pilgrim's Opera*. Amid the smell of candles, incense and smoke, The Authenticator proudly declared: "Questi sono gli eterni pellegrini. Devono viaggiare senza sapere il perché." ("These are the eternal pilgrims. They must travel without knowing why.") Thus echoing the Drummond dictum of: "If we knew why, we wouldn't be doing it." Standing beside Esperide, Daisy Campbell (The Bricklayer) gleefully introduced the *Pilgrim's Opera*, pointing out that this was to be performed by a bunch of people who had mostly never met before the trip, who had been on a bus throughout the whole of the previous night, following a six-hour journey on a ferry. Oh, and she added that they had only time for a one-hour rehearsal. With that, the show was underway.

At the Gates of Chaos, The Authenticator introduced the proceedings (again in Italian), as a straggly bunch of grotesquely garbed figures entered

like a "Dance of Death" (Danse Macabre). The Discordian Accordionist as the Devil, dressed in a filthy Ronald MacDonald costume, enters playing a soulful tune, with Serialism chained by his neck in tow, hairy in face and body, stooped almost double.

Over the next 40 or so minutes, we experienced The Chanteuse singing her recurring refrain of *Is That All There Is?*, attracting a lively clap-along; a robust re-enactment of Jung's dream of Liverpool as the pool of life that included a flexible manhole cover and a most magnificent expanding magnolia tree; an exposition of the entire Cerne to CERN journey, complete with a display of all the pilgrims' tarot cards; and a luscious Clamjamfrie-led performance of an ancient British time dance, with leg-over crossings, accompanied by filmed images of the Cerne Abbas celebrations from the previous day. All this was delivered with vim, vigour and gusto that easily made up for any slackness of technical expertise.

Michelle was corpsing outrageously as she attempted to count in a boisterous version of *Rock the Hard-on, Rock the Hadron*, sensationally received by the enthusiastic audience. A re-written version of David Bowie's last recorded song, "Blackstar" was the foundation of the next section, gloriously manifesting itself as a Jodorowsky-inspired fable of mysterious intrigue. Pilgrims vogued and did strange trance dancing, becoming increasingly ecstatic as the song went on.

> On the day before the eschaton,
> On the day before the eschaton
> All the pilgrims come to call.
> Ah, ah,
> Ah, ah.
> Show us so we can understand.
> Show us so we can understand.

The dance that had been taught would be performed. Danza Sacro. The mystical "Dance of Shiva and Kali" filled the stage, complete with the truly magnificent sight of Kermit the Moment Maker as the many-limbed Shiva. The Lion, The Yoko and The Firestarter, all dressed as Kali, danced wildly and terrifyingly around Shiva.

The whole thing was brought to a dazzling climax with a sing-along rendition of "Is That All There Is?" led by The Chanteuse. The *Pilgrim's Opera* had certainly been a raucous piece of rumbustiousness that Ken Campbell would probably have termed "slung-on theatre", meaning that as a compliment, as a celebrated confirmation of something truly magical.

And that it was, for sure.

The ensuing and much-anticipated DJ mash-mix dance event was much enjoyed by the travellers and the Damanhurians alike, as it took us late into the night. A wholesome and joyous shared experience. The visit to Damanhur seemed to have been an unqualified success. The pilgrims were appreciative of the way we were welcomed, the amazing Temples of Humankind, the way the *Pilgrim's Opera* had been appreciated, and the camaraderie engendered in the dance event.

Afterthoughts were summed up by LouLou Whalley (The Runner), stalwart of the Liverpool Arts Lab and an active participant in the first of the Toxteth Day of the Dead celebrations, who had made all manner of things for this trip, including a large fabric vagina and a wonderful flowering magnolia tree for the *Pilgrim's Opera*. She was never to be seen without a needle and some fabric in her hands. Her perspective on Damanhur was essentially practical:

> The most strikingly beautiful, calm place on Earth. The smiles are different here, even the local villagers who are welcomed into the local Damanhur shops, have a welcoming beautiful peace around them. I felt honoured to be shown the temples. No words can describe. We 69 people, some of whom hadn't met before our trip, put on a *Pilgrim's Opera* for the Damanhurians, and they made us glow at giving them such obvious pleasure. I will never forget such a special place and with such amazing people and I will return, even though I still feel I am there.

As we said goodbye to Damanhur, our magical tour bus would take us to what, for me, would prove to be the most difficult part of our journey. Our trip took us up through the gorgeous scenery of the Alps to the CERN 27-kilometre tube of gnothing that straddles the French and Swiss border. Here, the Large Hadron Collider, the world's largest and most powerful particle accelerator, which has the enormous underground ring of superconducting magnets and accelerating structures to boost the energy of particles, whizzing them around the tube close to the speed of light.

On the way to CERN, Daisy helped us all prepare the dress she would wear. It was the fantastic dress that her mother, Prunella Gee, had worn as Eris in the stage production of *Illuminatus!* It was 20-foot long and in the show, as Eris was delivering a speech, she started to rise on a hidden forklift truck, the dress getting longer and longer as she rose in stature. It was an incredible image. Daisy intrepidly cut the skirt of the dress into 23 strips and we all devised our own sigil that had to have a personal association. These were then applied to the strips of skirt, all before we arrived at CERN. After a short stay at the visitor centre, we then drove as far as we could towards the absolute centre point atop the 27-kilometre tube. The rest of the journey was to be undertaken on foot.

The day was hot, the terrain was rough, and the journey to the centre of the gnothing tube was long. Very long. We were organized into groupings and told to look out for each other. The long walk began – 23 of us were chosen to hold one of the fabric strips. I'm old and slow but did my best to keep up. Holding onto the skirt helped. I was hot and sweaty. My feet were suffering from their enforced efforts. John Horabin (Aye) gave me a cap to help keep some of the burning sun off. After what seemed like the long march of Hannibal across the Alps, we finally arrived above the centre of the Large Hadron Collider.

Daisy stood in the centre and the 23 who held the strips of her dress gathered around her and started walking in a large circle. The rest of the 69 gathered in a larger circle around all of us and they danced the sacred dance learned at Damanhur, delivering the message "show us so that we can understand".

We walked round and round and round, I'm guessing it was 23 times, but I'd lost count. The ground was as rough and rugged as the walk towards this place had been, my feet were failing, my legs were aching, my body was just about holding together. All this time Daisy had been reciting, sighing, moaning, exclaiming, until her utterances reached redolent orgasmic proportions and as she ultimately climaxed... we all stopped and released our fabric strips. In this way, we had accomplished our aim and IMMANENTIZED THE ESCHATON and the world would never be the same again.

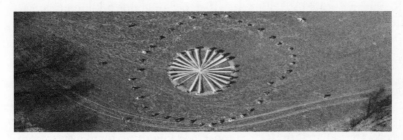

It was a great relief for me that it was all over. I tried my best to walk back the way we had arrived, but I'm afraid my body gave out and I collapsed. I was vaguely aware of people helping me to get up, to walk, and lay me down on a river bank. I was dowsed in water, became more aware, as kindly people took off my shoes and socks to reveal toes that had turned black. All sounds a bit dramatic, but I tell you, I would not have missed this total experience for the world. My body soon got over it and the rich memories were all that I'd ever needed.

Back on the bus, everyone was elated and joyful. Onwards and upwards to the next part of our adventure, further into Switzerland and in search of Jung's house. Jonathan Harris (The Money Burner) had been our mentor, guide and tour manger extraordinaire. He had hassled us on and off the bus, often shouting, invariably swearing. Yet everyone loved him, realizing the trip would not have been happening without him. He had been kneedeep in the organizing of this adventurous tour for months. Here is a piece he wrote after the event, about the next part of our pilgrimage, the part that took us to Carl Gustav Jung's garden at Bollingen:

During the months of planning, Daisy and I loved the idea that we should do a long walk on the final day of the pilgrimage. It wasn't easy to keep it in the itinerary. The final day was the trickiest of all days to organize. A 90-minute walk is easily traded off against some other activity. The walk got put in, shortened, taken out, and then put back in again several times.

Eventually, just a couple of days prior to the start of the pilgrimage, as our plans were about to cross the threshold into reality, we realized that the walk was actually a hugely significant part, not just of the day, but of the whole pilgrimage.

"What's the path like?" Daisy asked.

"It looks really good. It's like a stone chip path running right alongside the lake", I replied. The path would take us from Rapperswil-Jona to Bollingen, a distance of about 5 kilometres.

"Stone chip?" said Daisy.

"Yeah. Why?"

"Well, it's just that if we were real pilgrims, we'd do it barefoot, wouldn't we? Walking 5 kilometres on stone chip might be pushing it a bit, though."

"Barefoot! Yes. We must go barefoot. The crown of thorns had been carried barefoot. It's the most valuable thing that's ever existed and the king had to humble himself to carry it. It just nearly got burned up in the fire at Notre Dame. We gotta go barefoot."

"Wait. You mean, as in what Jesus had on his head? How do I not know about this?" asked Daisy.

I thought I'd best tell. "Just how King Louis IX of France came to possess the crown of thorns is complicated. The pious King Louis had great wealth and power, but an even greater desire for Paris to become the 'New Jerusalem' – the heavenly city on Earth (he too, wanted to immanentize the eschaton!). When his opportunity arose, Louis found a way through the complexities and gave over half his entire annual budget to secure the crown of thorns for France. The amount of money the king paid makes the crown the most valuable single object to have ever existed. In August 1239, stripped to the waist, he removed his shoes and walked into the city of Sens carrying the Crown, an ultimate act of self-subjugation. Walking barefoot was for Louis an act of the greatest humility and the highest possible veneration of the crown, which was then taken by river to Paris and placed in Notre-Dame."

Daisy and I agreed that the pilgrims would be asked to do the very final stretch of the walk barefoot.

We arrived at the entrance to Bollingen Tower tired from the 5 kilometre walk that had taken much longer than it should. I checked the time. We were running well behind schedule. We would drive directly from Bollingen back to our ferry at Caen. It would take about 13 hours. To be late would be a disaster.

I knew we had 90 minutes to do the Bollingen rituals and no more. Really, no more. But I also knew that rituals take as long as they take. And some take even longer.

For one of us, this moment we spent at Bollingen would mark the culmination of a 40-year journey. Larry Sidorczuk would plant a magnolia tree brought from Liverpool into Jung's garden. Jung had a dream with a magnolia tree at its heart, which was both the source of, and reflected within, its own light. The counter-cultural events this dream inspired were woven through Larry's life. He had been part of them since he was a teenager. And now those events, and Jung's dream, were part of him.

Larry from Liverpool planted his magnolia sapling and we all celebrated the pool of life that Jung had dreamed about. Then came one of the highlights of the whole trip for me, when Eric Maddern (The Omphalos) recited a long extract from *Merlin's Prophecy*, a dramatic epic poem,

originally written in Latin as the *Prophetia Merlini*, a 12th-century poem by John of Cornwall, which he claimed was from a lost manuscript in the Cornish language.

Here is part of Eric's powerful recitation.

The Dragons are awake.
There is a disturbance in the Land.
The red dragon is the people of Britain, the bearers of tradition Those
who come from the beginning.
The white one is the Saxon invader, the greedy, grasping newcomer.
And so they will chase each other back and forth across this land Until
such a time as arises the Boar of Cornwall.
Only then will peace and harmony be restored to this land.
He will be the noblest king,
And tales of his exploits will be as meat and drink
To the storytellers who relate them in ages to come.
Though the Goddess be forgotten
There will come a time of plenty
When the soil will be fruitful beyond man's need. The Fatted Boar will
proffer food and drink,
The Hedgehog will hide his apples in London.
Underground passages will be built beneath the city. Stones will speak;
the sea to France will shrink
And the secrets of the deep will be revealed.

With the poetic folklore still ringing in our ears, our pilgrimage was drawing to a close. Another night on a Swiss campsite, where The Money Burner organized a cosy little chalet for me, and the following morning a gorgeous sunrise over the lake that looks across at Bollingen. Then, the bus sped us to Caen, where we made the boat on time. Gentle sea, lovely comrades, a special journey. In the twinkling of 69 pair of eyes, we were back in Blighty, back into all the Brexit fiasco, homeward bound in our cars, but with fabulous memories of our journey and a bucketload of new friends.

The idea of the superindividual had permeated our journey, from the article that pilgrims had enjoyed in the guidebook, through our collective collaborations and adventures, the experiences of Damanhur, the rituals we had performed. One of the last things we all did together was to contribute to a jointly written poem. This was compiled by Michelle

(La Chanteuse) who asked us all to contribute one line, right off the tops of our heads. Here is the result, a poem by the superindividual:

The Road To Gnowhere

Shit doesn't just happen
Discordians make it happen
Walking the Planck into the gnothing
Digging the fuck in
To an emotional spiral
Confusion and revelation intertwined
A verdant wonder call
To an uberworld
Through death and rebirth
Infinity the safeword
Purging the anarchism
Transforming the cataclysm
Trans everything
A transcendental humbling
A shush to noisy serendipity
No fixed numinous
Wordless epiphanies
An awesome frequency
Of humour
Grace
Simplicity
And connectivity
A reboot
Channelling to clarity
Astoundingly
Through collective determination
And grit
Where soul and eye unite
Letting love transform time
A persistent energy of connection
Profound Beautiful
Challenging
Susurration
Sigilization
Astral gyration

Release
All astonishingly scintillating
A garlic dipped artichoke utopia
Of trust
In trust
On top of trust
Held
The sugar
Bliss
Beautifully woven togetherness
Plastic the fnord
Mu the truth we call for
Feets don't fail me now
The hoppers returned
First mission done
Many more to come

THE QUESTS

The Quesiti have been developed as a set of principles and are established as the basis by which Damanhurians live their lives. This word (Quesito is singular) has no direct equivalent in English as its meaning is somewhere in between a "question" and a "quest". The Quesiti are dynamic formulas, themes that can be used for meditation and applied in everyday life. Their formulation is a direct result of the collective achievements of Damanhur, but each person can interpret them according to their own talents and characteristics.

The First Quesito emphasizes the importance of action and choice, living life fully and with purity of intentions:

- Complete and aware action
- Purity of intent
- To live the synchronic moment to the full

The Horusian Path is a School of Initiation which has action as its basic foundation. Action means: to work responsibly and with purity of intent for the spiritual progress of others, because only by doing this does one have the premise for one's own evolutionary growth.

One has, moreover, to live fully the synchronic moment, which means "to live in the moment": not to be bound egotistically to the fruit of the action carried out. To act also means "to choose", with living in the moment being "continuous choice", instant by instant. This quest is the highest expression of free will. Action is the physical and moral prerequisite for identity. Action is our way to differentiate ourselves and assume a position relative to the continuum of things. To live the synchronic moment to the full, it is necessary to not expect a result of our actions It requires you to choose and intervene in reality with pure intentions and without calculating on the things that you do.

This is the beginning of the transformation, it is the passage which makes it possible to act upon synchronicity, exercising positive and optimistic thought in the search for a thread that is able to string events together. A thread able to pull the apparent negativity of some moments around into the necessary pre-condition for the successive realization of favourable circumstances.

Synchronicity renders it possible to insert the power of our thought among the probabilities which link the unfolding of events, such that we can increase the possibility that what we want to happen actually does without the need of hanging on to expectation.

The Second Quesito calls for constancy and continuity, to give meaning and importance to choices that have been made. It emphasizes the importance of keeping one's word:

- Coherence and continuity in action
- Continuous choice, instant by instant, to give substance to Quesito I.
- Respect when giving one's word in faith whatever the cost

Spiritual choice, once made, is to be coherently and continuously kept going in time. The lamp that has been lit should not be put out, because "to be put out", in esoteric terms, means that it may never be lit again. The second quest gives substance to the first. The first talks of action; the second calls for a change in logic to welcome new visions of self, life and the sacred dimension of existence. This is the first step in creating a civilization and culture. If we live constantly in the moment, the possibilities of this second passage open to us. To live in the moment does not mean to limit oneself just to a specific instant, but presumes action continues through time. The second quest is a sort of programming, so that living in the moment is not an event, which happens by accident. Action must not be ephemeral, but consistent and constant. One needs to have a deep respect for oneself: only thus will one have the inherent strength to keep one's word.

The Third Quesito concerns the application of a will to change. That is, the direct use of a different logic that makes it possible to turn a purely hypothetical idea into an objective reality, through the application of the first and the second quests. The effect of a continuous and consistent action leads to self-transformation and to the capacity to accommodate new ideas and modes of interpreting reality. This consists of:

- Inner transformation
- Rebirth to the sacred
- New logic and a qualitative leap
- Formation of a new people
- Formation of a new culture

This is the quest of inner transformation and return to the sacred.

Humanity must grow, must lift itself from the state of matter in which it has been restricted and rise on high, towards those spaces that once were its own domain due to its divine position. This requires, above all, that each individual transforms himself or herself and works so that even others might complete that inner alchemical transmutation which leads, through a new culture, to the creation of a people, the primeval cell of the future reawakened humankind. This is the real importance of the return to the sacred, to that mystical vision of life, which permits one to overcome pride and individual egoism and ensures that the single pieces of the mosaic take their rightful place assigned to them in the great divine plan.

Thought is not a "something" that each one of us produces, but it is like a great flow in which we are constantly immersed. Everybody elaborates thought according to their own cultural, religious and economic characteristics. To similar social backgrounds, to the same experiences and conditionings correspond similar ways of thinking, the same behaviours, the same "quasi-real".

Quasi-real is the subjective perception of an event. Reality is coded through a series of data determined by birth, age, sex, learning, language, relations and history. Any event we go through is filtered through the character and disposition and as a consequence can be perceived only in a subjective way.

A very significant example is that of physicists who entertain different theories on the same phenomenon. They study it according to the same procedure, using the same instruments, but they still reach opposite conclusions. This happens because they read the event through the filter of their education and expectations.

The Fourth Quesito, specifically feminine, encourages men and women to discover their feminine side, with openness and availability and the profound awareness of representing a stable element of union:

- Aware availability, not egotistical, of oneself
- Dignified progress towards perfection and respect for completion of femininity
- To be an element of union, the feminine stabilizes

This quest indicates those premises that are indispensable for overcoming the bound condition of woman. The road passes through awareness of a feminine self, which manifests in continual giving and thus constant presence. It also deals with the completion of the gifts usually attributed to man's companion, opening up new characteristics which unite gentleness with strength. These are conditions that every woman can rediscover or find again in her peers, when searching for the completion of her own missing parts, even among masculine elements, with respect for diversity.

Woman is the weaver and source of friendship, understood as an element of union, able to bring back together in a single thread the "scattering" of humanity and so put back together the secret symbol of mankind, shattered into pieces in the distant times of its undeserved defeat. The fourth quest is chiefly feminine, because it has within it the formula for overcoming the subordinate condition of women, but it also speaks to the feminine side of every individual.

According to the philosophy, which is at the basis of this path, every human being has a feminine and a masculine part. It is true that there are functions, which are totally masculine or feminine, for instance in procreation, but social roles are interchangeable, and it is only society which imposes fixed roles for men and women.

The reawakening of humanity requires an equal respect for the dignity of women and men. Men and women are different and by extolling their differences they reach wholeness. The feminine character from a social and spiritual point of view makes it possible to build and consolidate any situation. If we compare men to bricks, then women are the mortar. Thanks to the specifically feminine capability of cohesion, of keeping a wider knowledge and of facilitating deeper relationships between individuals, we obtain stability with a different strength than that of a pre-eminently masculine one.

The Fifth Quesito brings attention to the masculine energies present in each one of us, to the capacity to live in constant and harmonious inner revolution:

- Stability and firmness
- Harmonious inner revolution
- Intelligent discovery and rediscovery of habits, and looking again at them, with the aim of overcoming the conditioned habits (creating, therefore, a stable and continual, harmonious inner revolution)

The elements of stability and firmness, belonging to the masculine, should be permanently strengthened, through continual inner evolutionary movement. Making use of the intelligence he possesses, man should know how to eliminate conditioned habits, the so-called "taken for granted", in order to rediscover or re-choose as conscious ritual strength, able to give a vital rhythm to his own actions. That means overcoming the conditioning required from one's education and environment, through a voluntary and conscious expression of free will.

Thanks to the steps we have taken we have now reached our inner point of balance. But how much of us is in this centre? How well do the values it contains represent us? How much do we act out of habit, out of fear of ridicule or judgement, out of respect for conventions we do not subscribe to? Let's look for our real identity, our own personal values and let's slough off our skin, but still remain the same person.

Habits are false friends, a result of the conditioning of our education and our environment. By the use of the intelligence he possesses man must learn not to take things for granted. The masculine capacity to invent, to drive, to move, must bear fruit through a conscious expression of free will in order for tradition not to become a habit, but a springboard to create new ideas and effect change and growth.

This is the quest of resolution, in which the elements of stability and firmness of man must become stronger through a continuous inner evolutionary movement.

The Sixth Quesito invites us to unite the masculine and feminine principles within ourselves, to activate our power of creation, not only of life itself, but also of its representations through art and creativity, generosity and kindness. The sixth quest may be summarized as follows:

- Inversion of the fourth and fifth quests, the former becomes masculine, the latter feminine
- Union generates life
- Rituals born of silence
- Rituals causing everything to grow and mature
- Prayer by working with the preceding quests
- Imagination, fantasy (in the sense of art, life)
- Generosity, goodwill
- The search for unification within human forces is the measure of things (dimensions) between them
- Spiritual fractals

This quest deals with life itself. Life is well and truly creation: substantiation of "nothingness", and not simply moving energies from one reservoir to another. It is the "anti-entropic" principle par excellence which shifts the concept of a "closed system".

Humanity is an aspect of the great divine fractal and even that which "substantiates" cannot be other than God's own imprint. We must mix the various ingredients in just measure: generosity, goodwill, action-form, education, art, imagination and fantasy. Only thus will the divine spark fill the creation of humanity and give life to matter. The first law of magic – as above, so below – is the formula of the sixth quest.

People who do not limit themselves to developing only those characteristics that their culture attributes to their sex, but try to really know themselves and to explore their every wish and inclination, realize they possess much greater riches than culture tells them. The difficulties in communication between the sexes cannot be solved by trying to create uniformity of behaviour, ways of thinking and attitudes, but only by welcoming the difference of the "other".

Equality of dignity does not mean to be the same, but to accept the wealth diversity brings, because it reflects a part of ourselves. If we do not respect difference in the other sex, we kill a part of ourselves too, between partners, in the family, in society. It is a game where there can be no winners, only losers.

According to Damanhurian philosophy, the human being must reconquer the original condition of androgyny, the primordial unity of masculine and feminine inside every one of us. Every man or woman, while keeping the specificity of their sex, will then have the key to reawaken inside themselves. This will make us really free and able to express ourselves with an infinite variety of shades and emotions. The sixth quest is an invitation to the individual to be above all a vital part of society.

"Prayer" in this quest represents an element of concentration towards oneself, a way of getting one's characteristics and talents to operate, a form of mental tidying up. Through prayer it is possible therefore to obtain a schema of one's own energies, the possibility of having an objective that we could not individuate before exercising this power.

The Seventh Quesito calls for the use of doubt and adaptability as research tools to abandon all dogmas and certainties, to discover what is true inside of us, beyond appearances. In summary:

- Uncertainty, doubt and adaptability to create the true real, moment by moment
- Demolition of certainties to edify every existence in constant mutation and evolution, where the real form is a bubble of appearance
- Solidity built instant by instant

This is the quest that indicates continuous transformation as an objective to aim for. This is the capacity of always reconsidering everything in order to reach a superior order. Only change makes it possible to see new roads, to elaborate innovative ideas. The seventh quest is a vision of the world, which allows us to face change without fear.

If life is constant change and truth is a crystal with many facets, then no human being and no one philosophy can contain the whole truth. True solidity can be created only when all certainties are demolished, as any certainty is only partial. When we are looking for a new balance it is okay to feel a bit disorientated, because all our existence is based upon the acquisition of information, elements and knowledge. If we feel too certain, it means that we believe that we have understood everything, and then we are really silly. We cannot ever comprehend everything, but we can always understand more.

Continuous change does not mean a chaotic situation, but guided transformation to a better situation, reaching a superior result with fewer means and less expenditure of energy. In continuous mutation, there are no fixed parameters, there is no need for a dogmatic philosophy: it is a method that everyone builds for themselves respecting ethics and the basic moral elements inherent in humanity. In the process of becoming we are always in the present. Only if we are constantly becoming can we live in the moment, as proposed by the first quest.

This is the quest of true and complete inner freedom, which can be conquered only when we are really in harmony with ourselves and all the parts that comprise us. Every one of us, in fact, is not formed just by a masculine and a feminine part, but also by several personalities. In Damanhur's philosophy, in fact, the human being is a being of multiple personalities, of different characters that are the great wealth each one of us has inside, that we have to learn to harmonize and tap into. Due to our cultural education and genetic inheritance, we are used to considering ourselves as one unique person, but we have many different parts, many different ensembles of memories and ways of interacting with the world around us. When we learn to recognize and recall them, they give us enormous riches in talents and possibilities.

The Eighth Quesito, finally, invites us to project our attention towards others. It speaks of love and teaching as instruments to transform the world around us; study as spiritual necessity; the irreversible choice of our own ideals to achieve the reawakening of our divine principle and be in service to the world.

The eighth quest is the integration of all the quests. All that is learned can now be brought out to nourish others. Do you share? After enlightenment, metamorphosis:

- Irreversible choice of the ideal: discipline not blackmail
- Reproduction, love
- Path towards inner divinity: study of emotion as spiritual necessity

The eighth quest "opens to others", a phrase dear to Falco, and integrates all the previous quests. It speaks of love and teaching as a means to transform the world around us, of study as a spiritual necessity; it invites us to respect the ideals we have chosen to follow so we can use our energy to help others and reawaken our divine principle. Let us remember, by the way, that the divine principle, as such, is very much awake, it is we who must become aware of its presence inside ourselves!

By giving to others we make a further leap in quality, as the good teacher who by transmitting knowledge to the pupils with passion is not deprived of it but grasps new aspects of it and enriches his/her learning process. Love is the extra element we have to include in our actions in order to create a link between us and the others, no matter whether they ask for it or we think they deserve it or not. It shows our ability to adapt ourselves to the environment.

A specific point of the eighth quest states that our life choices become irreversible: we must continue to discuss, verify and confirm our choices within ourselves every day with the aim of improving their content and practical implementation, never more to doubt them. In this regard, do you remember the difference between searching and finding? As the distinctive element of human beings is our free will, every choice we make must be honoured, namely made right through our subsequent, coherent actions.

For that reason, we must respect our initiatives, which can be perfected to suit us better but never rejected in their basic concept. Obviously, if we discover that some choices we made in the past have turned out to be wrong, as they were detrimental to us and others, this quest does not compel us to maintain them. On the contrary, it invites us to move away from them through a further act of transformation of ourselves rather than a rejection.

All that we have learnt through the path of the previous quests can now be brought outside to nourish others and the world. Transformation must not just function as a support for ourselves, but it must become a factor of evolution which finds its maximum expression in reproduction. Reproduction here is defined as knowledge, as the capacity to create something superior to oneself in the direction of evolution.

This work on the development of the quest has its own logic. It is related to being an individual within a larger entity called the People, where the individual is important, but so is the development of the People. One relates purposefully to the other; they are not contradictory.

APPENDIX 2
THE DAMANHUR FOUNDATION

The Damanhur Foundation is a not-for-profit organization, founded in 2017, and based in the Netherlands by arrangement with a group of friends there. It has ANBI status, the non-profit tax designation in the Netherlands issued by the tax office (Belastingdienst) in accordance with general tax laws. ANBI stands for Algemeen Nut Beogende Instelling. The mission of the Foundation is to be an example and inspire people to take actions that can change the world for the better. The organizers are a group of people devoted to sharing ideas, discoveries and social and spiritual technologies to support the evolution of humanity, collectively, individually and in connection with the living intelligence of this planet and the cosmos.

It is important to note that the governance of Damanhur, through its king guides and a well-developed social structure, is not to be confused with the Damanhur Foundation. The latter exists to support, maintain and raise funds for the future development of Damanhur as it strides out into the world. Whereas the governance of Damanhur is concerned with its day-to-day functioning and ongoing activities.

The core of the knowledge of Damanhur Foundation is the result of several decades of shared living, studying and transforming of the Federation of Communities of Damanhur. Originally born in Italy as a social experiment and spiritual movement, the Federation now has affiliates all over the world. At the core of its philosophy, rooted in the ancient wisdom of the West with a visionary approach to the future, is a commitment to be an example and inspire people to take actions that can positively change the world.

The principles of Damanhur are built around creation, commitment and knowledge. Creation, to resonate with the needs of our time and give birth to a new humanity, connected, engaged, compassionate and curious; commitment, to take actions to change the world for the better, and inspire others to do the same, day after day, with dedication and radical optimism; knowledge, to open minds and hearts, to inspire understanding of the language of the cosmos and create a new culture of harmonious interconnection.

The Damanhur Foundation is active in fundraising initiatives to support its main projects in the areas of:

- Respect for Earth, the environment and exploration of interspecies communication
- Fostering of spiritual awareness through the arts, education and the creation of sacred spaces
- Intercultural dialogue and support of indigenous peoples' wisdom

The main purpose of the Foundation is to manage fund-raising, gifts and donations in the future development initiatives of Damanhur.

The ANBI system means that qualifying organizations are entitled to certain tax advantages related to inheritance, gifts and donations:

- Inheritance: exemption from inheritance taxes
- Gifts: exemption from gift tax
- Donations: donations of goods or money to a good cause may be tax deductible for the donors

The Foundation, like Damanhur, is dedicated to the uplifting principles of creating sacred space and connecting to universal wisdom. Ashok Khosla, the former Indian Minister of the Environment, and former President of IUCN (International Union for the Conservation of Nature), declared:

Damanhur and the Temples of Humankind are for the 21st century what Assisi was in the time of Saint Francis – both represent the deepest commitment to the well-being and the dignity of all our fellow human beings, and the highest respect for other living things and indeed for all of creation.

The creation of sacred space is a practical manifestation of the highest collective ideals. Building spaces with a symbolic and transcendent meaning gives a feeling of development not only in material, but also in spiritual and artistic terms. This, in turn, feeds community members with continuous and renewed inspiration that leads to new ideas and optimism. A positive attitude and a sense of self-realization are indispensable ingredients of a society that is thriving and not just growing.

The sacred spaces of Damanhur are not monuments of the past, but rather an answer for the future of the world. They are sacred mirrors that amplify the inner light of every human being and reflect it from Earth to the heavens.

It is to oversee such aims, ambitions, expectations and dreams that the Damanhur Foundation has been set up, to help provide a safe and vibrant future. I spoke with Rinoceronte Giuggiolo, the king guide elected as head of the governing body, and asked him to tell me about the Foundation:

> The Foundation is the first step in opening up Damanhur to the world. We needed a fresh container to place all our assets in. But there was a shift and we allowed the Foundation to become a reference point for the whole world, not only for fund-raising on our project, but as a repository of knowledge. We really have the authority to share the knowledge with the whole world, not just through the initiation path. But a lot of what we do is a universal language and involves the whole planet. In this moment, we are starting to use the Foundation as an instrument because we are almost ready to do it. But we are taking the necessary steps so it can really take off. And we are on a good path now. We have revisited the board members this year and most of all we have started to create a scientific committee, perhaps more correct to say a spiritual committee.

This committee is open to people who are not Damanhurians but are relevant to what is being done in the world. Rinoceronte thought that it would take perhaps 12 months for the Foundation to really take off. It was still a little bit of a struggle. But the whole of the Foundation really will be shared by all the Damanhurians, the initiates of Damanhur in the world and everybody that has an affinity with this project. In a similar way, the Foundation would like to participate in the work of other organizations. The latest thing we have been discussing is the idea of a container for a project where many communities of the world can participate, if they want to. It could be a useful territory like the web. Rinoceronte again:

What is important is the real exchange of ideas, projects, knowledge, energies and other things. A comprehensive network. And we would like to think that it is our Foundation itself that triggers us to accomplish this.

The Foundation is dedicated to starting a training programme, which would be run by initiates in Holland and then shared with everyone who wants a spiritual journey. Such a programme would not be like teaching but transmitting active training to people who want to start new communities.

Even though Damanhur is not perfect, we have been a community for 45 years and we are a reality. A lot of people ask us, how can we create a community at home? So, through the Foundation we can create the organism to do this. And I like to think of the Foundation as something that inspires joy and happiness. And I would like the events organized by the Foundation to be based on the principle of joy. As well as creating a scientific committee, I am thinking how we can get in touch with all those entities inspired by joy and playfulness. So, we are devising a project that I hope is going to work like an art club that we start here in Damanhur and then export it throughout the world. Art is our greatest gift, both as an expression of who we are and as a gift that we can give.

If you want to share this exciting adventure, in whatever way you wish, you can contact the Damanhur Foundation at:

www.damanhur.foundation

BIBLIOGRAPHY

Accorti, Rinaldo (Gnomo Orzo), *How Many Holes Does a Ring Have?*, Devodama, Vidracco, 2017

Accorti, Rinaldo (Gnomo Orzo), *I Make Things Happen: Selfica, Spiritual Technology for the Third Millennium*, Devodama, Vidracco, 2020

Airaudi, Oberto (Falco Tarassaco), *The Myth of the Sapphire Masks*, Federazione Damanhur, Baldissero Canavese, 2001

Airaudi, Oberto (Falco Tarassaco), *Dying to Learn: First Book of the Initiate,* English edition, Oracle Institute Press, Baldissero, 2012

Airaudi, Oberto (Falco Tarassaco), *Reborn to Live: Second Book of the Initiate,* English edition, Oracle Institute Press, Baldissero, 2013

Airaudi, Oberto (Falco Tarassaco), *Seven Scarlet Doors: Third Book of the Initiate,* English edition Oracle Institute Press, Baldissero, 2013

Airaudi, Oberto (Falco Tarassaco), *Liber S: Prophecies of the Age of Aquarius*, Devodama, Vidracco, 2016

Airaudi, Oberto (Falco Tarassaco), *Prophesies of the End of Times*, Edizioni Horus, Baldissero, Italy, 1980; English edition, Devodama, Vidracco, 2016

Airaudi, Oberto (Falco Tarassaco), *Stories of an Alchemist: The Extraordinary Childhood Years of the Founder of Damanhur in 33 Tales*, Niatel, Vidracco, 2012

Airaudi, Oberto (Falco Tarassaco), *The Synchronic Lines: The Energy Streams of Planet Earth*, English edition, Devodama, Vidracco, 2016

Barker, Eileen, *Stepping out of the Ivory Tower: A Sociological Engagement in "The Cult Wars"*, Department of Sociology, London School of Economics, *Methodological Innovations Online*, 2011

Bennis, Warren, and Biederman, Pat Ward (*Organizing Genius: the Secrets of Creative Collaboration*; Ingram Publishers, US, 1997

Blackadder, Jill Slee, *Shetland: An Island Guide*, Colin Baxter Publishers, Lerwick, 2007

Bramwell, David, *The No. 9 Bus to Utopia: How One Man's Extraordinary Journey Led to a Quiet Revolution*, Unbound Publications, London, 2014

Buffagni, Silvia (Esperide Ananas) & Benzi, Roberto, *Damanhur: Temples of Humankind*, North Atlantic Books, Berkeley, 2006

Buffagni, Silvia (Esperide Ananas) & Palombo, Silvio (Stambecco Pesco), *The Stories of Damanhur: The Chest of Memories and Checkmate to Time*, Devodama, Vidracco, 2016

Buffagni, Silvia (Esperide Ananas) & Palombo, Silvio (Stambecco Pesco), *The Traveller's Guide to Damanhur*, North Atlantic Books, Berkeley, 2009

Buffagni, Silvia (Esperide Ananas), *Spirals of Energy: The Ancient Art of Selfica*, Devodama, Vidracco, 2013

Calati, Fernando (Unicorno Arachide), & Palombo, Silvio (Stambecco Pesco), *Journey into the Temples of Humankind*, Devodama, Vidracco, 2016

Campbell, Daisy, *Pigspurt's Daughter*, Mycelium Playscript, Brighton, 2019

Campbell, Ken, *Violin Time, or The Lady from Monségur*, Methuen Drama, London, 1996

Cardo, Coyote, *Spiritual Physics: The Philosophy, Knowledge and Technology of the Future*, Litoprint Editioni, Emilia Romagna, 2014

Deutsch, David, *The Fabric of Reality: Towards a Theory of Everything*, Penguin, London, 1998

Einstein, Albert, *Ideas and Opinions*, Folio Edition, London, UK, 2010 (Crown Publishers, London, 1954)

Faruolo, Mario (Coyote Cardo), *Spiritual Physics*, Litoprint Edizioni, Emilia Romagna, 2014

Harari, Yuval Noah, *Sapiens: A Brief History of Humankind*, Penguin Books (Vintage Imprint), London, 2015

Harari, Yuval Noah, *21 Lessons for the 21st Century*, Penguin Books (Vintage Imprint), London, 2019

Harari, Yuval Noah, *Homo Deus: A Brief History of Tomorrow*, Penguin Books (Vintage Imprint), London, 2017

Harris, Jonathan (editor), *Burning Issue Magazine, Vol. 1*, Burning Issue Publishing, Welwyn Garden City, 2018

Hawking, Steven, *Brief Answers to Big Questions*, Random House (Bantam Books imprint), New York, 2018

Introvigne, Massimo, "Damanhur – a Magical Community in Italy", *Journal of the Communal Studies Association* 16, 1996

Jones, Tobias, *Utopian Dreams*, Faber & Faber, London, 2007

Koziol, Carol Ann, "An Exploration of Four Ecovillages through the Ecoresilient Lens of Spirituality", PhD thesis, Laurentian University, Sudbury, Ontario, 2020

Lyon's, Matthew, *Impossible Journeys*, Folio Edition, London, 2009

Melo, Coboldo, *Secrets of the Damanhur Political System*, Devodama, Vidracco, 2017

Merrifield, Jeff, *Damanhur: The Real Dream*, Harper Collins (Thorsons imprint), London, 1998

Merrifield, Jeff, *Damanhur: The Story of the Extraordinary Italian Artistic and Spiritual Community*, Hanford Mead, 2006

Merrifield, Jeff, *SEEKER! Ken Campbell: His Five Amazing Lives*, Playback Publications, Sandwich, 2011

Merrifield, Jeff, *The Perfect Heretics: Cathars and Catharism*, Enabler Publications, Lyme Regis, 1995 (Revised Playback Edition, Great Totham, 2018)

Moore, Alan, *The Jerusalem Trilogy*, W W Norton (Liveright imprint), London, 2018

Orzo, Gnomo, *How Many Holes Does a Ring Have?*, Devodama, Vidracco, 2017

Palombo, Silvio (Stambecco Pesco), *A Day in the Life of Damanhur*, Devodama, Vidracco, 2016

Palombo, Silvio (Stambecco Pesco), *A Temple in the Green: What the Sacred Wood Temple is and What it Represents*, Devodama (Con Te Series), Vidracco, 2017

Palombo, Silvio (Stambecco Pesco), Calati, Fernanda (Unicorno Arachide), & Crapanzano, Mirella (Ciprea Calandula), *A Popolo of Artists*, Devodama (Con Te Series), Vidracco, 2017

Paragio, Roberto (Coboldo Melo), *The Damanhurian Version of Risk*, Devodama (Con Te Series), Vidracco, 2017

Paragio, Roberto (Coboldo Melo), *Secrets of the Damanhur Political System*, Devodrama, Vidracco, 2017

Paragio, Roberto (Coboldo Melo), *The Faces of the Crystal Damanhur*, Devodama, Vidracco, 2017

Parks, Alexia, *Rapid Evolution*, The Education Exchange, Eldorado Springs, 2002

Prete, Tiziana (Piovra Cafè), Buffagni, Silvia (Esperide Ananas) & Guasti, Niccolo, *I Templi Dell' Umanità: La Roccia, L'Arte e La Luce (Temples of Humankind: Rock, Art and Light)*, Scripta Maneant, Bologna, 2019

Ray, Josh (The Rework), editor, *The Pilgrim's Guidebook*, Liverpool Arts Lab (private publication), Liverpool, 2019

Read, Herbert, *Education Through Art*, Faber & Faber, London, 1961

Robinson, Ken, *The Element: How Finding Your Passion Changes Everything*, The Penguin Group, London, 2009

Sagan, Carl, *Planetary Exploration*, University of Oregon Books, 1970

Salter, Kara Margaret, *Structure and Anti-Structure: Communitas in Damanhur, Federation of Communities*, Doctoral thesis, University of Western Australia, 2015

Shea, Robert & Wilson, Robert Anton, *The Illuminatus! Trilogy*, Dell Publishing, New York, 1975

Silva, Freddy, *The Divine Blueprint*, Invisible Temple Books, Portland, Maine, 2010

Valenta, Eraldo, *Oberto Airaudi: Quadri Selfici*, ValRa Damanhur, Torino, 2004

White, Michael, *The Pope and the Heretic: The True Story of Giordano Bruno, the Man Who Dared to Defy the Roman Inquisition*, Harper Perennial, 2003

Wilson, Robert Anton, *Cosmic Trigger: Final Secrets of the Illuminati*, Dell Books, New York, 1977

INDEX

Note: page numbers in **bold** refer to illustrations